FLY TALES

Also by Scott Sadil

Lost in Wyoming: Stories

Cast from the Edge: Tales of an Uncommon Fly Fisher

Angling Baja: One Man's Fly Fishing Journey Through the Surf

FLY TALES

Lessons in Fly Fishing
Like the Real Guys

Scott Sadil

BARCLAY CREEK PRESS
Bolton, Massachusetts

ISBN-13: 978-1-936008-03-2
ISBN-10: 1-936008-03-3

Barclay Creek Press, LLC
PO Box 249
Bolton, MA 01740-0249 USA

www.barclaycreek.com

Publisher: James D. Anker
Page design: Dutton & Sherman Design
Jacket design: Dutton & Sherman Design
Jacket art: *Back Porch*, watercolor painting by Fran Noel
Author photo: Carol Sternkopf

For Peter Syka

CONTENTS

CONTENTS

ACKNOWLEDGMENTS

Many of these stories were read and commented on by members of the Columbia River Writers, a covey of spirited talents who, during late nights punctuated with chocolate and red wine, learned more about fly fishing than any of them would have ever imagined. To all of these fine friends and writers I owe the deepest gratitude.

As well, I'd like to thank Richard Anderson at *California Fly Fisher,* Dave Hughes at the *Flyfishing & Tying Journal,* Jim Reilly, formerly at *Fly Rod & Reel,* Joe Healy, currently at *Fly Rod & Reel,* James Babb at *Gray's Sporting Journal,* and Steve Walburn at *American Angler* for choosing to publish these lessons, in somewhat different versions, when they first took form.

Finally, many thanks to Fran Noel for use of the art which graces the cover of *Fly Tales.*

INTRODUCTION

In a plastic crate I carry to classes, I have a stack of index cards, nearly two inches thick, with the names of the people I've taught to fly fish while I wrote this book.

I have mixed notions about this wealth of students. Had I finished the book sooner, for example, the stack wouldn't stand so tall. There's also the sense that I might have contributed to the problem of ever-increasing crowds, although that one washes out pretty quickly when you consider that few of us will even have local waters to fish if we don't multiply the number of people who care about rivers, watersheds, and healthy fisheries. Then there's the feeling that I've steered people down a path of dissipation: How many more lives do we need to see ruined by fly fishing?

And finally, there's this: Have I misled my charges, one and all, into believing I'm a Real Guy?

Real Guys, goes the logic, belong to an inner circle of expert anglers, a cadre of insiders whose skills and knowledge and perhaps fortunes of good breeding have positioned them in territory the rest of us can only glimpse or occasionally admire. Real Guys embrace the gravity of the sport toward which we're all somehow attracted. Real Guys live to fish— while the rest of us have fishing lives.

I'm anything but a Real Guy. And that's only one of my qualifications for writing this book.

Teaching, writing, and fly fishing share fabulous peril. All three vocations offer themselves up as harbors of sanctimony for mavens of deceit.

Anyone can get in on the act. Worse, still, is the consensus among the public at large that teachers and writers and fly fishers, say what you will, make careers out of telling lies.

Real Guys, on the other hand, stand above all that. They don't need to indulge in veiled rhetoric, slippery innuendo, and half-cocked theories based on changing weather patterns, private cosmologies, augury, and the color of their lover's eyes. Real Guys don't suffer the *need* to fabricate stories—unless, perhaps, they feel cheated somehow, removed from the grave humiliations dealt the rest of us on the water, in front of our families and colleagues and friends, and in the great arguments held with ourselves while seated in front of the blank page.

Unlike those of us short of the rank, Real Guys have learned their lessons—front and back, top to bottom, A to Z, one through ninety-nine. Let me hazard a roundabout example. Once, on the Deschutes, while conducting a field clinic for beginning fly fishers (illegally, it turns out—but that's a different story), I watched as a young woman intent on embracing the sport hooked a classic hard-running redside that immediately threatened to spool her. I thought she was overstating her case when she claimed the trout had most all of her line; but when I inspected her reel, sure enough, she had but a half-dozen turns of backing on the spinning large-arbor spool.

Then even that was gone.

The rod grew dangerously heavy in the woman's hand: all that line in the river, the famed Deschutes current, and somewhere at the end of her tippet a good trout still fighting with all its might.

My student and I looked at each other. The desert light drowned her eyes—and in a moment every teacher comes to face with uncertainty and often dread, I needed to say something.

"Run," I told her. "You have to run."

Run she did, chasing the fish downstream in awkward plunging lunges, recovering line in frantic bursts that seemed a kind of musical trope in a teenage anthem of love. Later, when we leaned together over the tired trout, while the sound of cameras whirred and buzzed from the row of students crowding the bank, while everyone present shared in the good cheer that seems so much a part of a good fish landed, regardless who has brought it to hand, it occurred to me that the young woman next to me had taken a step on her way to becoming a Real Guy. She had learned a lesson, passed the test. The only significant difference between her and me, I decided, was the number of lessons I've learned—some successfully, others less so—in the course of a lifetime fly fishing.

The difference between me and the Real Guys, I concluded, is essentially the same.

As I approached the end of this book, I faced one question that I never fully answered: How do you know if or when you've become a Real Guy? Failing to reach a definitive answer, I suffered the odd sensation of writing a story that never ends. As a writer, I appeared destined to retrace the same endless and oftentimes uphill path my fly fishing career has essentially followed.

Which might be the best lesson I have to offer. As long as you don't quite know where you're headed, at what point you can say you've arrived, you can let go of purpose and destination and stick to the business at hand. That is, you can keep fishing, keep casting for new stories, and keep coming up with something to say when an unsure student looks you in the eye.

There's a lesson there, too, I'd say.

Scott Sadil
Hood River, Oregon
February 2010

He was as unscientific and prone to voodoo in
selecting a fly as you and I.

—Thomas McGuane, on Roderick Haig-Brown

Lesson 1

CHEWAUCAN

On the Virtues of Streams

Long before Sheridan Anderson exhorted fly fishers to go forth and seek their own Curtis Creek, a small stream which to cherish while growing intimate with the ways of running water and wary trout, experienced anglers everywhere have sung the praises of little waters for their capacity to teach us, quite simply, how to fish.

Besides some dinky Sierra Nevada streams above Fresno and Kingsburg, visited once or twice each summer during childhood family vacations, my own "Curtis Creek" might really have been the surf at Black's Beach in La Jolla. Here, for the first time in my life, I had daily access to fishable water—initially plied most often, it is true, with a surfboard, not a fishing rod; yet eventually this short stretch of shoreline became proving ground for experiments—and fantasies—of fly fishing in the surf. Success, even limited success, demanded familiarity, attention, insight—the stuff of genuine education, forcing the questions how and why, answers to which will serve a fly fishing career, in whatever form, until one's dying days.

Nowhere do small waters offer greater opportunity for this kind of learning than the creeks of Lake County, Oregon, just over the California border as one heads north beyond Goose Lake on Highway 395. Here, more than a dozen different streams and diminutive rivers thread their way out of the Fremont National Forest, many of them destined to disappear into the shallow, alkaline sump lakes that mark the northwestern edge of the sunbaked Great Basin. Draining the western reaches of the county, two of these little rivers, the Sycan and the Sprague, do their best to mimic the illustrious trophy-trouted Williamson, which they eventually join, making them worthy, it seems to me, to a story all their own.

For it is the hidden, unheralded Chewaucan River, flowing north for much of its length toward the tiny outpost of Paisely, that epitomizes Lake County trout fishing: remote, unexploited, unrefined. At the same time, the Chewaucan speaks to the notion of a cherished small stream—a Curtis Creek on which to school oneself in the delicate demands of fly fishing while also learning to recognize, by way of intimacy, what Mr. Anderson and others like him have referred to as, appropriately enough, "the hot spots."

Of course, this is entirely about fishing. Isn't everything? So when I bring up a sun-lashed morning on the Chewaucan during which my youngest son and a friend of his, both twelve-year-olds, were back in camp tucked in the tent sleeping after a late night roasting marshmallows and feasting on S'mores, I don't want to dwell too long on the pleasures of the scene, the sage and juniper setting, wildflowers splattered on benches above the floodplain, even though that's the Chewaucan, too, and I do believe that by the time either of my sons has children of his own it will be a rare place indeed where one can drive out West to the end of a road and camp along the banks of a river, free of pavement, numbered sites, mortared fire pits, and chained-down picnic tables, not to mention pit toilets and tap water and, well, I hate to say it, any other pilgrims within sight or shouting distance.

The fly was a yellow Humpy. The previous day the boys and I had noticed, among other things, lots of little, immature, yellow- and lime-green-bellied grasshoppers; bursts of Pale Morning and Pale Evening Duns; plus the Little Yellow Stonefly, *Isoperla* or *Isogenus*, I don't know which. Does it matter? Yellow, anyway, was in the air—and the stout, chunky Humpy, a size 16, looked especially good on the water as an impression of those tiny hoppers, blunt and angular and appendaged in a way that so-called realistic flies rarely do.

The trout were fooled, too. The first one surprised me by rising in the middle of the pool, on a cast made before I took my best shot at the sheer, undercut bank, its shadow spread opaque as an olive over half of the stream. That first fish wasn't alone. More unusual still was the repeated willingness of each fish to rise to the Humpy as it made its way, casually as a poet, down the length of the pool. *This isn't the way small streams work at all,* I kept thinking, recognizing that it is precisely this like-never-before occasion that makes streams what they are, as time and again I lifted tight to the sight of the last place I had seen my Humpy before the water erupted and that silly little fly disappeared.

Another case, anyway, of being in the right spot at the right time. So much of this escapes the beginner. Despite all the attitude and hoopla, there are two truths in fly fishing that can serve as bookends to hold the rest of the sport's knowledge. One, you catch fish where fish are. Two, you don't catch fish without your fly in the water.

I don't mean to sound glib. It took me an awful long time—a regrettable amount, really—to understand just how profound these truths are. Yet without experience on the likes of a Curtis Creek or Chewaucan River, fly fishers often fail to grasp this kind of gravitational verse. Teaching newcomers to the sport, I am often surprised to discover students who have little or no fishing experience—of any sort—behind them. To me this seems a formidable handicap, like designing clothes without knowing how to sew.

Again I'm reminded of growing up around surf, frolicking in waves long before I had opportunity to paddle out on a board. By the time I did, I had been a serious bodysurfer for years, so that I was well acquainted with the temperament of waves, when and where and how they break, how they're affected by tides and the structure of the bottom, why waves from a north swell are different than those from, say, the south. All of this—and a lot more—felt like second nature by the time I began borrowing boards, so that even as a rank gremmie I had the wherewithal to say to myself, when a set came, "*There's* one I want." Or, as often as not, "Uh-oh."

Which, naturally, went hand in hand with casting flies in the surf. It seems to me, as well, that much of this kind of foundational experience is lost to fly fishers who have spent entire careers on big rivers and famous, *productive* waters. Very often such anglers have learned the sport from experienced friends or "professionals"—guides or teachers who put them over fish and tell them what to do and how to do it. No doubt this is a great way to begin. I recall a friend's future wife catching a twenty-inch cutthroat on her first trip to Yellowstone and saying, "Hey, this is fun!" I sensed the romance serious enough to refrain from pointing out how this lighthearted response, to what might well have been called a momentous occasion, proved just how little she really knew.

For the Chewaucan, like any Curtis Creek, will rarely reveal its secrets easily. Knowledge is invariably hard won. Patience, diligence, and observation mark the small-stream aficionado and his willingness to accept the moment, come what may. Other fly fishers, faced with the subtle problems posed by a creek, simply throw up their hands and dismiss such waters as beneath them—missing out, in the process, on the chance to do the kind of fishing that would go a long way in making them that much more competent back on bigger, more renowned waters.

"Plentiful game," noted Roderick Haig-Brown, "never yet made an excellent sportsman." The sage writer's observation also contains a nugget of truth about small-stream fishing, the wisdom available from experience stalking little waters. Results are rarely spectacular. The so-called lunker runs a pound, at best maybe two. Nothing comes readily. Which is precisely the point: There is simply too much to learn in fly fishing to get it all at once, from a teacher, from reading, from a class. Better by far is to come to know a stream over time, know it in such a way that from this point forward, everything else in fly fishing will point back, somehow, to what you saw and learned and did here before.

Time, I suspect, is the critical factor. The Chewaucan goes on and on, meandering through miles and miles of meadow before tumbling through a bouldery oak and ponderosa canyon, every piece of it inviting your attention, although it's easy to imagine one part interchangeable with others. But of course that's absurd. Every hole is unique. You learn to fish them one at a time. Fail to do so, treat one the same as the last, and the next thing you know you're painting by numbers rather than creating ideas on your own.

I had an old guy once in a beginner's fly fishing class I was teaching, an experienced fly fisher who had decided to take the course to brush up on skills he had let slide during a decade of steelhead fishing with hardware and conventional gear. Following our "field trip," two hours spent casting on moving water and looking at bugs, without any designs on catching fish, I asked this guy about small streams he might know of, and we got to talking about how important such places had been in each of our respective careers, how spending time on small streams, lots of time, proved crucial to learning how to fly fish. Then the guy glanced around at other students in the class, many of whom were middle-aged and just beginning. "I wonder if they can get there," the guy said, without trace of malice or condescension. "I don't know if they have enough time."

Odd though it may seem, the smaller the stream, the more time it often takes to discover its true character and virtues, the more time required to become acquainted with its hidden treasures and subtle joys. You show up at a big famous river with big famous trout, and immediately you understand what you're here for. See a guy land a trophy rainbow and your heart cries "Gimme!" While on a small stream you can't be sure, at times, whether there are even fish in the water. Usually, on the Chewaucan or some other Curtis Creek, there's no one else to even point the way.

You're in it on your own. And like so much real learning that requires you submit to the subject, rather than try to master it, learning to fish a small stream demands you slow down and pay attention, take your time, falling back on what you already know while remaining open to the discovery of something new.

For the Chewaucan is, after all, just another trout stream.

Little Yellow Humpy

Hook: TMC 900BL or Mustad 94845, size 14–16
Thread: Yellow waxed 3/0 monocord
Tail: Dark elk hair or moose body hair
Body: Yellow tying thread or yellow floss
Wing: Natural deer or elk hair
Hackle: Brown and grizzly

Tying Notes

The Humpy is not an easy tie. Deer hair requires the touch of experience. Jack Dennis exploited the floating capabilities of deer, elk, and moose hair in his *Western Tying Manual*, still an excellent reference for learning how to manipulate these invaluable materials for patterns so appropriate to our region's swift, unruly streams. Foam rubber and aerospace floatants have reduced the allure of hairwing and hair-bodied flies—but there remain among us those who never tire of fingering swatches of fur, searching for that alchemy of color, texture, pliancy, and durability that we recognize, with all our senses, as *The Stuff*.

There are actually two fundamentally different approaches to tying a Humpy. I prefer Dennis's method, in which the wings are formed from the tips of the same deer hair secured before the body and then pulled forward to form the distinct humped back of the fly. Randall Kauffman, and others, suggest tying in the wings first, and then using the long clipped butts from the tail material to eventually cover the body. Each method offers its challenges. The Humpy, especially in smaller sizes, is one of the great all-around patterns on Western rivers and streams—yet you can fish weeks without running into anyone fishing this verified classic. And that's not just because serious dry fly fishing has diminished so radically. The Humpy begs practice and repetition. Results reward the effort.

Step 1: Secure the hook and start the thread. Clean and stack the elk or moose hair. Tie in the tail. Trim the butts. Make sure tail is secured tightly. Advance your thread to the center of the hook shank.

Step 2: Clean and stack your deer (or elk) hair for the wing. Hold the hair so that the tips extend just beyond the tail. Take one wrap around the hair at the middle of the hook. Without releasing the hair, trim the butts at the halfway point of the hook. Taking loose wraps at first, wrap the thread back toward the bend of the hook. Work back and forth over the deer hair until it is covered completely by the yellow thread.

Step 3: Return the thread to the front of the body at the middle of the hook. With thumb and forefinger of the right hand, pull the deer hair straight up, giving it a slight twist. Pull the deer hair forward and, with the left hand, wrap the thread over the deer hair, creating the fly's distinctive hump.

Step 4: Take a couple more tight wraps behind the tips of deer hair. Pull back the tips, which will now become the wing. Advance the thread and make several wraps to hold the wing in an upright position.

Step 5: Divide the wing using figure-eight or crisscross wraps of thread. Take further wraps at the base to keep the wing vertical or cocked slightly forward.

Step 6: Once the wing is divided and positioned, tie in a pair of saddle hackles—grizzly and brown or any other combination. Secure both hackles with pliers. Take two turns of hackle behind the wing and another two turns in front. Ideally, the wing stands right in the middle of the wound hackle.

Step 7: Tie off the hackle and trim. If you've tied the fly correctly, you should have plenty of room to whip finish a small head. I often fail to leave myself near enough room.

LESSON 2

BLUE-WINGED OLIVES

Despite the glamour and elegant fandango, there are many of us drawn to the sport of fly fishing for the simple surety of failure. If you've spent time at all at the sport, you cultivate a history of futility in what should well have been moments of unqualified success. I like to believe there are circles of Real Guys—men and women of rarefied gifts—to which such things never happen. But I doubt this to be true. In my mind I have created a society of secret practitioners who beguile fish, especially trout, with the flair of stooping harriers—while on the water I recognize the earthly countenances of fellow fly fishers who know what it means, time and again, to fail.

Yet failure, goes the logic, is good. It teaches us, profoundly, that we are unable to master the world, that there remain forces beyond our knowing, that even our most splendiferous insights leave us far short of understanding the mysteries that propel both man and fish across the surface of this expiring orb. Such reasoning, of course, can also go a long way in helping to escape feelings of stupidity when faced with a river of rising trout, none of which appear remotely interested in the sublimities of your drifting fly.

Nothing, in any case, teaches us more about the inadequacies of our game than feeding fish that refuse our flies. Responses to these occasions are as varied as fly fishers themselves. Recently, I listened to a detailed description of the classic scenario: big fish rising, tiny flies, the mounting frustration of the speaker as he had sifted, to no avail, through the contents of his boxes beside a river we both know and love.

"What do you do then?" the fellow asked, his voice edged with a trace of the moment's recent hysteria.

"I don't know," I answered. I looked him squarely in the eye. "It's never happened to me."

Mostly, however, I confess my shortcomings. The point of all this—and I don't think I'm talking just about the fishing—is to pay attention to what is. On a scale of orders, that seems as tall as they come. On the rivers I fish, that also means keeping your eyes out for Blue-winged Olives, the little mayfly that very often is exactly what is—that is, what is hatching, what trout are feeding on, and what'll break your heart if you haven't figured out how to fit it into your game.

For a long time—certainly a lot longer than I care to admit—Blue-winged Olives belonged to a type of hatch that befuddled and frustrated me. I'd see some little mayflies and try to decide if their wings were really blue (they aren't), their bodies actually olive (sort of), and then I'd put on a fly I thought seemed right when I'd tied it, only to find, after a cast or two, the color or size or profile all wrong. Sometimes I'd see fish rising; sometimes not. My flies, anyway, never drew much attention. Later, I'd hear someone along the river mention Blue-winged Olives, and I'd think, "Oh no, here we go again."

Usually, however, I just chalked up these moments to experience, further instances, I felt, of what makes the sport, at times, so difficult.

But if you come to any greater understanding about fly fishing—greater, that is, than it's a hell of a lot of fun—you'll eventually conclude that if fish are rising, you should be able to catch them. No matter what. Rising fish are feeding fish, and feeding fish can be fooled with flies. I'm not arguing I can do it. I'm not arguing anyone can. Not always. But the fact is, you *should* be able to catch rising fish—or at least get them to bite your flies.

You can't be serious, anyway, about casting to rising trout in the West unless you've put together some sort of strategy for fishing over a blue-winged olive hatch. The bugs can come off practically year-round, although on any one river there's normally a spell in late winter and another in fall when the hatches are heaviest if not downright predictable. Given all of the usual variables that keep any of this from becoming airtight, you can actually plan your fishing around a blue-winged olive hatch, making it the focus of a day or even a series of days on the water.

I'm not sure how it happened, but eventually I figured out a few things—and I don't just mean learning a little scientific nomenclature so that I can refer to this thing as a *Baetis* hatch. In time, I even began to look forward to fishing over Blue-winged Olives. I would never claim to have anything in my fishing actually dialed, but I recognized recently that my feelings toward Blue-winged Olives had come one-eighty. I had a string of weekdays lined up on a river where, come spring break, the hatch can settle into a daily routine. City errands kept me tied up Monday morning, and by the time I reached the water I was pretty sure I wouldn't see any Blue-winged Olives that day. Still, I was there to fish. Scouting water from the railroad tracks, I crossed paths with a guy who said he had stood, an hour and a half before, in the midst of a river full of rising trout while "these little bugs" went floating past all around him.

None of the trout had cared for his flies.

"Little gray kind of things?" I asked, holding up thumb and forefinger as if to indicate *that* close.

The guy nodded. "I'm from the Midwest. We used to call 'em 'Trout Flies.'"

"Like these?"

I drew a small box from its own separate pocket in my vest. Inside I showed off the neat rows of tiny dries, Parachutes and Comparaduns, Sparkle Duns and Hairwing Duns, CDC thises and thats—all with the usual tweakage and material variations that make even one of my single-bug boxes look, no matter how well ordered, as diverse as a classroom of high school sophomores.

But, damn, these suckers look good, I thought.

The guy confirmed my opinion, pointing to a row of sparsely dressed size 20s. I reached out and gripped the sleeve of his wading jacket.

"That's what we're here for," I said, saliva floating my tongue.

March *is* a good month for Blue-winged Olives. The weather can be lousy, which Blue-winged Olives seem to love, and if you get lucky, this sort of nasty chill will keep a lot of other guys off the water. Midweek you can probably get a pool or run all to yourself, although that might mean arriving an hour or more before the hatch so that you've staked out your territory, thereby letting any other anglers who happen by know that they can look for water someplace else. Not everyone agrees, but I've always felt that if you've positioned yourself on good water, you should be able fish that water—and fish it by yourself or with the others in your group—throughout the rise and fall of a hatch.

Of course, if you came up and just asked me, I'd probably invite you down to water's edge, tell you what I know, share the fishing, and maybe we'd end up becoming lifetime friends. But most fly fishers desire a certain distance between themselves and strangers—although even that can break down pretty fast if you're hammering fish and the pair upstream are changing flies like a couple of dogs worrying a gopher hole.

If we did talk, however, I doubt I would tell you anything you don't already know. For me, the big difference when fishing over Blue-winged Olives—or over any other predictable hatch as far as that matter goes—has been a gradual realization that these are the moments that matter most. Now, instead of treating a hatch as an incidental occurrence in a day's fishing, I'm willing to direct a good deal of my attention and energy to the moment this thing comes off. I'm going to prepare for that moment—learn the hatches, learn the flies—and be ready for those first splashy rises that indicate the little guys getting first licks before their bigger brethren decide this flood of bugs is for real. By the time the hatch reveals itself as flies on the water, I want to have my fly amongst them, and I want to feel I have as good a chance as anyone to move fish to my every cast.

I guess the real question is: What took me so long to figure out *that*?

I'm sure I'll struggle with this question, too.

BWO Dun

Hook: TMC 100, Mustad 94845, size 18–20
Thread: Rusty Dun 8/0 UNI-Thread
Tail: Light Dun Microfibetts
Body: Dark olive dubbing
Wing: CDC, natural white or dun
Hackle: Grizzly or dun, undersized and sparse

Tying Notes

This is only one of about four different styles of small mayflies I tie. If I also included different wing materials, plus those flies I pare back and think of as either emergers or cripples, I could point to at least a dozen different Blue-winged Olives alone I carry in their own separate box.

Step 1: Secure the hook and start your thread: 8/0 is essential for flies this size. I think I can cover most BWO hatches with a size 18 fly, but I always carry size 20s as well.

Step 2: At the front third of the hook, tie in a wing made from a tuft of CDC, tips pointing forward. Stand the wing straight up, building a base in front of it with the thread. Take a few turns around the base of the wing in the manner of a parachute post. (Later you can adjust the cant of the wing with a turn or two of dubbed thread.)

Step 3: Wind the thread back toward the bend. Tie in a tail, the length of the hook, made out of three to five Microfibbets. Take one turn of thread underneath the tail, which is usually enough to separate the fibbets and give them that distinctive mayfly tilt.

Step 4: Twist just enough dubbing onto the thread for making a body as thin as possible. (Sometimes I use only thread for the abdomen, adding just a pinch of dubbing to form a distinct thorax.) Stop the body directly behind the upright wing.

Step 5: Tie in your undersized hackle feather. Of course, I experiment with colors. Before winding the hackle, add a bit more dubbing material and build a thorax that extends in front of the base of the wing.

Step 6: Wind two or three turns of hackle. To tell you the truth, up to this point I might still not have decided whether I was going to wind the hackle conventionally, around the base of the wing parachute style, or mostly in front of or behind the wing. I'm sorry, but I'm just not ready to commit to one single pattern for a hatch as prevalent—and thus potentially idiosyncratic—as Blue-winged Olives.

Step 7: Tie off the hackle, clip excess, wind a head, and add a dab of cement.

Lesson 3

STONED AGAIN

I'm pretty sure it was John Gierach who noted that practically every fly fisher, throughout the West at least, carries around a box of oversized, rarely used flies tied to imitate the region's ubiquitous but devilishly unpredictable stonefly hatches. The bugs in question excite both anglers and trout alike. Stoneflies, when you find them, are generally the largest insects of any season on a river or stream, from the little brown and black stoneflies of winter, to the fabled giant salmonfly of late May and early June, creatures so preposterously large that their imitations—some bold as bats, butterflies, or hummingbirds—require that special stowage that Mr. Gierach noted. For the angler, of course, both the real stoneflies and their diverse imitations inspire a kind of hallucinatory zeal, visions of happening upon a scene of said bugs falling to the water like so many feathers jettisoned from above; while at the same time, foundering in the water, one after another stonefly disappears, inhaled by the river's biggest trout—always the river's biggest trout—feeding as carelessly as drunken sailors.

The point of Mr. Gierach's observation, however, is that relatively few fly fishers find real opportunities to fish such flies. Rarely do any of us encounter these mythic moments of gadwalling lunkers gobbling stoneflies like so many bluefish blasting bait. Many fly fishers can go entire seasons without seeing stoneflies in or around the water—or, certainly, trout feeding on them. And even when we do hit it right—or at least come close enough to justify opening that special box with its tangle of flies big enough to adorn a sombrero—even then we often discover, with something approaching regret, that we still catch most of our fish, big ones included, on the likes of a Soft-Hackled Caddis or a #14 Gold-Ribbed Hare's Ear.

And yet.

Those two words, simple and short, reveal the nearly primordial level at which the magic of stoneflies works on us. And yet. For every fly fisher knows someone, or someone who knows someone, or recalls the occasion himself, or herself, when the stoneflies did fly, and the fish did feed. And yet. I like one told by the father of kids my sons have played sports with over the years, the time on the Deschutes that fish kept grabbing his orange strike indicator above a nymph until he finally switched to a big Sofa Pillow . . . (and here the father's palm is held out, and upon it thumb and forefinger from the other hand suggest a fly tied on a sixteen-penny nail) . . . "and the fish just kept getting bigger. Not longer. Just . . . bigger."

And yet. For in that box of big stoneflies that so many of us carry around, or at least maintain a spot for in our complicated preparations for another stint on the water, there lies the and-yet hope of something that could just happen, even if it has never happened—for us—before. A box of big stoneflies says *I believe.* And even if our faith wavers, we have the flies themselves to remind us what—and yet—might be.

I've tied so many stoneflies, and failed so many times to catch trout with them, that I'm reluctant to dispense information under the pretense of know-how. And, anyway, the whole fantasy of encountering a bodacious stonefly moment includes the associated drama of a bunch of big trout acting dumb. It won't matter what you throw at 'em! But if there is one thing the sport teaches everyone, it's that it's rarely *that* easy. In our dreams we expect logic to loose its terrible grip, while experience teaches us that much of what happened yesterday will happen again today.

One stonefly I have had success with of late, however, is the midsize Skwala Stone of late winter and early spring. Skwalas used to be sort of a secret, the kind of off-season hatch that locals knew about and watched for and now and then caught just right, keeping it all to themselves. In some places, skwalas were not only obscure, they were also misidentified, called little golden or just golden stoneflies, which didn't make much sense, considering the true golden stonefly will generally follow the big salmonflies sometime in early summer. But the two insects, skwalas and golden stones, look more or less the same, and by whatever name guys called them, skwalas could be imitated with a good-sized, tan or yellow-bodied, hairwing dry. Such a fly can make for a memorable day of March fishing, the trout rising willingly to the surface, breaking into view beneath the still-bare willows, proclaiming winter's end as they mistake your faulty imitation for the real thing.

Of course, now there don't seem to be any secrets at all. An angler glimpses a solitary skwala and fuels an online forum. A dozen different websites detail where and when to find your next neighborhood skwala delirium. Pronouncements prompt predictions. Patterns abound. Step right up. See trout eat skwalas *now*.

And yet. The point of this endeavor—casting flies for trout—does seem to be to pay attention and notice what is going on. And a half-dozen rises to your favorite Skwala Stone in March can locate you within a seasonal context as firmly as gray whales, tanagers, or calypso orchids. You may be reminded, once again, that all of this—the fish, the river, the stoneflies—orbits within its own cosmology, your presence here, amidst the splendor, as superfluous as it is to the stars in deep space. By the looks of things, you don't matter. No, really. Not at all.

And yet without the fishing, the stoneflies and trout, some of us are prone to forget such truths.

All of my stonefly patterns, like all of the patterns I tie, are rip-offs of other people's flies and ideas. My Skwala Stone is essentially a Stimulator, Randall Kaufmann's enormously popular, swift-water, crossover pattern, originally designed for Deschutes River salmonflies. Depending on size, color, and density of materials, Stimulators can cover just about any stonefly hatch anywhere, as well as a good many caddis hatches. I like a Stimulator the way I like an Adams or a Hare's Ear. The fly says *bug*, and you can take it from there.

To turn a traditional Stimulator into a Skwala Stone, I make one fundamental change: Instead of elk hair, I use moose mane for the tail and wing. Unlike either elk or deer hair, moose mane rarely flares when secured to the hook, allowing you to create a wing that lies practically flat along the length of the hook. This low-profile, horizontal wing comes closer than the typical flared hair wing in mimicking the adult stonefly, wings at rest, lying atop the water. Of course, the argument made for the more impressive wing on most traditional stonefly patterns has always been that such wings do a better job of representing the vibrant blur of wings when the actual insect flies, most significantly the females releasing their eggs on the water. Yet I'm convinced I see more stoneflies on the water with their wings in the flattened at-rest position—although what trout see in these moments, and how and why they respond as they do, must remain in the realm of conjecture and speculation.

Certainly, moose mane doesn't float as well as either elk or deer hair. Sophisticated modern floatants, however, take care of much of the problem of keeping dry flies where we want them; and, anyway, one complaint many anglers share about the traditional Stimulator is that in slow, flat water, the bushy fly floats too high. Hence, the lower-riding stonefly patterns such as Clark's Stone or even a Mormon Girl. The nearly flat wing of the Skwala Stone can actually suspend the fly directly in the surface film, the bulk of the body submerged, an attitude of vulnerability that I feel demands less risk on the part of a feeding trout. Expecting trout to rise to the surface has always seemed to me more reasonable than that they breach this profound boundary between the media of water and air—although here again I'm venturing into that realm of fishy perceptions, the depths of which I suspect I'm only minimally qualified to fathom.

And yet.

Despite all my reservations, the hackneyed truths and hyperbole, there are some things we do know. I feel this is an important concession. The skwala and other stoneflies, like all varieties of seasonal hatches, offer the opportunity to recognize ourselves as linked to rhythms falling outside the clumsy particulars of school years, holidays, six-month checkups, palm pilots, and daily planners. Like the trout itself, the experienced fly fisher maintains a state of watchful readiness, prepared to abandon himself to the unlikely moment when the biggest trout flies he owns suddenly demand center stage. Even then he knows it's not a sure thing. If it were, he might be happier; but never—when he hits it right—so completely justified by time squandered on the water.

Skwala Stone

Hook: TMC 900BL or Mustad 94845, size 10
Thread: Brown Danville Unwaxed 6/0 Flymaster
Tail: Moose body hair, tied short
Ribbing: Undersized brown hackle
Abdomen: Pale yellow or tan dubbing or synthetic yarn
Wing: Moose mane
Hackle: Brown, palmered over thorax
Thorax: Yellow floss

Tying Notes

Step 1: Secure hook. Unlike most stonefly patterns, the Skwala Stone is tied on a standard dry fly hook, rather than hooks with longer shanks.

Step 2: Clean, stack, and secure the tail. Unlike deer or elk hair, moose body hair lies so straight and flat that I work the thread back toward the tips and then give one good cinch, flaring the hairs slightly rather than trying to avoid the radical flaring of other hairs.

Step 3: Secure the undersized hackle just in front of the tail. Create a slender abdomen using your favorite dubbing material. Leave plenty of room for the wing and thorax. Rib the abdomen with three or four evenly spaced turns of hackle.

Step 4: Clean and stack a slender bundle of moose mane. Tie in a low-profile wing that extends just to the tip of the short tail. Clip the moose mane butts short; cover with an even layer of thread.

Step 5: Tie in a second brown hackle feather just in front of the wing. Tie in a short length of yellow floss. Wind the floss forward, building up the thorax over the moose mane butts. Secure the floss and clip just behind the hook eye.

Step 6: Take two or three turns of hackle over the thorax. Clip excess hackle; finish the head and coat with cement.

Lesson 4

CADDIS PAEAN

The river I fish most is famous for salmonflies.

There's also the ubiquitous blue-winged olive hatch and, on occasion, a pretty good diet of both pale morning and evening duns.

Green drakes and March Browns have their seasons.

The more time you spend on the water, the more hatches you see.

But if you're like me and you fish when you can, not only when the class hatch blooms, you find yourself thinking more and more about caddisflies.

We're talking the blue-collar bugs of the West.

And if you're also like me, and you like to catch fish when you go fishing, you may start thinking caddis before you tie on any other flies, although that might be the sort of simple-minded thinking that garnered you a chance to go fishing in the first place, in the midst of these troubled times.

Of course, nothing new can be written about caddisflies.

Gary LaFontaine exhausted the subject in his monumental treatise, *Caddisflies*.

Shortly before Gary called me, out of the blue, to say he wanted to read a manuscript of mine, I started fishing his Deep and Emergent Sparkle Pupas, patterns I had resisted out of some vague objection to novelty and synthetic materials.

I will not take this opportunity to go into my thoughts about the way the world works.

The Sparkle Pupa caught fish, demonstrating to me the workings of a creative and insightful mind.

There was also a remote, spectral weirdness to Gary LaFontaine's thinking.

Why else would he be interested in publishing a book of mine?

And just like his most famous caddis patterns, Gary seemed void of pretension or guile, utterly lacking in self-consciousness, a quality I admired because of my own inability to shake, as a middle-aged father, the insecurities and self-doubts of a teenager.

At the same time I signed a contract with Greycliff, Gary LaFontaine's publishing company, I found out he was dying.

Closer friends and associates have since shared their respect and admiration.

I was a bit player in a great man's drama.

Which leaves me conjoined in some unfathomable manner to a fraternity of fly fishers circling this mudball like so much cosmic dust, linked by impressions of a fly as pragmatic and elegant as a light bulb, and each one of our own private visions of hungry trout grabbing a swimming caddis rising secretly at the end of a mended line.

I can see I've already gotten ahead of myself.

My intent here is to write a simple account of how caddisflies can play an essential role in the successful trout angler's approach to Western waters.

It is useful to know the stages of the caddisfly lifecycle—egg, larva, pupa, adult—and that most caddis prefer swift, well-oxygenated, riffly water, although the trout that feed on them may often hang out downstream at the head of the pool above which the larvae and pupae reside.

Emerging caddis—that is, the mature pupa headed for the surface to shed its pupal shuck, spread its wings and, if a trout doesn't eat it, fly—are usually good swimmers, making it necessary for trout to grab them aggressively.

Some caddis are also helped to the surface by the formation of gas inside the pupal skin, the impression of which is so accurately represented by the Antron bubble-like overbody of the LaFontaine Sparkle and Emergent Pupa.

Like other aquatic insects, the only real purpose of the adult stage of caddisflies is to mate in the relative safety of flight or streamside foliage, and then for the females to return to the water to lay their eggs, either on the surface or by swimming to the bottom of the river, another risky journey.

None of this is rocket science.

And there's a certain generic quality to most caddisflies and their behavior to allow for a lot of overlap in the fly patterns that represent the different families and even stages of their lifecycle.

As I suggested, this is blue-collar, public school, populist fly fishing.

Leave the airs at the lodge.

Tactics can be as delicate as fishing a #22 spinner fall.

Or as coarse as the bounce of a crappie jig.

And I hope you don't mind, should it come to it, squeezing a little lead on your line.

It was Dave Hughes who opened my eyes to the possibilities of the soft-hackled fly as an elegant and highly effective representation of pupal, emerging, and even egg-laying caddis.

I resisted him as well.

Maybe it was the fact that he wrote clear, articulate, straightforward, informative, how-to books.

That was the last thing I was looking for when I read about fishing.

Don't ask me what I *did* want.

Let's just say I found it in Roderick Haig-Brown, Tom McGuane, Jim Harrison, Russell Chatham, and eventually John Gierach.

And Faulkner.

Besides *Moby Dick*.

Yet at times it did occur to me that I might catch more fish if I knew more about what was going on in the river, and the methods serious fly fishers used to fool trout into biting their flies.

Dave Hughes's *Wet Flies* appealed to me in ways that other technical books didn't.

Perhaps it was the pictures.

Here, finally, were flies I could tie—with a little practice—that spoke to my own sense of impressionism, simplicity, and life.

Plus tradition.

I didn't want to believe I had to represent the exact number of abdominal segments to fish an effective *Rhyacophila* emerger.

Nor, that old-timers would necessarily be "inferior" anglers because they didn't have certain patterns available today.

On the other hand, I recognized certain technological advances in both materials and design.

No doubt there would never be a better surfer than, say, a David Nuuihiwa.

But you put him on a longboard at Jeffreys Bay, even during his prime, and he wasn't going to make it down the line through those long, long barrels that enfold the modern rider for ungodly stretches of time.

Soft Hackles, as we now know them, are the rediscovered secret of the well-versed modern fly fisher.

His or her grandfather would have told you precisely as much.

Presented in and around caddis riffles, your modest Partridge and Green, Partridge and Orange, or Hare's Ear Soft Hackle offer a potent stimulus to holding or feeding trout.

In deft hands it is astonishing what good fish can be teased by a swinging Soft Hackle out of shallow or otherwise seemingly marginal lies.

During periods of genuine caddis emergence, when trout move into a riffle and feed with the slashing abandon of pelagic jacks, the takes to your humble Soft Hackle can be felt deep in the fly angler's forearm and snap even the stoutest of tippets if line is not immediately allowed to peel at a high-pitched rate from the reel.

Whoa, daddy.

It must have been those days last week after the salmonfly circus departed.

Let me explain.

Twilight on a back eddy is another place to fish your caddis flies.

I like them now in pairs.

Slightly modified versions of the Emergent Sparkle Pupa (Krystal Flash or glass bead underbody; peacock herl head) and a Partridge and Something soft hackle.

Or, as surface feeding increases, a lightly dressed #16 Hare's Ear and a slightly smaller grouse-and-Antron-winged Diving or Wet Caddis, or the elegant Starling and Herl.

It's all pretty unsophisticated, despite the convoluted nomenclature.

Presentation *is* the name of the game.

This is the slurping and snout-poking and fish-rolling scenario of my emerging haunting dreams.

Light is fading.

Fish are on the feed.

It's the Caddis Hour.

Good drifts are difficult because of the mixed-up currents.

Brush and steep banks make backcasts tough.

But a long rod can steeple cast or roll cast into the seam beyond the boils, and if you pick up most of your line from the surface you get a decent drift before the flies finally drag.

Leave the cast there a while longer.

You probably can't see exactly where your flies are anyway.

There's a swirl that might or might not have been you.

While you're still thinking about it, your line bows like a kite string, then a dog leash, the reel whines, and upstream a trout that seems slightly smaller than you would imagine, considering the pull, hangs silhouetted in the gauzy night air.

Oh, and make sure your knots are sound.

I seem to have strayed again.

Is this the fault of an undisciplined mind?

The effects of a reprobate life?

Perhaps this is the appeal for me of pitching a brace of retrograde flies into a nondescript riffle or run and snugging up tight to a throbbing take.

My numbers are up this year and I wonder if this June has been better than usual or I've just figured out a few new things.

I did get a copy in winter of Sylvester Nemes's *The Soft-Hackled Fly Addict* from my buddy Ed Simpson in Oceanside, a book that should be looked at if only for its cover ("The 15th color page"), a selection of flies that had better resemble many of the ones in your own caddis fly box.

I mean a whole box of these babies.

I'm also using a dubbing loop to tie the thorax of all of my Gold-Ribbed Hare's Ears, spinning in the very darkest fur and guard hairs from the mask to get the effect of larval legs and the head.

The use of a dubbing loop brings to mind the work of the great Polly Rosborough, not because I learned it from his book, *Tying and Fishing the Fuzzy Nymphs*, but because the concept of fuzzy nymphs set the standard for my impressions of a successful subsurface bug.

Only when I began using a dubbing loop was I able to get *that* look.

Before using the dubbing loop, my Hare's Ears were just another nymph.

Now I look at them and think *caddis*.

Apparently trout do, too.

Which may or may not be what this is all about.

Have I been getting more fish this summer because I know more?

Tying better flies?

Reading better books?

Or is it simply a matter of noting that caddisflies are in and on the water day in and day out, all summer long, and if I keep flies that look and behave like them in the river, too, I catch more fish?

I do know it helps to go fishing.

Perhaps such insight proves *I'm* pupating at last.

I also think it important to recognize you don't put all the pieces of this puzzle together overnight.

I like to fish my caddis flies in the fast stuff, the deep, the shallow, and the slow.

One thing leads to another.

A trout in summer is never startled by a little caddis.

There's more to it than that, on your river and mine.

But all summer long they're out there, the trout and the caddis on which they dine.

Selected Caddisflies

Deep Sparkle Pupa
Emergent Sparkle Pupa
Gold-Ribbed Hare's Ear
Partridge and Green Soft Hackle
Partridge and Orange Soft Hackle
Diving Caddis
Starling and Herl

Lesson 5

PARTRIDGE AND GREEN

Halfway up the mountain I quit. Wind and waves of rain rushed in at harsh angles, obliterating resolve. Lightning. Rolls of thunder. Mud on the trail grew dangerously slick—in other stretches, sticky as warm peanut butter. Straps from my float tube worked against my shoulders like naked shins. Those football-shaped rainbows I'd been thinking about for a decade, ever since a buddy finally got around to tracking down the rumor he'd carried for years, those spectral trout would just have to wait.

The river rose. By the time I returned, refreshed if not actually relaxed, wadeable riffles had disappeared beneath dark, treacherous runs. Rocks normally exposed now revealed themselves as twisted currents and terse, sucking whirlpools. You could see into the river but just barely. The texture beneath the surface seemed a shadow the thickness of blood.

There were salmonflies in the sage and head-high grasses—but not in numbers large enough to generate the sort of confidence I need to tie on a fly the size of an owl hatchling. Not yet. And there was also the matter of those illusive, stillwater rainbows. Who can risk his failures in pair? So I based my fly selection on this: When the water rises and darkens, or drops and clears, or stays pretty much the same, and trout remain sequestered beneath the surface, offering no visible clues as to what they might be feeding on, I find it prudent, if not also elegant, to rely on tactics that have nearly always worked before, stroking the river with a well-greased leader and the swing of a soft-hackled fly.

Partridge and Green. The name itself recalls a simpler time, when flies were often designated solely by the materials from which they were made. Gold-Ribbed Hare's Ear. Copper and Peacock. Starling and Herl. Now we have the Bitch Creek Nymph, Turck Tarantula, Chernobyl Ant, and Gulper Special. Of course, a look back into fly catalogs from any era, no matter how remote, will make clear that fly tyers have inevitably fallen prey to a brand of poetic license that rivals Linnaeus's own Latinate nomenclature. Who was Lady Caroline, anyway?

The fly in question, Partridge and Green, is a model of simplicity: the floss body, nondescript fur thorax, two or three turns of wispy partridge feather. I also like to rib the silk abdomen with a strand of fine gold oval or round tinsel, suggesting the appearance of segmentation that I believe makes all impressionistic flies more effective. Maybe. Maybe not. For at the heart of all soft-hackled patterns, an entire genre of flies that comes again and again into style, as if pinstripes and pleated pants, at the center of soft hackles lie the quixotic elements of artful design that speak more to alchemy and shape shifting than to the axiomatic claims of hard science.

What does—or doesn't—the fly represent? The common wisdom indicates an approximation of the green rock worm (*Rhyacophila)*, either the caseless, free-living larvae, or the pupal stage of this widespread caddis, so prevalent in the swift, rough, riffly freestone waters of the West. Some genericists, myself included, also believe the fly, like most soft hackles, can suggest the egg-laying females as they return to the water, swimming or crawling for the bottom and, when finished, swimming back or drifting to the surface—all the while fair game for feeding trout.

It is, of course, this all-of-the-above nonspecificity of the Partridge and Green and other soft hackles that recommend them so highly to a breed of fly fisher who believes as much in the behavior and impression of his flies as he does in the details of their appearance. Adult rhyacophilids, in some places referred to simply as the green sedge, fall into but another of the basic categories of caddisflies that dominate summer hatches on many Western rivers and streams. The so-called green of the rhyacopholid adult becomes, by way of impression, merely dark. The myriad tan caddises are called, predictably, light. Rhyacophilids are also a medium-sized caddis: that is, "about a #14." Small caddis translate into a size 16 or 18; any smaller and fly fishers will refer to them as something like "those tiny little suckers," the disdain in the voice inspired by fears of trying to tie, in fading light, a size 20–24 fly to a hair-thin tippet.

But wait: In mentioning the common association between the Partridge and Green and the family of rhyacopholid caddis, I may have given the wrong impression. For this same fly could very well also represent a stage of some other type of caddis, be it the hydropsychids, the brachycentrids, or the glossosmatids. Or no caddis at all. Which is really why fly fishers of a certain bent return again and again to patterns like the Partridge and Green and other soft hackles: Such flies suggest a mix of foodstuff on which trout feed, be it emerging, egg-laying, or drowned stoneflies, mayflies, or caddis, things that trout see and feed on day in and day out, and that, given half a chance, trout will accept again as viable fare.

Granted, fooling trout with flies is usually harder than merely tying on a generic soft hackle and tossing it in the water. Usually a lot harder. But a pattern like the Partridge and Green (or, say, the March Brown Spider, a Hare's Ear Soft Hackle, or the countless unnamed soft-hackled patterns that fly fishers create on their own) provides the fly fisher looking for trout a pattern he knows can work—even when he finds no sign of feeding trout—so that he keeps his fly in the water, the only place any fly will actually catch a fish.

Partridge and Green

Hook: Standard wet fly or dry fly, size 12–16
Thread: Green Pearsall's Gossamer silk or Brown 6/0
Body: Green floss
Rib: Fine oval gold tinsel
Thorax: Hare's mask fur
Hackle: Gray or brown partridge

Tying Notes

Step 1: Secure hook. I tie all my soft hackles on both stout standard wet fly hooks and fine-wired dry fly hooks so that I can fish the pattern at various levels in the water column in various speeds of current.

Step 2: Start your thread. Soft-hackle advocates Sylvester Nemes and Dave Hughes suggest the use of Pearsall's Gossamer silk, in the appropriate colors, for traditional floss-bodied flies, eliminating the need to tie in a different body material.

Step 3: Both Nemes and Hughes also recommend tying in the hackle first. Hold the hackle at the hook eye, stem toward the bend, concave side toward you. Strip the fibers off the top side, then tie in the feather by the stem, leaving it to be wrapped later. Wind the thread to the hook bend.

Step 4: Secure a short length of tinsel. Tie in your floss. (If you are using Pearsall's silk, you will build the body out of thread alone.) Advance your thread; create a slender, even floss abdomen. Rib the abdomen with three or four evenly spaced turns of tinsel.

Step 5: Wax your thread and twist on a pinch of hare's mask fur. Build a small, distinct thorax with a couple of turns of dubbing, leaving plenty of room for the hackle.

Step 6: Hook your hackle pliers to the very tip of the partridge feather. Wrap the hackle, starting from the eye of the hook and working your way back to the thorax. Two or three turns is enough. Then secure the hackle, winding the thread through it and up to the hook eye. Clip the excess hackle and tie off the thread.

LESSON 6

TWO FLIES

I hesitate to offer advice. My credentials, or lack thereof, are a matter of public record. Of late, I feel the equivalent of fly fishing's red-haired step-child. Every opinion I voice raises suspicion, eyebrows, debate.

But now and then I do happen upon a fly or two that works. Not that I've ever created one that was actually new. I recall the wonderful listing in *Flies for Steelhead* of Bob Griese's distinct, but in no way unusual soft-hackled wet fly, the Herniator, a pattern he claims to have named after being admitted to the hospital for a hernia caused by the strain of catching so many steelhead the day the fly was introduced. New colors, but hardly a new fly. Still, there's a man after my own heart.

New flies are rarely new. We tinker, nudge, recycle. We modify and tweak. We fiddle and fool around. Who does, in fact, want to crank out a hundred dozen of the exact same fly? Why not employ the same techniques the government uses for stamps, currency, and schemes for educating our young?

I think most of us fell into the game for something other than that. It's not about duplicating the other guy. We want to think, examine, discover, explore. We want to fit pieces together on our own. We want to come away from a good fish believing we had a problem—catching one!—that we just solved.

You would be hard-pressed to come up with a fly more ubiquitous than the Gold-Ribbed Hare's Ear. For that reason alone, I might have ignored it for years, if there wasn't also the minor detail that anytime I happened to tie on the pattern, I caught squat. The fact that my nymphing techniques were as sophisticated as bowling strategies would also argue innocence for my failures when fishing this famous fly. Let's just say I knew about the pattern, had tied up my share, had even fished them. But they were forever descending into that fly box netherworld where one encounters queer experiments, Matuka streamers, navel-lint nymphs, and that set of keys from an old Volkswagen van.

How all this changed I can't exactly say. But sometime during the summer, when I found myself tying Hare's Ears by the dozen, not just a few here and there, but entire rows of them, parading like infantry side by side, I realized I have come to rely on the pattern—or at least my version of it—more than any other fly in my subsurface box. More than the Stone Nymph. More than my soft hackles. More than all the sophisticated caddis stages combined. And this a pattern that a year before I considered a "classic" only because it was easy to tie.

It didn't help, late in the season, when my pal Fred caught a steelhead on this same pattern, the fly tied on a size 16 hook, no less. By then he had started calling it my Wild Hare, or sometimes his own, depending on the subtle inflections of material produced spontaneously at the vise. Needless to say, neither of us wants to give the other too much credit. This kind of pattern can make your teeth ache, such confidence do you have in it when short-line nymphing through promising water. Fished shallow on the swing, or even retrieved as an emerger, this is a fly that trout often hit on the run. Many of those marching dozens this summer were tied to replace casualties of heavy-handed strikes or other instances of operator failure.

But is it really a new pattern? Or did I just finally figure out how to fish it? Or did I start casting this fly in earnest when I did things to it to make it "my own"? I do recall the moment, while showing bugs in a net to a group of students, when I first noticed just how closely the prevalent caddis larvae resembled that same size 16 Wild Hare I had been using with such success. I was especially impressed with the slender, segmented abdomen, the pronounced anal hooks, and the dark, leggy thorax, all of which seemed mirrored, if only impressionistically, in my own scraggly pattern.

Wild Hare

Hook: TMC 3761, size 12–18
Thread: Brown 6/0
Tail: Small tuft of stacked deer hair
Abdomen: Light tan or gray "furry" dubbing from a natural hare's mask
Rib: Fine gold Mylar or varnished French tinsel
Thorax: Darkest fur and guard hairs from the hare's mask, first spun into a dubbing loop

Tying Notes

I aim for a slender profile, more along the lines of a Pheasant Tail Nymph. Keep the tail stubby and sparse. I store the light-colored, furry dubbing from the hare's mask in one container, the spiky, dark stuff in another. Twist on just enough abdomen to hide the thread. Two or three wraps of tinsel is enough. I want my dubbing loop to hold lots of guard hairs. When I wrap the thorax, it's almost like winding a very short soft hackle. I brush back the guard hairs as I take two or three turns forward, leaving just enough room to tie off behind the hook eye.

I was on the Deschutes, trying to figure out my new hand-me-down Spey rod, when a guy pulled up in the campsite next to me, dragging enough gear to launch an assault on a polar ice cap. His wife got out and tried to direct him into the parking spot. The tongue of the four-wheel trailer kept bottoming out behind the tottering, garage-sized camper. You know it's touch and go when the woman keeps shouting, "All you gotta do is . . . !" and the guy's hollering back, "You don't understand!"

I didn't have a lot of sympathy. Just how much gear do you need, anyway? Besides, I had my own problems, trying to learn how to wave that fifteen-foot stick without strangling myself with fly line.

When he finally got his camp put together, my new neighbor came over and apologized for all the ruckus. "I was starting to lose my patience," he said. "She just didn't see what was going on." He nodded, eyes rolling, in the direction of the camper, a gesture as old as language itself. Then he noticed my Spey rod leaning up against the bushes beside my van.

Turns out he was the genuine article, years spent on the Snake, the Clearwater, the Grande Ronde. For the past decade, all of his steelhead fishing had been with two-handed rods. "It was a big deal in the eighties," he reported. "Now everybody uses them."

He asked about my flies. I was feeling relatively good about such matters, having raised a single fish four different times that morning before finally getting it to grab, only to miss the hookup, probably by pulling the fly out of its mouth instead of first allowing it to turn downstream. There's always a reason. Still, for one of the few times in my life, I had evidence that flies I was fishing could move steelhead. The first had been a lightly dressed Coal Car, the one that finally got the grab, a fancy Spade, right out of an article in a magazine. After the unsuccessful take, I switched to a smaller version of the same pattern, a line of logic that failed the remedy by blown attempt at hooking my first steelhead on my new, third-hand rod.

"So. You're using small flies."

We went and looked at his. I had never seen anything quite like them. At least not in the box of someone who was used to actually catching steelhead. They were beautiful. They were simple. They were tied on big, fine-wire hooks, 2s and 4s, with slender bodies only half the length of the hook and sparse, equally proportioned deer-hair wings and loosely spun heads. I had toyed with Muddlers—especially Bill McMillan's classic Steelhead Caddis—the previous season, my first as a genuine steelheader, and although I caught a few fish on them, I was far from confident in their alleged effectiveness, often because I couldn't get them to fish in the surface the way I wanted them to.

But these flies spoke to me in a new way. I could see exactly how they were meant to be fished at the end of a well-mended line, swinging through the surface film, controlled as only flies can be controlled by the matchless efficacy of a rod as long as a flag pole. A voice inside me said *Yes*.

And for once in my life, that voice was right. Over two-dozen steelhead in a six-week stretch—with at least twice as many rises and grabs—left me jittery with success. I had a fly that worked! I tied the short, slender bodies out of floss, employing black and bright butt color combinations from Randal Kaufmann's popular Deschutes patterns. I ribbed all of the bodies with the narrowest of flat silver tinsels. The crux of the fly became the spun deer-hair head with but a dozen or two strands straying back over the body, rarely extending beyond the point of the hook. After experimenting, I ended up using the softest deer hair. I didn't like the fly to skate on top of the water, finding it more effective, instead, waking in the surface. At times, after a fish or two, nearly all of the hair broke off, leaving a nearly wingless fly that would still stimulate rises. Often, I took these flies back to the vise, stripped what was left of the deer hair, and simply spun on more. That tactic, plus the fact that the pattern is basically a recycling of others' ideas, prompted the less than elegant name, which should secure the fly's anonymity, an appropriate rank in the sport's crowded lexicon.

Remuddled

Hook: Wilson dry fly, size 6–10, or TMC 7989, size 4–8
Thread: Black 6/0
Butt: Either yellow, red, orange, or two of these colors paired, one-sixteenth to one-eighth of an inch long
Body: Black silk floss or nylon/rayon UNI-Floss
Rib: Fine flat silver tinsel
Head and wing: Loosely spun soft deer hair, with approximately one- to two-dozen strands left extending back over the body, butts trimmed to form the head

Tying Notes

The body of this fly is barely thicker than the hook; I layer the floss only enough to maintain color when the fly is wet. I now use only genuine tinsel, not Mylar, because the latter rarely holds together beyond a single grab or fish. I experimented with turkey quill underwings a la McMillan's Steelhead Caddis and the original Muddler, but I found the fly to be just that much bulkier and less effective, so I eliminated what came to seem an unnecessary step. The trick with the deer hair is to get an even distribution of hair completely around the hook. Fred, a professional tyer, holds the tuft of stacked hair at a forty-five degree angle to the hook, tips pointed downward toward the point. He then takes two loose turns of thread before finally cinching tight. The hair usually revolves all the way around the hook, flaring evenly throughout. If I'm not happy with the look, I do it all over again, if only to give myself complete confidence in the fly, an aspect probably just as important as any of the actual attributes of a steelhead fly.

Lesson 7

LITTLE OLIVE BUGGER

My son is twelve years old and afraid of water. Not so frightened that he won't go fishing, wading knee deep over slippery freestone through heavy, capricious riffle. But ever since he was a toddler, Patrick's had that look in his eyes that says if you lower him into the deep end, or drop him in the middle of a lake, it will not be a pretty picture.

I take all the blame. Mostly, we've just never spent enough time goofing off in swimming pools; around rivers, lakes, and streams; or, most significantly, at the beach. The imperative remains inflexible: *We're here to fish!* Yet somehow I also want to link this negligence to the long decline of my marriage, a disheartening process that embraced a goodly portion of my second son's early childhood. Hanging out at water's edge does seem to me a family activity—at least in healthy, functioning families; while securing a haven in books, video games, friendships, or even solitude has probably felt vastly more important, in the face of another family shitstorm, than perfecting one's crawl stroke or dead man's float.

There was also the time, when we did manage a family outing on the water, that the canoe capsized in heavy current sweeping against a dock, beneath which canoe, children, and well-intentioned parents disappeared like so much jettisoned cargo. Moments before this mishap, when it became apparent to me from the stern that we had misread the current and the placement of the dock (a configuration, we found out later, due to a change in the river during winter high water), I had stated emphatically to my wife that she needed to paddle as hard as she could. She turned in the bow seat and began to argue a different course of action—so I guess we weren't exactly an episode of *The Brady Bunch* that day on the Calapooya River. A sentence or two into my wife's case, questions, of course, were no longer an issue: We approached the dock broadside, and when we pressed our paddles against the weathered timbers, the upstream gunwale tilted into the current and the canoe immediately filled with water. The canoe, and my family, vanished. Pressed tight by the current to the edge of the dock, I held myself long enough to realize I wasn't strong enough to push against the current and climb free of the river, and then I looked left and right, saw no one, and thought, *Okay, here goes.*

The part my son can laugh about, more so today, is when he noticed, floating just downstream from the bobbing wreckage of his family, the unbitten apple his big brother had asked for moments before I realized our error in direction and suggested to my wife that she get her paddle in gear. "There was Riley's apple," he likes to point out, relishing the juvenile irony. "The only thing we lost!" The rest of our gear lay trapped inside the overturned canoe. Myself, I also recollect images of my ex-wife dragging herself out of the river and back to the van, enacting a wet T-shirt performance of the sort that would have been rare during the best of times. Such nuances, however, are probably lost to a child who has just escaped—if only theoretically—his own drowning, impressions of which were certainly strengthened by the panic coursing, at that moment, through his veins.

All of which contrives to trouble my son when I propose we try fishing from float tubes. I tell him to get over it. Such pronouncements, however, from a father still unable to dislodge the bitter pill of his failed marriage, lack conviction. And, anyway, with a decade or so still left to consider the possibility of procuring, say, a drift boat, I need to make sure I haven't permanently alienated one of only a handful of fishing partners who would put up with my nonsense should the occasion arise.

We end up borrowing a second float tube. All winter I make motions to spring for an outfit to complement my own, but on each occasion Patrick suggests we wait, that my teacher's salary minus hefty child support payments forwarded to the boys' mother might be better spent some other way. I recognize his game. As long as we own only one float tube, Patrick is free from facing his deepwater demons, relieved of pressures to climb in and set sail.

Still, he is tempted. The previous summer, during a one hundred-degree heat wave, we ventured up to a cluster of pothole lakes, seeking relief from the heat while, in the process, flushing a few brook trout. Both notions proved marginally prescient. Despite bugs, the altitude eased our discomfort, and though we did find them, the fish possessed the grave profile of undernourished survivors in shallow, eutrophic lakes. I caught sparrow-sized brookies on an unweighted Hare's Ear, finally getting Patrick interested in taking a turn in the float tube. We had trouble securing my oversized flippers to the soles of his boot-footed waders, and while trying to propel himself through the shallows, he felt one fin pull free. I helped him struggle out of the tube; we readjusted buckles and straps. Wading through muck and weeds, Patrick maintained his balance by resting his weight on the float tube. Then he stumbled, went down, and in a clever maneuver probably impossible to replicate, he ended up beneath the overturned float tube, trapped there for several heartbeats, his rod projecting as if the antenna of some enormous, squashed bug.

Yet there remained a moment, sometime before this pratfall, when Patrick experienced the sudden sensation of breaking free of the bottom of the lake, that seductive thrill of finding oneself, as if released from gravity, floating atop the water—the closest thing to flying anyone gets. He liked that. Liked it enough that he did engage in the winter discussions about allocation of our sorely reduced fly fishing budget, stretched to the breaking point should we decide to get a second float tube and appropriately sized fins.

We chose not to. I found deals, instead, on Patrick's first pair of neoprene waders, new fly lines all around, plus sink tips for lakes, a couple extra reel spools, all that fly tying material—the usual assortment of stuff that does in fact constitute necessary equipment if you're going to play the game for real. Which had come to seem, to me, the only way to play it, after fifteen years, while married, of trying to convince myself that there are other things more important in this world than fly fishing.

The float tube we borrow is nicer than mine. The other reason I decide I should use it, and not Patrick, soon escapes me. Maybe something about replacement costs should anything go wrong, a greater possibility, apparently, for an undersized twelve-year-old than for a chubby, middle-aged man.

Up at the lake, an irrigation reservoir restricted to flies and lures, we put up rods and climb into our waders and haul our tubes and fins down to water's edge, a decidedly different approach than the usual wading caper. I resist the urge to holler "Anchors aweigh!" Patrick has grown quiet, his gaze sweeping the rippled blue surface, a light chop pushed by breeze in our faces. *How deep is it?* his eyes ask—as if it matters once you're in over your head.

Yet as soon as he settles into the sling of the float tube's seat, suspended, as it were, from the skin of the ruffled blue lake, a look of amused relaxation passes over Patrick's face. This isn't going to be nearly as hard as fighting the current of a brawling river, bushwhacking along stream's tangled edge, or walking, walking, walking—through rattlesnakes, heat waves, and poison oak—to that unimaginably fecund fishing hole, somewhere just around the bend, that his father always has his far-flung sights on.

Still, there is the matter of propelling these things. Patrick leans back, the tips of his fins jutting into view. He tries kicking this way and that, pivoting back and forth as if a teenager checking out girls from atop a stool at a fifties diner. He glances over at me; clearly he has been had. Relegated to the old-style inner-tube type float tube, he experiences firsthand the inferior handling of the circular design in comparison to the more sophisticated U-boat we borrowed. I look away, concentrating on my line, stretched out in front of me as I kick backwards across the water. *Oh well*, I think. *Either him or me.*

But he has his fly in the water, the very best of my Little Olive Buggers, a pattern I still fiddle with enough to rank some better than others. Not that trout, often stocked, in a mid-altitude reservoir, seem to care. Dragged behind a float tube on the end of a sink-tip line, or cast, allowed to sink, and retrieved, the fly, in whatever permutation, produces a higher percentage of fish I catch on lakes than all my other stillwater patterns combined. Of course, a Little Olive Bugger is often the first fly I tie on if I don't see fish feeding on the surface. Once there, affixed to my tippet, this is the fly that usually begins catching fish, at which point I'm reluctant to switch to a pattern of a different kind.

Maybe it is Patrick's erratic, swiveling progress across the lake, a course as kinky as a caddisfly's mating flight; maybe it is the suddenly relaxed attitude, an almost nonchalant presentation of his unevenly swimming fly; or maybe, just maybe, the angling gods do favor children of fathers who try to appear, in the name of sport, less selfish than they really are.

But for whatever reason, Patrick hooks the first fish of the day, lands it smartly atop the float-tube netting suspended above his submerged lap, and he continues to outcatch me throughout the sunshot morning—although we never, ever, keep track of numbers closely enough to qualify as an accurate tally. Unless, I suppose, you're the one getting skunked.

Or, maybe, Patrick just gets lucky—a notion all but heretical in these times of technical wizardry promulgated within the sport. He certainly doesn't always make it look easy. Despite their cocktail posture, float tubes present a number of challenges, especially to anglers new to the equipment. The big question, obviously, is where to set anything down. Rods—complete with reels, lines, and the rest of it—are not the only items float-tubers lose to the bottom of lakes. Cameras, sunglasses, Pakistani needle-nose pliers, those sexy English-made aluminum fly boxes, with flies—any of it can disappear if it's not buoyant or somehow tied down as you're swallowed by the excitement of feeding fish or merely bob bob bobbing along.

I know.

Halfway through the morning the breeze stiffens, confining us to a narrow strip of water along the bouldered dam. It doesn't seem to make a difference. Fish take our Little Olive Buggers whether we troll them or retrieve, a few spirited native cutthroats, their adipose fins unclipped, but mostly hatchery-grown rainbows, eight to fourteen inches, several which share the ghostly pallor of dead fish lifted from ice. *Not exactly The Last Great Trout Place*, I think. But it occurs to me, as well, that maybe that's been my mistake from the start, believing we need to always skirt the edge, stalk the most challenging water, when what a son is is just a boy who would like to fool around on the water, playing with sticks and string and even goofy rubber rafts, while maybe catching a few fish, besides.

Back near shore, the wind now painting the lake a paler, avian blue, Patrick guides another fish to hand. He hoists it into view, a wriggling slash of silver, then grabs hold of the fish and grips it to the front of his waders. He struggles to free the fly.

"You need some help?" I call from a cast away.

"I've got it."

Behind him, glaciers hang like sad laundry from eleven thousand feet of volcanic rubble, challenging the claim that this is anywhere but paradise. And it strikes me, too, that Patrick is suddenly no longer afraid of the water. He will be, again, I imagine, some other time. But not just now. He's got his hands full—which seems to me the very best way to get over our deepest fears.

Still struggling with the fish, Patrick, in wraparound sunglasses and Sherlock Holmes headgear, offers the impression of a boy with no idea, at the moment, that there's a world beyond the sphere of his immediate experience. Maybe I haven't done such a bad job after all.

"Here, let me help!" I holler, turning my back to Patrick so that I can head his way.

"I've got it!" he repeats. Although at the rate he's going I'm afraid, watching over my shoulder, we might be taking this one home.

Then suddenly the fish spasms, falls from Patrick's hands, and flops into the lake, leaving Patrick with his Little Olive Bugger, displayed between thumb and forefinger, the fly already snapped from his line.

"There," he says, looking over at me. "That's one way to finish the day."

Together we spin around, pointing our backs toward shore.

LITTLE OLIVE BUGGER

Hook: TMC 5263, size 10–12
Thread: Black 6/0
Tail: Olive marabou or yellow grizzly marabou with or without a few strands of olive Krystal Flash
Rib: Fine copper wire, optional
Body: Dark olive Possum Plus or similar dubbing
Hackle: Olive India hen back or similar soft hackle

Tying Instructions

Step 1: Secure hook in the vise and start thread.

Step 2: Tie in tail materials so that they extend past the bend of the hook, about the length of the hook shank. I waffle on the Krystal Flash: Is your faith in the attraction qualities of sparkle or in more drab, lifelike coloration? I do like dyed grizzly or any other multitoned materials, as they mimic, in my eyes, the uneven hues and segmentation of most living creatures.

Step 3: Tie in a short length of copper wire just in front of the tail. Because I like the look of tidily wound hackle, I sometimes skip the wire ribbing, even while knowing that I then risk having the hackle unravel if its stem is severed by a toothy take.

Step 4: Prepare the hackle feather by holding it tip down, bright side out, and stripping the fibers from the side to your right. Tie in the half-stripped feather by the tip. Leave it there, with the ribbing material, to palmer forward after you wind the body.

Step 5: Wax the thread and spin on a slender noodle of dubbing material. Wind an even body about twice the thickness of the hook, quite unlike the body of typical Woolly Buggers, tied with chenille. The palmered hen hackle is what actually gives the body of the fly its substance and bulk.

Step 6: Wind the half-stripped hackle feather forward, maintaining an angle that keeps the fibers swept back along the hook. If you use India hen back feathers, the hackle will start off mottled and fairly free of web near the tip and then become progressively webbier as you wind toward the stem, eventually appearing much like marabou, a transformation that I take full advantage of. Make two or three tightly spaced turns of this marabou-like material just behind the head of the fly. Tie off and clip excess.

Step 7: If you are ribbing the fly, carefully wind the copper forward, trying not to disturb those neatly arranged, rearward-sweeping hackle fibers. Because I hackle the fly with a half-stripped feather, I try to keep from squashing as many fibers as possible. Do the fish care? Tie off the wire at the head of the fly and clip the excess.

Step 8: Build an even, tidy head with the thread, whip finish, and cover with head cement.

LESSON 8

MIDGES

I used to be afraid of midges. The fishing I associated with these inde-
corous bugs seemed draped in its own dark logic, tinged with secrets
held deep beneath the surface of waters both still and, at times, unclean.
Midges are, after all, essentially mosquitoes—true flies (Diptera) but
without the penetrating proboscises. I recalled the dapping we did in the
westslope Sierra drainages above Shaver and Huntington lakes, dancing
a size 18 Mosquito knotted to six feet of level leader in brook trout-
choked meadow streams while the real bugs whirled and screamed about
us, turning our hands and faces into tortured lumpy red flesh, no matter
the amount of *Cutter*'s or *Off* we lathered on ourselves. By the time I
could manage a reasonable loop in my forward cast, I felt entitled to more
refined traditions of the sport, casting over hatches of elegant mayflies or
oscillating caddis rather than swarms of malarial bloodsuckers. Midges,
all in all, seemed as charming as gnats, fleas, or no-see-ums, the latter the
pesky biting flies that have driven surfers from beaches in Mexico and
Central America when nothing else can—not even bandits, *federales*, or
intestinal disorders.

Then there was the size. Not all midges, of course, are small: My
friend Fred Trujillo ties up tens of dozens of those half-inch long ice
cream cone midges for customers headed to the Kamloops lakes of British
Columbia. And this spring I cast over shallow weed beds for two-foot-
long rainbows alongside a fellow using a green midge tied onto a hook
large enough from which to hang a coffee mug. But mostly midges are

tiny insects, imitated on hooks the size and breadth of eyelashes. Once, for kicks, I piled a hundred midge flies, size 22, on top of a dime; the neat little heap recalled a quarter-teaspoon of black pepper for seasoning a favorite jerky recipe, or a pile of cigarette tobacco loosed, long ago, from an unfiltered Camel before being mixed with something stronger. Imagining tying such tiny flies to the end of a hair-like tippet—especially in day's fading light—forces many anglers to confront the limits of their otherwise adequate vision. Those of us no longer new to less exotic disciplines and the routines of domestic life may also be inclined to question other aspects of our declining physical powers.

Yet if you fish anywhere in the West, sooner or later you will understand the necessity of coming to terms with the ubiquitous midge. I'm thinking, especially, of the multitude of tailwater reaches that stretch from the foot of dams built to stem the flow of the region's limited agricultural waters. Trout feed on midges between hatches of other insects, when other food sources aren't available, or when conditioned by angling pressure to avoid larger flies, both natural and artificial. As Gary LaFontaine pointed out in discussing the effectiveness of a fly like the Adams, a midge pupa is never wrong: That is, trout will nearly always accept a midge as plausible fare, rarely rejecting it as unlikely or too good to be true. And there are times, of course, when trout feed exclusively on midges, even on one stage of a midge's life; and at such times casting anything other than a midge pattern—or casting any fly you can actually see on the water—will soon seem as futile as trying to fool fish with a beachball tied to a length of baling wire.

Now I'm going to lie. It shouldn't really matter, because all I'm tweaking is a name, calling someplace different than it appears on maps. It's not that the river is a secret; you've heard about it, although you probably haven't been there yet. Those who have are maintaining unusual restraint; no one wants to be known as the guy who divulged the inside dope, no matter the notoriety. And, anyway, we all recognize the long tradition of writers masking the names of cherished or pristine waters, a practice that still seems relatively innocent when set against the painful self-confessions of these therapeutically public times.

Call it Wolf River. The name, though fake, recalls a distant era, remote as the animals of those all but forgotten times. Condor Creek? Grizzly Meadows? Wouldn't it be something, too, if one day—should we turn this thing all around—we have names from a bygone, vaguely remembered era that include Aqueduct Falls, Ditch Creek, Reservoir Fork, Strip Mall Pond, Interstate Channel? Wouldn't it be something if we honored our restored waters with the irony of wisdom gained from this epoch during which streams and rivers and oceans alike have suffered our irrepressible greed and abuse?

Dam Strait.

Yet the animal in question is not the all but lost predator of the West, but instead big brown trout that only behave as if they were wild, marauding canines. The fact that brown trout themselves are a perversion of the region's natural order, thriving in the so-called Wolf River solely because of an artificial environment created by tailwaters below an irrigation dam, merely confirms a growing sense that the sport of fly fishing is no longer innocent—if it ever was—of problems that afflict the West today. The dam that created this remarkable tailwater trout fishery is the exact same one that stopped salmon from continuing upstream and spawning in Nevada. *Salmon in Nevada.* Get your minds around that, my lovelies. This is supposed to be a quiet, half-hidden piece about midge fishing, with passing mention—if I get there—of fooling gnarly brown trout with a fly hardly bigger than a fleck of dandruff. But suddenly it seems just as important to recommend we all pay attention to the fish at our feet today, the waters in which they swim and why, and the decisions each one of us makes, moment by moment, to create a world that retains some semblance to one in which the sport of fly fishing might still even matter.

Either that, I guess, or get it while you can. And on the Wolf, for example, that means getting good at fishing tiny midges in the slick gray waters of winter or in the pale, deceptive light at break of day. These are honest fish, I tell myself, when I see the chilling sight of trout the breadth of biceps leaving dimples in the surface of the river that extend to dimensions as if the result of depth charges. They will take a midge, I argue faithfully, if you present it to them as a midge should be presented—although what that means exactly remains open to interpretation. Hence, you have sport rather than "Recipes for Success." Hence, you accept the quiet desperation when, somewhere within the ring of the rise, you feel the miniscule hook hard against toothy flesh, and you snug up just firmly enough to persuade the trout that its midge feeding has gone amiss, an assertion on your part that may come to seem, during the brown trout's full fury, an act of pronounced hubris.

If there's a trick to midge fishing it's this: Find a pattern you believe in and then keep your fly in the water, attempting to replicate the behavior of the insects at the stage on which trout are feeding. Sound familiar? In other words, in my mind it's a presentation game: "Midge pattern" is all but an oxymoron; the flies tied to represent both midge larvae or pupae, the stages of the insect's life on which trout usually feed, are really as simple as any a tyer will produce. Ed Engle talks about no-frills guide-fly midges created entirely out of thread. Most of us approach the vise with a need to create something slightly more sophisticated. Yet I'm inclined to believe I could do much of my midge fishing with a bare hook—although that's a theory, unlike those as severe about dog- and child-rearing, that I haven't yet had the audacity to test.

The pattern I've settled on, anyway, has nothing to recommend itself over a dozen others, besides the fact that it works and I believe in it. There are, nonetheless, a few critical elements to the fly worth noting. For one, the thread body (that's 8/0 material, nothing larger) allows for the slenderest of profiles, crucial, I believe, for imitating these slightest of wormy critters. (Would a painted hook—ribbed with copper wire—work just as well?) At the same time, I do prefer a dubbed head rather than one built solely out of thread, as it's the pupal stage of the midge that I find most effective, and with a small twist of dubbing you can approximate the larger thorax and head area with a clear indication of wing pads. I also like how you can grease the dubbed head to get your fly to hang beneath the surface film, that curious attitude of the natural that a pattern like the old Serendipity so effectively mimics. Yet I'd be hard pressed to argue the superiority of any midge pattern—be it a Thread Midge Larva, Engle's Miracle Nymph, the Disco Midge or Larva Lace Midge or the tried and true Brassie. The trick, as I mentioned before, is presentation, not representation.

More than anything else, I like to fish a midge pupa down and across, not quite on the swing, but at that spot on the end of a straight leader where the line influences the fly without actually affecting its drift. This is subtle almost beyond words. But for anglers who have explored the sophisticated presentation possibilities of soft-hackled surface flies, those in which the fly approaches fish before line and leader, the down-and-across approach to midge fishing is merely an extension of practiced techniques. We are talking here about the tiniest of wet flies on a microfine tippet; you can't drag the fly, but you must strive to keep line and leader one iota short of taut. At this point your midge is swimming; it looks alive. At the same time, a midge at the end of a nearly straight line allows the angler to respond to the quiet, even disturbingly gentle takes so often associated with big trout intercepting drifting midges. Knowing the precise position of your invisible fly, you watch for the appropriate movement of a feeding fish, or any microscopic twitch in leader or line, and you gently swing into the take, in a manner not unlike greased line fishing for summer steelhead.

All of this makes for challenging sport. Yet I know just as many anglers who simply drop a midge pattern tied to a couple feet of tippet behind nearly every fly they fish, be it dry, wet, or nymph, and who end up feeling they catch a lot more trout than while fishing a single fly. I like two flies as well. Yet I must add that when fish seem keyed into one insect or one stage of one insect's life, I feel a second fly can work against my primary offering, and in the case of midges I often resort to the single fly, believing I need to avoid any possible disturbance to the appropriate look and drift of my cast.

Of course, in lakes or stillwater, where midges often play such an important role, issues of drift and drag might seem less relevant. But I will often contend that the angler must still influence the attitude of the fly so that it appears alive in the water rather than a fleck of organic detritus decomposing toward oblivion. I know what *I* think looks good enough to eat. And though fishing a tiny midge can often seem at the extreme range of fly fishing possibilities, an attempt to entice trout to feed on little more than the hint of a fly, I recall images—real or imagined—of bears feeding on ants, lifting them one by one on the end of a single, extended claw.

Or wolves nipping at shadows.

Wolf River Midge

Hook: TMC 100BL or Mustad 94845, size 20–24
Thread: Black 8/0 UNI-Thread
Body: Same as tying thread
Ribbing: Fine copper wire
Thorax/head: Black rabbit fur

Tying Notes

Step 1: Secure the hook and start the thread. Let me interject here and add that if you are trying to tie midges without some sort of magnification (I use +1.75 reading glasses), you are fighting an uphill battle. For twenty-five years I did it and thought I could see just fine. Once I tried reading glasses I realized that even during the decades of my best vision, I didn't see everything I might have.

Step 2: Wrap an even layer of thread to the bend of the hook. Tie in a piece of fine copper wire. Wrap an even layer of black thread forward to just short of the hook eye.

Step 3: Rib the body/abdomen with the fine copper wire. Tie it off and trim.

Step 4: Add a pinch of dubbing to the thread and wrap a small but distinct thorax and head. Whip finish and clip the thread.

That's it—although you might also want to take those reading glasses to the water, to help tie your midge to a 7X tippet.

LESSON 9

MARCH BROWN

I'm getting better at this hatch business. In the old days I used to just show up and go fishing, catch some fish one way or another, and when a hatch came off I'd frantically try to figure out what was going on and usually end up with a few fish more. Later, someone might mention Blue-winged Olives, or this or that kind of caddis, and I'd think *Yeah, something like that*.

It all seemed sort of hit and miss. Probably because it was. I prided myself on being a generalist, or genericist, one who didn't need to get fussy about details because, after all, these were just fish and bugs, and this was just fishing. I suffered frequent humiliations, but such moments seemed balanced out by instances of remarkable sport as well. Which proved, of course, that I was right: It *was* just fishing.

Any fool could get it right.

But if you keep at it long enough, fly fishing will eventually lead you to the conclusion that whenever you see rising fish, fish that are feeding on the surface as insects either leave or return to the water, you should be able to catch those fish. It's that simple. That's the name of the game.

Simple, that is, as an organizing principle of the sport. Fish are feeding, coming to the surface to eat bugs, you should be able to fool them with a fly. Should, of course, is the operative word. You should be able to fool rising fish. Anything else is just an excuse.

I know. I've used them all.

This is a story I like to tell. The part about catching fish doesn't much matter, because by then you can see it's inevitable, the problem's been solved. Up until then, even though it's a fish story, so you're pretty sure how it'll turn out, there's the element of mystery, which every good story demands. There's also a lot to be said for telling a story in which, on the brink of failure, you stumble on an answer so obvious—yet previously unseen—that no one can bark at you for hotdogging, even though there's always a little of that when things work out in your favor in the end.

Of course, I wouldn't tell any of this if I came off looking like a complete idiot. I've tried that. Just doesn't work. The screwball act makes people nervous.

Anyway, this was in March on one of those rivers we all have in our lives that's a little too far away to visit any weekend you choose, but not so far away that you have to mount a full-scale expedition to get there. On your own, these places can take years to sort out. That's part of the beauty. You're never there long enough to see hatches come and go, and as soon as you learn a couple of good drifts, you're reluctant to do much exploring during the prime hatch hours. Also, there's the simple matter that when a hatch does turn on, you can't be ten places at once, which means you're never really sure what's happening anyplace but where you are—a fairly profound perspective, although certainly no different than that of a lowly trout.

But this time I ventured upriver, determined to try someplace new. I stopped in town for a boot-sized draught of coffee, drove east a half hour on the interstate, then wandered around the edges of a revitalized hamlet, looking for access to the water. Later, wadered and casting, I settled into that slightly daffy mood of methodically covering a series of likely look-ing pools and runs, waiting for something to happen without a clue of the existence of a single trout in the water.

Two hours passed. By now I was checking my watch, nervously scan-ning the water. Could the Blue-winged Olives I'd seen in such numbers downriver the day before fail entirely to materialize here? I rejected the impulse to plunge off to a new stretch of river. On both sides of me a shallow feeder creek gurgled over a broad tongue of bread loaf-sized free-stones, spilling into a deep run where the river swept back into a single channel after separating above a narrow island. I could have prayed and not devised a better trout hole.

I mean, come on, I thought. *If there are fish anyplace, they're here.*

Then they were. They started up in the usual sporadic fashion, although right away I could see the good fish were positioned along a pair of tight seams in the conflicting currents, as precisely as sequins on a plunging bodice. Confident, because I had been waiting for this to happen, I lengthened my leader and knotted on the prettiest of my little Parachute Duns; then, for good measure, I tied on a slender CDC Emerger that had worked so well the previous day, cinching it to the tag end I had left, for just this purpose, on the bloodknot to my tippet.

Fish began to rise in earnest. Along a faint, jagged foam line, where dead water pooled between the currents, bright trout plucked at the surface, starting visible waves that drifted downstream. Here and there I saw bugs on the water. I got my flies in amongst them, retracing the good drifts I had found and been practicing the past hour.

But nothing happened. I adjusted my cast, my position, the angles of my drift. Nothing. By now fish were feeding in steady rhythms, coming up with confidence. I tried a half-dozen more casts. A dozen. Two.

Now at this point the sage advice is to stop casting and try to see what in God's name is going on. And on this occasion I took that advice, a practice I've finally adopted with some regularity, against a tendency toward insidious flailing. If we return to our original thesis—feeding fish can be fooled with flies—then casting to said fish and failing to entice them to bite your fly suggests that you should change your fly—as long as you can say with absolute certainty that your presentation is also adequate.

Or, another way to look at such moments, when fish are rising and you don't stop, is the trite but not inaccurate definition of insanity: doing the same thing over and over again expecting to get different results.

Anyway, this time I stopped. There were bugs drifting through the pool, the fish were rising, but as is often the case, I couldn't keep my eye on a single bug long enough to see one actually get eaten. Yet while trying to track a fly here and a fly there, I began to notice that not all of them were the same. They were all mayflies, with those distinct, upright, sailboat-sail-like wings, except some of them were about twice the size as the predominant Blue-winged Olives. Hmm. Not only were they big mayflies, they were brown, or maybe kind of rusty tan, but they certainly weren't that cloudy gray that makes the little *Baetis* unmistakable, if only because I've studied it so many times on failing, in the past, to catch fish during a blue-winged olive hatch.

Now, this is the part of the story I really like. It's silly but so what? You think anything about fly fishing isn't? I kept looking at those big brown mayflies, and I thought *Brown . . . March . . . March Brown.*

Oh.

I get it.

I didn't have an actual March Brown pattern. But I did have some size 12 and 14 Parachute Adams that I had tied the previous summer for stillwater *callibaetis*. The trout didn't seem to notice the difference. I like a post on my parachute flies tied out of deer hair, and on a size 12 that sucker stands tall. Amidst the little Blue-winged Olives, it looked like a flagship surrounded by a bunch of pleasure craft—until a flash the color of flesh swirled against the current, opening the surface of the pool, and that big fly quietly disappeared.

The hatch didn't last as long as I would've liked. Does anything that's that much fun? Four on the beach, just as many missed grabs, one that slipped the hook at the end of a blistering run, a couple more half-hearted rises after the bugs had all but disappeared. Say an hour, tops. Of course, if you could bottle this stuff, or put it in a capsule, available whenever the mood strikes, you could make a killing online. But I guess that's pretty much what's already there.

While I was making a few last casts, trying to hold on to what had just happened, a drift boat came by with a guide and a client. They stayed out of the good water. We exchanged greetings. Below the pool, the guide let the boat swing round in the eddy.

"Did you see any March Browns?" he asked.

"I did," I said. "A whole bunch of them."

The guide looked at his client. They both had those silly looks on their faces like they had just been into fish. I'm sure I must have looked the same.

"You don't see that every day," added the guide.

"*I* don't, that's for sure," I agreed.

Pulling on the oars, the guide nodded toward a seam in the currents. "Did you try right here?"

March Brown Parachute Dun

Hook: TMC 900BL or Mustad 94845, size 12–14
Thread: Brown 6/0 Danville Flymaster
Tail: Light Dun Microfibbets
Body: Tan to rusty brown dubbing
Hackle: Brown and grizzly or dun mixed
Wing post: Rusty brown deer body hair

Tying Notes

Step 1: Secure the hook and start the thread, leaving it about a third of the length of the hook shank from the eye of the hook.

Step 2: For the wing post, clip, clean, and stack a slender tuft of deer hair. With the aligned tips pointing past the eye of the hook, secure the deer hair to the top of the hook. Clip the butts. Stand the deer hair tips and advance the thread in front of them. Wrap the base of the post, allowing the tips of the deer hair to remain slightly flared. Use thread wraps to secure the upright position of the wing post.

Step 3: Wind the thread just short of the bend of the hook. Secure several microfibbets for the tail. Take one turn of thread under the fibbets to cock the tail slightly upward. Clip the fibbet butts.

Step 4: Wax your thread and twist on a slender noodle of fine dubbing material. Build a tapered abdomen, stopping directly behind the wing. Advance the thread in front of the wing post.

Step 5: Secure the stripped butts of two hackle feathers in front of the wing post. (Use two feathers only if you are mixing colors; one feather is much easier to wind.) Before winding the hackle, complete the body by adding a bit more dubbing in front of the wing. Wind the two hackle feathers simultaneously, taking the first turn highest on the post and working your way back down toward the body with three or four complete wraps. Tie off the hackle feather, clip, and wind a neat head. Add cement.

LESSON 10

PALE MORNING DUNS

In my efforts to become a Real Guy, an angler who approaches the task of catching fish with assurance and skill, not the reckless crapshooting of the frenzied wannabe, I imagine myself capable of distinguishing the subtle differences between *Ephemerella inermis* and *Ephemerella infrequens*, the Pale Morning Duns.

You find PMDs—whichever species—in early summer, June or July, midday, not necessarily morning at all. Which is one of the problems, one of the telltale deceits of so many of these famous mayflies and their traditional, misleading, old-school names. Pale? Okay, I'll buy that, if a soft yellow not unlike the color of a sun-bleached page from off the top of a legal pad is indicated, and nothing that tends toward tan, cream, or gray. Dun? Well, this proves a little trickier. The word can signify either color or the first of the two-winged stages of the airborne mayfly—although the earlier indication of color probably does point us to the latter entomological meaning, the *subimago* stage of the winged insect, not the gray of horses, expensive hackle, or Shakespeare's dark mistress's breasts.

These fine lines fuel my despair. I believe such distinctions matter, that the ability to recognize one species of mayfly from another offers yet another layer of insurance against finding feeding fish and failing to fool them. That's the goal, the grail, the illusion. Know enough and never again will your lack of aptitude and talent—your lack of genius—be revealed. Never again will a pod of feeding trout proclaim, if only metaphorically, *You suck, dude.*

There's a curiously transformative moment in the lives of most fly fishers when they suddenly recognize, for the first time, insects that heretofore they've known only as flies tied to their leaders. Some recall these moments in tones typically reserved for first tastes of love. What is shared by either event is the clarity of foreknowledge, an assuredness that promptly disintegrates with the abrupt affrontery of a bouquet of summer wildflowers wilting in one's fist. You thought you knew something. And now—this.

The magic of the moment fuels the giddy surprise of a toddler caught short by a jack-in-the-box. All this time you thought your March Brown was just a big bushy dry fly, something to float through a bouncy run, where now and then it sparks an aggressive rise, usually by a fish only half the size you're after. Then, one day—in March, perhaps—you spot these big brown mayflies drifting like couch stuffing down the middle of the stream, while here and there one lifts from the water, pirouetting like a frisbee-snatching terrier freed from the confines of gravity.

With any luck at all, trout in the neighborhood have noticed this occasion as well. Evidence of their attention arrives in sudden partings of the waters, whirling orifices into which the large but clearly overmatched mayflies disappear like so many raindrops in sand. Inspired by this show of carnage, you hazard a calculated conclusion: "Guess I'll tie on one of these . . . *March Browns!*"

You feel like a flipping Einstein. No one can call you a charlatan this time. Maybe you won't need the Groucho glasses after all. Be good, finally, to give up the bit with the rubber chicken, waved while genuflecting up and down the stream.

Pale Morning Duns are like that, too.

You've heard about them, and someone someplace told you something about some pattern or another you need to squeeze into your box just in case you stumble on a hatch. Probably a Light Cahill. It's a handsome fly, traditional in the manner of all Catskill dries, with those upright, divided, wood duck wings, and you feel pretty good about having them ready just in case, even if you haven't ever seen a mayfly that looks quite like it. Now and then you tie one on, because sometimes the light on the water makes all the bugs look kind of pale, and of course there are always caddisflies that seem creamy and small and, anyway, shouldn't anything you put on the water that gets a good drift and looks sort of real get something to come up and grab?

If you're like me, your Light Cahills probably grew rusty before you ever really needed them. Or they just sort of disappeared, like your old high school friends, or that bottle of port you were saving for a date who somehow slipped off your plate. What was the point of the fly in the first place? You certainly weren't going to tie many—not with those damn tricky wings.

But the thing about fly fishing is, if you keep at it long enough, you eventually see the stuff guys have been talking and writing about for the past century or two. I mean, when you get right down to it, trout streams are a pretty restricted affair; it's not like all of a sudden you're going to need a pattern to imitate a praying mantis, a scorpion, or a tsetse fly— although, come to think of it, if you had a decent imitation of any one of these, you could probably get a gnarly old brown trout interested in attacking it. But day in and day out, you know you're bound to see the insects that require the exact same cool, clean, oxygenated water that trout need—your mayflies, your stoneflies, and your caddisflies.

What a concept.

And so one day you *will* see some PMDs—probably east of home, probably midday, these little yellow suckers—although not nearly as small as a trico, not even as small as most Blue-winged Olives—just a lovely little mayfly that, if all goes well, the trout are keyed into and feeding on in the manner of teenagers sharing a bowl of popcorn.

For a couple of years, when I first started seeing PMDs, I felt I did pretty well with a yellow-bodied Adams—which means it wasn't really an Adams at all, but just the sort of tweaked pattern that insinuates its way into fly boxes everywhere. This was the same fly, in fact, that I would reach for when I encountered Yellow Sallies, the funky little stonefly that can light up summer days on mountain streams throughout the West. But a fly capable of covering such disparate hatches has its limitations— even if it does remind us, yet again, that precise imitation is rarely the crucial element in a fly fisher's success.

Yet if you get into a spell of serious PMD fishing, a stretch, say, in late June, with the bugs coming off every day right after lunch, and the trout feeding on them with the deliberate attention of pieceworkers in the midst of a good harvest, you're probably going to want—or need—a fly that covers the hatch specifically. Of course, what that means in terms of the fly you choose to actually fish says as much about you as it does about any pattern that claims to fit the bill for what is really nothing more than a "little yellowish mayfly."

Which begs the question: Does it ever need to get any more complicated than that? Does one really need to know, in other words, the difference between *E. infrequens* or *E. inermis*, the Pale Morning Duns?

Curious about the matter, I emailed Dave Hughes, author of those countless books that will make you a better trout fisher if you will just sit down and read a couple of them. Traveling as much as he does, seldom fishing the same waters over and over, Hughes makes the claim that he has no choice but to be a generalist—and his feeling is that it doesn't make much difference to the fish, or the fisherman, which species you're talking about.

"But," he added, like the good teacher he has always been, "the size and color of the fly should be right, and what is right will depend on one you scoop off the water and hold in your hand, the day you're fishing."

Sound advice—from a guy who ought to know. Yet there's always something more to it with Real Guys—they didn't get where they are by knowing what everyone else knows. So Hughes offered up another piece of advice, catching me squarely between the eyes: "Always remember that trout don't speak Latin."

Mea culpa.

Quill-Bodied Parachute PMD

Hook: TMC 900BL or Mustad 94845, size 16–20
Thread: Lt. Cahill 8/0 UNI-Thread
Tail: Light Dun Microfibetts
Body: Biot from turkey quill dyed PMD (yellowish with hint of green)
Wing: Turkey flat quills, cream
Hackle: Cream

Tying Notes

Step 1: Secure the hook and start the thread just behind the eye.

Step 2: From a single turkey flat, clip a tuft of quills (approximately fifteen to eighteen quills), keeping the tips aligned. This tuft of quills is tied in to create your wing post. Secure the quills, tips forward, at the front third of the hook. Unlike deer hair, turkey flat quills are forgiving, relatively easy to keep from spinning around the hook shank. Clip the butts and then advance the thread back to the tie-in point. Stand the quills and wind a dam of thread to hold them upright. Wrap the base of upright quills in the manner of typical parachute wing posts.

Step 3: Wind the thread to the bend of the hook. Tie in a tail of microfibbets. Rather than a three-part tail, I use five or six fibbets for added flotation and, if truth be known, a disdain for anatomical fussiness.

Step 4: Clip a single biot from the dyed turkey quill. Cut off the delicate tip of the biot. At the root of the tail tie in the biot by the remaining tip. Advance the thread, building a tapered abdomen to the base of the wing post. Hold the butt of the turkey biot with hackle pliers and wind a quill body. Secure the biot with the thread and clip excess.

Step 5: Advance the thread in front of the wing post. Secure the stripped base of a single hackle feather in front of the wing post. Use the thread to create a full-size thorax.

Step 6: Hold the tip of the hackle feather in your hackle pliers and wind it parachute style around the wing post, starting higher up the post and working your way down. After your last wrap, tie off the remaining hackle feather and clip excess. Whip finish, turn over the fly, and apply a drop of head cement to the thread.

LESSON 11

CALLIBAETIS

Nothing gives more pleasure to fly fishers and fly tyers alike than a hatch they feel they effectively cover both on the water and at the vise. After all of the mystery, the quibblings and postulates, the divinations of cosmic vibrations, you can finally settle down to the business of effectively duping the pea-brained fish that have made you look so silly over the years. It's a stirring moment in a fly fisher's career when he recognizes that there are certain hatches, seen repeatedly, that he can count on seeing again—and if he ties flies that replicate the stages of the hatching insect's entire life, he can approach the water during the season of the hatch with as much confidence as his slippery sport ever concedes.

Rarely does any of this work out quite as planned. The vagaries of sport, weather, time, chance—of life, dammit—do in fact elevate the fly fisher's enterprise above the drear discipline of arithmetic, verb conjugations, or a more precise definition of the abdominal six pack. I've claimed in the past that there are those of us drawn to the sport for precisely this surety of uncertainty, the impossibility of knowing nearly enough to avoid failure. Which is only to say that while fly fishing, at least, we feel reminded that humiliation is not necessarily disgrace, and that in the face of failure we can still recognize that life, by all counts, is more interesting for being lived than mastered.

Still, we aim to improve. And if you spend any time at all nosing around trout waters in the West, you eventually come to realize that there are a handful of hatches around which you can devise a pretty sophisticated campaign for catching fish throughout the year. None of this is a secret to anyone; all it really boils down to is that you know at least as much as the other guy. The curriculum itself is fairly stable. It's not like all of a sudden the trout are going to band together and take up living on vegetable protein in order to reduce stress, cholesterol, and competitive behaviors.

This restricted diet, however, doesn't make your job easy. Trout, we must remember, are wild and wary creatures. They didn't get to the size you want them to be when you catch them by neglecting to pay attention to the dangers all around them—no matter how reckless they act with insects streaming through their vision like debutantes in a gaffer's dreams. Or when drawn themselves, randy and hued, to annual assignations on the spawning gravel. We all of us know, as well, that most trout would be far less difficult to catch if we hadn't made them gun shy, invading their turf like bikers at a prep school dance. Trout will, in fact, eat practically anything. But they learn pretty quickly to stick to what's on the menu, shunning anomalies as if penguins offered roast beast.

Of course, *learn* is often dismissed these days as the wrong word. Sticklers keep reminding us that a trout's brain is too small for doing anything that can be classified as genuine learning—the same claim I make about what's inside the heads of some of the students in my sophomore English class. But we all know that something goes on there—and in the case of trout, fishing pressure transforms their behavior in profound ways. Although this change may not be accurately described as learning, that's probably because we have little evidence of what's at work in a trout's brain, beyond impulses governed by laws as pure as those in chemistry, physics, and the play of shadows on a moonlit night.

Of the hatches I expect to run into every year, none seems more widespread—nor predictable—than the stillwater *Callibaetis* mayflies. Nearly every trout lake in the West—and a few notable slow-moving rivers and streams—harbors a *Callibaetis* population, and those lakes with extensive weedy shallows can produce extraordinary hatches and the big trout that flourish from feeding on these insects, often for months on end. Most noteworthy to both trout and angler alike is the ability of this mayfly to produce multiple broods throughout the warmest months of the year, with some generations passing from hatched egg to mature nymph in less time than it takes to grow a bumper crop of bush beans. Successive generations grow progressively smaller adults—duns in autumn can be as much as two hook sizes smaller than those hatched early in the season. Yet this repetition of the *Callibaetis's* complete life cycle ensures the presence of this mayfly throughout the season, and anglers who learn to fish the hatch can approach most lakes with a proven game plan rather than the chuck-and-chance methods employed by so many stillwater fly fishers.

Beyond this ready availability, another appeal of the *Callibaetis* hatch is its patently civilized hours. Emergence never challenges the midnight reveler, and even late risers are afforded ample time to muscle up on their favorite eye-opener. Often, the entire hatch follows the schedule of a Sunday summer picnic, even those that sprawl into happy hour. Over the course of the season, hatches usually start later and later as the heat of summer gives way to the cool of autumn. The sole restraint on *Callibaetis* hatches from descending into sickening congeniality, in fact, is the insect's affinity for sketchy weather. Like so many mayfly hatches, the length and intensity of any day's *Callibaetis* hatch will be enhanced by overcast skies, chill temperatures, even rain. Foul weather is fine if you hope to enjoy serious *Callibaetis* sport.

Fishing the hatch is straightforward as song. An hour or two before emerging, nymphs begin to leave the weeds, swimming upward and then repeatedly settling again until they finally head directly for the surface. Trout feast on these nymphs, drawn to them as if children to bubbles. I like a simple soft hackle for this stage of the hatch, relying on the movement of the supple partridge quills and swimming action imparted through rod and line more than any specificities of pattern. Consider the behavior of the nymph and fish accordingly. Using a floating line, allow the fly to sink to the weeds, rod tip lowered to the water. Wait. Then slowly raise the rod tip. After lifting the tip, strip in slack line and allow the fly to sink again. Later in these early stages of the hatch, slowly retrieve the sunk fly to the surface, then allow it to sink again, repeating the process until the fly is at your feet. Both of these methods produce petulant grabs. Although often as not fish take the settling fly, a grab on the lift or retrieve is often felt in the kneecaps, a jolt that recalls the shocking strike of fish in the surf.

Once emergence begins in earnest, trout reveal themselves by leaving boils from subsurface feeding. Duns start to lift from the water. The rising, swimming nymph remains your best bet—but at this stage I like nothing better than to tie on an emerger, a cripple pattern, or a floating nymph. This is not a universal preference. The widely professed short-comings of dry flies in contrast to nymphs and other subsurface patterns have prompted countless anglers to all but forgo topwater presentations in the belief that they must deliver the fly to the fish rather than entice the fish to move to the fly. This seems to me at great cost. Besides offering the obvious delight of witnessing evidence of fish taking the fly, surface patterns exploit the profound threshold between water and air, where so much foodstuff collects and frequently expires. There may be more to it than that. Steelhead anglers who employ skating and waking patterns talk about "breaking the glass" of this window between the fish's world and the sky above, an analogy that could well be more literal than met-aphorical for explaining why steelhead respond in so many interesting ways to surface presentations. Little is written anymore about fish rising to or biting the fly for any reason but to feed. I can't help but think this is a limited view of things, as one dimensional as papist insistence that the point of sex is creating more of our own kind.

Now where was I?

Duns on the water, fish on top and feeding, I like a parachute pattern or comparadun—again something that floats in the surface rather than on it. This is fishing that requires its own kind of patience. Instead of casting here and there, trying to cover rise after rise, you're better off sim-ply delivering the fly toward feeding trout and allowing it to rest quietly on the water. The only good thing any cast does is put the fly where fish can eat it. Bad things about casting include a waving rod, line in the air, line falling on the water, line lifting off the water, and so on—all of which disturb trout, often spooking them into retreat.

After the heat of the hatch, anglers anticipate the celebrated *Cal-libaetis* spinner fall. Or so they say. To tell you the truth, I've never seen a spinner fall of any real consequence, at least not the sort that John Gierach describes in the essay that gave him his most famous title, *Sex, Death, and Fly-fishing*. These are the questions, understand, that Real Guys address while standing near the water as darkness falls, awaiting the expiration of mayflies in numbers that will preempt, at least momentarily, the need for conclusive answers.

Spinners, of course, are the final, sexually mature stage of mayflies, a molt beyond the hatched duns. Mating takes place in airborne swarms, and in the case of *Callibaetis*, the fertilized females then head for water-side foliage, where they wait up to five days for their eggs to develop.

After returning to the water to lay their eggs, spinners fall—spent to the point of dying. Naturally, trout exploit the opportunity to feed on these all but lifeless insects. Put enough of them on the water—a good spinner fall—and trout key into the exhausted adults, sipping them from the surface film with a delicacy more avian than aquatic.

I'm making this all sound simpler than it really is. I've never been certain, for instance, when exactly the males begin to fall, although we can safely assume it has something to do with when they run out of whatever they had that the females needed to produce their eggs. Those eggs, of course, are the whole point. After that, the adults become superfluous—much to the delight of feeding trout and fly fishers with casts that find them.

CALLIBAETIS SOFT HACKLE
Hook: TMC 3761, size 12–16
Thread: 8/0 UNI-Thread, Rusty Dun
Tail: Wood duck flank fibers
Rib: Fine copper wire
Body: Superfine dubbing, dark tan or Adam's gray
Thorax: Hare's mask, dark
Hackle: Partridge

Tying Notes

Nothing new here: Affix the partridge feather at the eye of the hook as per Sylvester Nemes and Dave Hughes and away you go. Aim for a sparse, slender body; a fine dubbing material allows you to keep these nymphs lightly dressed. Note as well that as with many mayflies, the wingpad of the *Callibaetis* nymph darkens as the nymph matures. The spiky stuff off the ears of a hare's mask is perfect.

CALLIBAETIS EMERGER
Hook: TMC 900BL, size 12–16
Thread: 8/0 UNI-Thread, Rusty Dun
Tail: Antron fibers
Body: Superfine dubbing, dark tan or Adam's gray
Shellback and wing: Deer hair

Tying Notes

The trick with this pattern is to use the right amount of deer hair tied in at the right place so that it eventually extends the right distance beyond the eye of the hook. Practice. I find that if the fly looks like a pretty good caddis pattern before I pull the deer hair forward to create the shellback, I've got it about right. Add dubbing to the thread to cover the clipped butts of the deer hair, creating a distinct thorax. Pull the wing forward over the thorax and secure the deer hair directly behind the hook eye. Whip finish around the hook, not the deer hair, by first pinching the tips of the deer hair and tilting them back out of the way.

CALLIBAETIS PARACHUTE DUN

Hook: TMC 900BL, size 12–16
Thread: 8/0 UNI-Thread, Rusty Dun
Tail: Microfibbets, Dark Dun
Body: Superfine dubbing
Wing: Speckled turkey flats
Hackle: Grizzly

Tying Notes

Again, there's nothing here a practiced tyer hasn't done before. I do like a segment from a turkey flat for a wing post (A. K. Best's "all-time favorite material" for the job, if you need a Real Guy's opinion), as it's so much easier to manage than deer hair or even calf body hair. But it's probably not as durable. I will also, at times, substitute medium dun hackle for the grizzly.

LESSON 12

SPEY CAR

Sometime in fall, at a moment more visceral than of mind, I give up swinging surface muddlers for summer steelhead and commit to a pattern steeped in tradition but no less sublime.

Like the fish in question, unless I'm mistaken, I am an animal, too. The light has changed, the weather grown chill. Leaves gradate and spiral to the ground. Showers distend. Finally, the river itself carries with it assertions of time, that deepening promise of diminished days, beyond which lies a new year that might very possibly fail to arrive.

This is not a moment, then, in which to feign cuteness or act without design. These fish and the fishing will not last. And though every season offers its own blend of voodoo and rhyme, this one—as a thousand others have spoken—is all we're sure we got.

The practice of relying on but a single pattern, upwards to months at a time, is common among dedicated steelheaders. If I read him right, Bill McMillan could go entire winters swinging his Winter's Hope, at least until he developed the Paint Brush, fished dead-drifted beneath a floating line, precursor to the eventual indicator/Glo-Bug rage. Nothing seems more hopeless to many steelheaders than a change of flies—nor more important than a fly one fervently believes in.

Yet only the radical traditionalist, unless also a steelheader who doesn't tie, can help but tinker with even his most trustworthy fly. Mine, in fall, is a Coal Car, or something quite like it, fished with the floating line as the muddler fails more and more to stimulate a rise, finally on a sink tip as the season advances and temperatures decline. This fly delineates for me a period of time, now imprinted graphically, as if primal memory. The Cal Car—my version of it—brings the last of the summer runs, rosy-cheeked and pink-sided, with darkening backs shaded olive and green. Each fish feels increasingly precious, spirited through a window that grows smaller with each passing day—until the season seems somehow complete, although never so much that you wouldn't mind just one more fish to call your last before the winter runs arrive.

It is Tom McGuane—who else?—in his essay titled "Tying Flies" who articulates the notion that whatever it is that attracts fish to a fly may well be connected to those aspects of the fly that appeal to the angler in the first place.

"An odd transference," writes McGuane, "occurs in the imagination. One holds up the fly and thinks both like a fish and like a fisherman, and perhaps as a species of prey, all at once."

Yet McGuane immediately questions this process as one of thinking at all—and here we begin to move in the direction that never plays well on the page, whether the subject be angling, art, gardening, or love.

Difficult for many of us is this notion that we *can't* figure out all we need to know. Or, more bothersome still, that "figuring out" precludes acts of imagination that bring us altogether closer to a better understanding of the problem at hand—in this case getting steelhead to strike a fly.

Naturally, you can easily run this line of reasoning too far. How else explain the scores of flies we buy and tie that never catch fish despite all the groovy feelings—if you'll excuse my French—that accompanied their creation or acquisition? And what about that paisely shirt still hanging in your closet? Yet in the matter of steelhead, that most mysterious of biters of the fly, one is inevitably compelled to conjure fabulous narratives, if for no other reason than that no one has a stinking clue what it is that really makes these fish grab one fly and not another. Experience is all we have to go on. What worked one time may work again.

And what works a handful of times, a dozen, and then more—well, thus begins the history of favorite or even career patterns for which steelheaders are renown. "While actual fly pattern," wrote McMillan, "means little in steelheading," he too felt it essential—especially in chill temperatures—to fish a fly one believes in. "If the pattern isn't attractive enough to the eye it won't stay in the water long enough to provoke that eventual, well-earned strike."

The Coal Car, of course, comes from the famous series of "train" flies developed in the 1970s by Randall Kaufmann for Deschutes River steelhead. Any number of these dark patterns—from Freight Trains to Ferry Canyons to Signal Lights—are now staples in fly boxes wherever steelhead are found. Yet like most patterns that withstand the test of time, the Coal Car is now tied from a variety of materials using assorted techniques, such that often all that remains is the original color configuration: black throughout, with but a segment of orange and another of red at the back half of the body of the fly.

Trey Combs made the Coal Car part of his "Winter Series," substituting marabou for both the tail and wing and using floss instead of yarn and chenille for the body. John Shewey created a waking version, the Coal Car Damp, by using fitch tail (European polecat) for both the tail and wing, the latter tied forward in the manner of other waking flies or Haig-Brown's famous Steelhead Bee. What I do to the pattern seems far short of remarkable, although when I look at my version I get that tingling sensation—if only because of the number of times, come fall, I've removed said fly from the lip or hinge of a steelhead's impressive mouth.

Coal Car

Hook: Bartleet CS10/1, size 6 to 1/0
Thread: Black Danville Unwaxed 6/0
Tail: Black hackle fibers
Body: Rear quarter: Orange silk floss
Second quarter: Red silk floss
Front half: Black silk floss
Ribbing: Small oval silver tinsel
Hackle: Black schlappen
Wing: Black marabou blood plumes

Tying Notes

I like the light-wire Bartleet hook and usually tie on a size 2; but I'll also tie this fly on heavy winter hooks, all the way up to the big 5/0 irons that McMillan uses for his Winter's Hope. After tying in the tail, I secure the oval silver tinsel, which I find more durable against abrasive teeth than the narrowest flat tinsels, even if you use the fancy French kind. For the same reason, I also use silk floss rather than nylon or rayon. Plus, I'm a fan of sparse, slender bodies. After wrapping the orange and red flosses to the middle of the body, I tie in the schlappen by its tip, having first stripped the side opposite I want to sweep back in the usual Spey manner. Before actually wrapping the hackle, I tie in the black floss, wind my thread forward, wrap the floss forward, followed by the tinsel ribbing over the entire floss body. The trick with wrapping the schlappen is to keep the angle of the quill such that the fibers lay back toward the rear of the fly rather than sticking out to look like a frightened Woolly Bugger. Winding the schlappen forward, I space each wrap about the same distance left between each turn of ribbing, until taking a tighter turn or two directly behind where I secure the wing. For the wing, I look for those straight, narrow blood plumes at the tip of marabou feathers, tying in the entire tip, center quill and all.

I've gone back and forth about whether or not to actually designate my modest Coal Car revision the *Spey* Car. I swing it with a soft, fifteen-foot Winston that Gary Bulla loaned me and will probably never get back. I fish the fly on a floating line until the weather takes on the bite of autumn; then I switch to a Type III sink tip. The swinging fly invites a variety of responses from steelhead, from the heavy stop that suddenly explodes as a fish crashing through the surface, to the tentative pluck that commands you continue to lead the fly, in hopes of securing that classic take that leaves the hook locked into the hinge at the corner of the fish's mouth. All of this goes far beyond the efficacy of any lowly fly pattern; the many mysteries of steelheading will always seem, subtly, just outside one's absolute grasp, especially as the window of summer-run fish in fall begins to close. Yet whatever the season, the success of any steelheader begins before he steps into the water, the certitude, real or imagined, that he has tied on the right fly, regardless of the name.

LESSON 13

DIVING CADDIS

I spent a long weekend on the water recently with Fred Trujillo, one of those professional tyers who is always fussing with patterns, trying to master fish by giving them the Right Fly. Unlike me, Fred's a no-nonsense fisherman; if fish aren't showing on the surface, he goes right down after them, never hesitating to load lead to his line. Not surprisingly, between his good flies and pragmatic methods, Fred catches a lot of fish—on this trip something like three or four to each one of mine.

Like I said, it was a long weekend—although, as a rule, I never do any serious score keeping, at least not when I'm on the short end. What was especially humbling, however, was that Fred was getting most of his fish on two patterns I first brought to his attention—or flies, at least, that I began using, years back, with enough success that Fred grew to favor them, too.

Naturally, as a pro, Fred has tweaked both patterns to his own liking. Yet there is nothing he has done to either the Diving Caddis or Wild Hare that seems significant enough to offer either fly a new name. Still, while he was outpacing me by a wide if imprecise margin, I was tempted to credit Fred's success to some freshly brewed potion, a new twist of ingredients that was attracting trout to this pair of old favorites as if children to agates and flames.

But I know better. Red wire ribbing on the nymph's abdomen? A tiny orange glass bead for the caddis's head? Come on: Catching fish is rarely, if ever, exclusively about fishing the Right Fly. We would like to believe differently—but it just isn't so. The last thing you change, goes the wisdom, is your fly—the very thought I recall having while I reached for my fly box as line again sizzled off Fred's reel.

There's an old story I suspect most fly fishers have heard since it first entered the literature in Tom McGuane's *The Longest Silence*. McGuane reports having asked "the greatest trout fisherman" of his era what percentage of his annual catch would remain if he were reduced to fishing only Adamses and Gold-Ribbed Hare's Ears. "Certainly over ninety percent," answered the famed angler. When asked, then, about the vast number of different patterns carried in his shop, the eminent piscator added, "I don't sell flies to fish."

Now and then I teach classes in beginning fly fishing, and when the subject of flies first comes up, I always share this story. When I finish, many of my students nod knowingly: they've been given some inside dope, weighty insight from a wily graybeard who really knows the sport. Better yet, their suspicions have been confirmed: All those different flies don't matter—just another ruse of greedy marketers.

Later, however, I open fly boxes of my own. Invariably, someone asks, in a voice pitched toward wonder, if I tied all those flies. And there's nearly always a fellow, a bureaucrat or middle manager, whose eyes reveal estimations of value based on rapid, cost-per-unit calculations. If only he knew the truth of a serious fly fisher's stash. Finally, someone addresses the question directly: If flies don't really matter, how come I have so many—and so many different kinds?

It's a telling moment. I often feel a shift in power, a crumbling of authority I recognize from high school classrooms when a student finally asks why, if I'm so smart, I've settled for a job putting up with the likes of him. I have many answers—about flies, that is. Mostly I seek to point out the multitude of insects, and stages of their lives, on which trout feed. There's also the Boy Scout argument: It's good to be prepared. But sometimes I descend into the heart of the matter, the psychological tendency of most fly fishers to fear, above all else, the absence in their fly boxes of that fly that will win the day, a single pattern, amidst the infinite choices, that will make fools of feeding fish when the Adamses and Gold-Ribbed Hare's Ears just won't do, when the tried and true standards won't touch that maddening ten percent of the trout that even "the greatest trout fisherman" of an era will fail to catch if he doesn't have the Right Fly.

The bureaucrat or middle manager is usually the first to wriggle. Or yawn. Or feign a polite, irritated cough. Once rolling, however, I find it difficult to stop. It's not about the fly, I repeat. Okay, it's *rarely* about the fly. You just want to have things covered. There are a lot of good flies out there, great flies, proven, traditional flies, classics and new takes on old ideas, old materials used in new ways, new materials used in old ways. It's not about the fly—but you do try to have one that works.

The bureaucrat or middle manager glances toward the ceiling. Sophomores, I'm reminded, aren't the only students I've ever pissed off. But I refuse to yield to perturbation.

"And like kisses," I add, "if a fly is good, a dozen of them isn't too many."

Let me make this as clear as I can. On the one hand, you have those who believe that the solution to the problem of catching fish is the Right Fly. On the other hand, you have those who contend that the fly is but a very small part of the solution, and what matters most is the presentation of the fly. Superior presentation is the reason why the great trout fishermen of any era would suffer only slight reductions in their success if restricted to a pair of generic patterns, a dry fly and a nymph, each tied, presumably, in a half-dozen different sizes. Then again, driven to the wall on those occasions when they really did need a more specific pattern, these same anglers might well have hucked their rods into the river, taken up permanent stations at the nearest bar, and left the trout for the rest of us with our crooked casts and overflowing vests and fly boxes.

Naturally, most fly fishers stand somewhere between the two extremes. Yet every fly fisher I've ever met leans in one direction or the other. It's tempting to generalize and say that newcomers to the sport gravitate toward the glamour of the Right Fly, while experience teaches most of us that our flies need be but approximate impressions, subjects to the demands of the accurate cast and efficacious drift. But we all know genuine hotshots who are shameless fly junkies, sober strategists and ruthless casters who would just as soon arrive at the river without a rod than without their library of flies.

Mostly, however, the cant of Real Guys favors the notion that what you do with your flies is more important than the flies themselves. In an article about fishing caddis hatches, Jim Schollmeyer makes no mention of the Diving Caddis, Gary LaFontaine's redoubtable wet fly, a version of which my buddy Fred was using with such success during our long weekend together. Schollmeyer offers several presentation methods for how to imitate the swimming or spent egg-laying caddis females, that important stage in the caddisfly life cycle suggested both impressionistically and effectively by LaFontaine's Antron-winged pattern. But not one of the thirty flies pictured in the article is specific to this stage of the caddisfly's life. Instead, Schollmeyer gives us the generic soft hackle and a couple of standard, emerging adult patterns as sufficient imitations when coupled with the appropriate, subsurface presentation.

This is in no way an indictment of Schollmeyer. On the contrary, I use his article as evidence of another Real Guy who concerns himself more with the behavior of his flies than the infinitesimal details of patterns. Nevertheless, in the caddis-rich waters I fish, the Diving Caddis fools as many trout as any pattern I use, and I wasn't surprised that weekend when Fred kept sticking fish with his version of Gary LaFontaine's famous fly. Sure, he had altered the pattern. But that wasn't why he was outfishing me, I kept telling myself, fiddling with splitshot, angles and lengths of casts, depths and speeds of drift, swings—all of the subtleties of presentation. The original Diving Caddis needs no improvements, I reminded myself. It's always worked in the past. It's not about the fly.

It's not about the fly.

I wake at first light to the sound of rain on the roof of the van. Somehow this gives me an excuse to fall back asleep, an act of omission that is repaid with nightmares featuring small aircraft, a subway tunnel, my high school surfing buddy, and gangs of post-apocalyptic necrophiles straight out of the movie *Mad Max*.

I blame the previous night's chili. Either that or a recent failure in romance that has left me all but sleepless two out of the past three nights. Or maybe I'm feeling the effects of watching Fred rope in a dozen trout to every handful of mine.

Fred's tying at the picnic table, protected from the drizzle by an overhanging juniper, when I finally stumble out of the van. Materials are arranged neatly around his vise; the product of his early morning efforts is separated into two tidy piles. I know what this means: Wild Hares and Diving Caddis, Trujillo style.

Even without coffee, I venture closer inspection. It's worse than I expected. Fred, who never talks much, less so in the morning, assumes the expression of a man who has received all the feedback he needs from a river full of trout. Or one who has been tying flies since dawn while his fishing partner oversleeps.

The flies, anyway, make my jaws hurt. I want to mention the elaborate sources of my troubled sleep. But this seems no time for theatrics. Fred's flies reflect perfectly an attribute that Gary LaFontaine searched for throughout his own life, "effective fly patterns instead of just precise replicas." Fred's Diving Caddis, especially, produces in me a clenching of the teeth that mimics the exquisite tension I feel when nymphing with flies I absolutely believe in. This, I understand, is why our efforts at the vise do matter: As McGuane, among others, has reiterated repeatedly, the most successful anglers are those who are capable of fishing free of doubt and indecision, who rarely suffer the temptation to reach for their clippers and gaze at the contents of their fly boxes.

But it's *not* about the fly, I remind myself, fumbling with my waders.

LaFontaine Diving Caddis

Hook: Mustad 7957-B (a standard wet fly hook)
Body: Sparkle Yarn: blend of clear and dyed filaments chopped into dubbing
Underwing: Soft-hackle fibers: grouse, partridge, or hen hackle
Overwing: Clear Antron (or Creslan filaments)
Hackle: Rooster hackle

Tying Notes

What's startling about this pattern is both its simple design and how quick and easy it is to tie. The fly itself appears almost crude, certainly one of the reasons it's never been particularly popular either commercially or for those who feel they need to tie sophisticated or "realistic" flies. Photos of the Diving Caddis tied by Gary LaFontaine himself inevitably prompt one to think, *Couldn't he have been a little neater?* Most tyers now use packaged Antron dubbing or a blend of Antron and rabbit fur for the body, eliminating some of the pattern's shaggy appearance, conceivably at a cost to the fly's overall effectiveness. The layered, two-part wing is as easy as wings come. A single turn of hackle—never more—creates a sparse collar, conveniently forced back toward the body with wraps of thread.

FRED'S DIVING CADDIS

Hook: Mustad 3906B, size 14–16
Thread: 8/0 Rusty Brown UNI-Thread
Beadhead: Dark brown glass bead, 11/0–15/0
Body: Superfine dubbing, tan
Underwing: Antron, cream
Overwing: Deer hair
Thorax/Head: Squirrel dubbing, natural tan/gray

Tying Notes

About glass beads I can only say that Fred and lots of other tyers like them, and they're always on the lookout for new sources, colors, and sizes. You usually need to pinch down the barb of the hook to slip the bead on. Fred uses Superfine dubbing, aiming for a realistic-size body. The big change-up on his pattern, however, is the use of Antron as an underwing; how this affects the pattern is anyone's guess, but clearly you still get the bubble-collecting properties of Antron filaments, the "magic ingredient" in all of LaFontaine's original caddis patterns. The deer hair overwing should be sparse compared to typical adult floating patterns. For the dubbing material used up front, Fred shaves the fur from squirrel skins with dog clippers. A commercial tyer, he hates fussing with dubbing loops, but he always seems to end up with just a few of those spiky barred guard hairs that look like both legs and antennae at the head of the fly, the same look created by rooster hackle in the original Diving Caddis.

LESSON 14

TRAVELS WITH CHARLIE

For a long time I disliked Charles Brooks. Not personally, of course—I never met the gentleman—but as the frank, forceful, and often dogmatic authorial voice in such books as *The Trout and the Stream*, *Larger Trout for the Western Fly Fisherman*, and the epochal *Nymph Fishing for Larger Trout*. Exhortations by a retired Air Force officer to study, record, observe, learn, practice and, above all else, concentrate, left me cold, if not thoroughly indignant. Charles Brooks made trout fishing sound like school. Or, worse, a job. In my mind, the sport offered retreat into a world without rules, schedules, authority, discipline—maybe even free of hard and fast facts and absolute truths. I waded through my early career as a fly fisherman armed with little more than innocence and wonder—and, on occasion, a doobie. Charles Brooks prescribed order and rigorous attention to detail. I wanted to go outside for recess.

I recognized all of this had changed, however, some years back while schooling my good friend Peter Syka in the subtleties of midday nymphing for Deschutes redsides. The Deschutes, as many know, can be tough—a big, brawling Western river churning through the basalt boulders of a steep-sided, high-gradient canyon fiery in a noonday sun. In other words, the kind of river that Charles Brooks loved and encouraged us all to master. It took me years of frequent visits to grow confident on the Deschutes—although that confidence, I should add, has more to do with finding and hooking trout than actually landing the best of the river's redsides, high-voltage trout that will bolt through heavy current, exposing as much backing behind your fly line as many of the river's higher-profile summer steelhead. The Deschutes, at times, is a superb dry fly river; its salmonfly hatch is legendary, and surface caddis activity is the staple of evening fishing for more months than all of summer. Yet the meat and potatoes of Deschutes trout fishing, especially beneath a midday sun, is some form of nymphing, adaptations of Charles Brooks's well-documented methods, all of which I've distilled for Peter into one simple lesson: "When in doubt, get the lead out."

It's not pretty. It's not necessarily even a whole lot of fun. But Charles Brooks argued the notion, radical at the time, that big nymphs—usually some form of stonefly—fished tight to the bottom at the end of an almost taut line offered the fly angler his or her best chance of catching most Western rivers' best trout. Brooks's methods were as subtle as a nightstick—and just as effective. I show Peter how to rig two flies with a single BB-sized splitshot in between, and after the usual casting problems at the start, he begins to guide his drift through the ledgy slots above Rattlesnake Canyon. Yet he comes up empty—until I tell him to pinch a second shot of lead to his line.

He breaks off the fish on the take. A classic error: At the same time you think you might be hung up on the bottom, you tug against the resistance, only to receive a jolt through the rod that feels as if produced by the hind hoof of a quarter horse. There's an instant when you think the fish—for that's obviously what was just attached to your line—might still be there. But at that deep place of real knowing, somewhere between your knees and your heart, you recognize with absolute certainty that you just screwed up and yet another big fish in your life just got away.

Rebuilding his rig, Peter glances over at me and states, with finely balanced sardonic irony, "We're nymph fishing for larger trout."

"Exactly," I say.

Still, I've been anything but a Charles Brooks disciple. Mostly, now, I abjure the big black stone nymph, favoring, instead, smaller subsurface patterns that imitate stages of the prevalent caddisflies, the workhouse bug on so many Western rivers and streams. More and more, as well, I fish soft-hackled flies on or in or just beneath the surface, a strategy that covers a wide range of feeding opportunities—be it stoneflies, caddisflies, or mayflies—for most trout. Of course, I also fish the true dry fly, more now than ever, every chance I get—although what patterns imitate, exactly, the newly emerged adult *Rhyacophila*, say, as opposed to the egg-laying female trapped in the surface film, grows more and more difficult to delineate every year.

All of which places me in direct lineage with Charles Brooks and nearly every other fly fisher who has called the West his or her home. If there is a "style" of Western fly fishing, it is the absence of restraint or conformity, a willingness to explore a full range of methods, experiments, and ideas, without the burden of—and sometimes even respect for—angling traditions. Fly fishing in the West is as democratic as public waters. Freedom can feed excess and abuse (note the countless newcomers servile to strike-indicating bobbers); but it is also the path to inspiration, innovation, and invention. Taken in full, Charles Brooks—despite his broad-shouldered six-foot frame, his stout rods, short heavy leaders, sinking lines, and lead-wrapped flies—was anything but a one-dimensional fly fisher. Examined over the breadth of his writing, Brooks reveals himself as the consummate Western angler, his work as indigenous to the region as that of writers as diverse as Russell Chatham, Steve Raymond, David James Duncan, Dave Hughes, or the exotic Roderick Haig-Brown. Charles Brooks embraced and enlarged fly fishing in the West, and he as much as anyone else helped us call the place our own.

Which is why this summer I decided to take my thirteen-year-old son and go search for Charles Brooks—or at least his ghost, drifting along the rivers of his fabled Yellowstone waters.

The Madison

I'm loath to confess the number of famous rivers I saw yet failed to fish in my youth. Raised in southern California, schooled in the fundamentals of fly fishing on dinky west-slope Sierra streams and alpine lakes accessible only by backpacking, I viewed big rivers as utterly incomprehensible, a sporting proposition reserved for Real Guys, not the likes of a sun-baked surfer adrift in a haze of metaphor and guilt. The Madison—broad and graceful in the park, one long vigorous bounce from Quake Lake to Ennis—seemed no more approachable than a movie starlet or a blooded glamour model. Or the Banzai Pipeline exploding across the reef.

Not that I was afraid—unless fear encompasses the morbid feeling that we are simply not good enough to suit up and play. Big water didn't scare me; my response to outsized surf was "Bring it on!" Instead, I looked at a big river like the Madison, weighed it against my experience and minimal expertise, regarded the well-equipped congregants (Where do they get that stuff?), and thought to myself, *Fat chance*.

I suffered a stab of this same juvenile anxiety as my son Patrick and I made our way upriver from camp at West Fork, looking for open water the evening before entering the park. The road from Ennis had revealed innumerable drift boats punctuating the famous "continuous fifty mile riffle" that leaves so many visiting anglers shaking their heads. It all looks more or less the same; where the hell do you start? We weren't the only pilgrims, either. Along the gravel road opposite the highway we found turnouts and parking areas full, anglers stationed knee deep at even increments a short wade from the bank. The best water we could find looked marginal at best—fast, choppy, monotoned. Old feelings welled up in me: This sucks. But on closer inspection I saw a river I recognized, if only vaguely, a powerful freestone river not unlike the Deschutes, textbook water for stoneflies and caddisflies and nymphing with the flies that suggest them.

"We know how to do this," I said to Patrick.

What worked best was to move downstream, passing quickly through the heaviest water until locating a break or pothole or shelf, some kind of obstacle, that softened the flow and the drift of your sunken flies. You learn to feel holding water: speed, depth, a void in the current. The upstream cast allows your leader to slice vertically through the water column; across the current and your flies will rarely get down to the fish, certainly not in the slots and tight channels you need to probe. Of course, you hook whitefish; I'm sorry, but that's nymphing in the West, too. But there were rainbows as well, a good one of which I knew would give me all sorts of trouble in such swift, heavy water, a promise I ignored and went right along fishing with a 5X tippet. Then, between a pair of garbage can-sized boulders, set a dozen feet apart directly in line with the current, that good rainbow grabbed the Diving Caddis, jumped casually a foot out of the water, did the same thing again so that Patrick also saw all eighteen or twenty inches of very redside-looking fish—and then it got down to business, boring off in the current, and made very short work of me and my ridiculously undersized tippet.

"Whoa," I said, turning to Patrick, his rod backlit by the cloudless evening sky.

"Whoa, indeed," agreed my son.

The Lamar

In the old days we used to do Slough Creek first. We felt it was relatively easy fishing, cutthroats in a meadow stream, plus the walk in offered hope that not all of the water had been pounded. We also liked beginning a Yellowstone visit in the relatively small, secluded campground there, in sharp contrast to the mega-facilities throughout the rest of the park. And Brooks claimed that First Meadow, two miles above the campground, lies "in the most beautiful part of the largest angler's paradise in the world," not a bad recommendation for a spot to commence one's Yellowstone stay.

Yet times change. A weekend, we found more than a dozen cars at the trailhead, after passing at least that many in turnouts above the meadows below the campground. The majority of the vehicles had Montana plates, presumably "locals"; I know I'd make regular visits if I lived—and worked—within striking distance of the Slough. You can't expect solitude many places in the park. But I wanted to put Patrick on water where we at least felt like we had fish to ourselves.

Slough Creek's destination, the Lamar River, is loved but rarely to excess. Traversing the northeast corner of the park, the Lamar remains off the beaten track. "Angler satisfaction is generally higher on the Lamar than other park streams," wrote Brooks, two decades ago, an observation that still rings true. "This doesn't mean that anglers catch more or larger fish, but that they are happier with the fishing and all that goes with it." The Lamar Valley itself is open, wide, and high; the river meanders through riffles and runs spread out over loose gravel and sand. Most places the river can't be forded, but nearly all of the water can be covered with a cast.

Fish in the Lamar are notoriously migratory, a response, probably, to fairly dramatic fluctuations in flow caused by summer thunderstorms. We found the river in perfect shape, a hint of green, the bars exposed. Patrick swung a Soft-Hackled Hare's Ear through the tail of a riffle; the trout grabbed in the seam between the current and the soft water, a textbook take as old as the sport itself.

"That's what we're here for," I said, while Patrick admired a chunky cutthroat that filled both his hands.

Later, in a deep, tight back eddy swirling beneath the remains of a high-water log jam, I pitched a size 6 salmonfly, a fly as big as a hummingbird, into the vortex of still water, right where you know the best fish in the pool will lie. The take was so slow, so deliberate, that at first I thought maybe it wasn't a good fish, somehow a tiddler had beaten out the boss and got its mouth around the audacious fare. Then the trout was on the reel—and I hollered at Patrick to come see what we were *really* after.

The Yellowstone

Lou Waar showed up at the park fifty years ago. He drove a trash truck and got paid $125 a month. Lou was from Alabama, and he never told anyone that he felt he was ripping off the park. Every day, before work or after work—or both, depending on his schedule—Lou waded into the Yellowstone River and caught cutthroat trout by the score.

It's an old story. Charles Brooks, along with every other writer who has described the Yellowstone, talks in phenomenal numbers, staggering quantities of fish rising, fish caught, fly fishers wading and casting in the most prolific piece of trout water in America. Lou Waar, sitting on gray log, shaking the sand and gravel out of his canvas Converse All Stars, still the only wading "equipment" he uses on the Yellowstone, a deep swift section of which below Nez Perce Ford he just crossed, soaking his khaki pants to the waist—Lou Waar confirms the descriptions of Brooks and so many others.

"There's just no way to say how good it was," says Waar, relacing the top eyes of a sneaker. "But five years ago something started happening."

I can't help but agree. In two days Patrick and I have seen but a handful of rising fish. Good fish, I should add, big fish, five of which we've brought to hand, colorful, immaculately handsome Yellowstone cutts stretching close to twenty inches, taller, top to bottom, than the breadth of my hand—great fish, really, that rose through the surface to crippled mayfly patterns and ran off through heavy current like summer steelhead, each one leaving us weary after long, teeth-grinding struggles, two of which ended a hundred yards downriver from where they began, another that demanded I grip Patrick by the back of his wading belt as I helped him cross deep current to the safety of an appropriate landing spot. *Good-as-it-gets fish*, I say more than once to Patrick—but we haven't seen a single trout, a Yellowstone cutthroat trout, between six and eighteen inches.

"They aren't here," says Lou, while we sit at river's edge, scanning the water for rises. "I don't want to sound pessimistic. But it might not come back in my lifetime."

Is there a problem? Certainly no one is catching fifty or seventy-five fish a day, "not at all uncommon," claimed Brooks, twenty years ago. For the first time in my life I waded into the much-ballyhooed tangle of anglers at Buffalo (now Nez Perce) Ford, which turned out to be but a handful of guys, none of whom moved a single fish during a steady midday caddis hatch. Whirling disease? A collapse of spawning success? Less than ten years ago Craig Mathews called this area "one of the most popular spots for catching trout that average 16 to 17 inches—and for watching other people catch them." I watched. I didn't see a single fish hooked.

The park has changed. Thirty years ago, when I first fished Pelican Creek, a main tributary emptying into Yellowstone Lake, you could kill two fish daily. Shortly afterwards, fisheries management instituted a park-wide catch-and-release policy, except for portions of the upper Gardner basin, where kids under twelve could use bait to fish for—and keep—brook trout, a policy still in effect today. Now, Pelican Creek is closed to fishing, a precautionary move to protect invaluable spawning waters for the Yellowstone cutthroat, while at the same time eliminating a major incentive to visit the drainage, a particularly popular byway for grizzly bears.

"You caught fish in Pelican Creek in September?" asks Lou. "I didn't know fish were even in there then."

"I guess we were too dumb to know they weren't supposed to be. But they were," I add.

Lou Waar stands, fingering a good looking Sage rod that contrasts dramatically with his all but nonexistent wading attire. Unlike a lot of old-timers bemoaning the loss of great fishing in the past, Waar—he's got to be close to eighty—is still in the game.

I offer him the run we're on, where Patrick and I have hooked and landed a handful of elegant but widely separated trout the past two afternoons.

"No, it's all yours," says Lou, heading off downstream. "You boys have found a few. You should be telling me what's going on."

The Firehole

The Firehole, it's always seemed to me, is where East meets West. Here, classic dry fly water recalls angling traditions from the first half of the twentieth century, in places like Pennsylvania, Michigan, upstate New York, all the way back to the cast-only-to-rising-trout ethics of historical England. Ray Bergman and Ernie Schwiebert, among others, fished and loved and wrote about the Firehole. Cliché-clear water, oil-slick runs, dainty bugs, and wary, persnickety brown trout all make for sport that can seem, to some of us out West, as foreign as silk lines, gut leaders, and horsehair tippets.

Anyone who's fished the Firehole also knows that it can be tough: As far back as the early 1970s, Brooks offered sobering results in *The Trout and the Stream* of a study showing that "only 18 percent of all fishermen catch any fish on the entire river, and only 5 percent catch trout of sixteen or more inches." Nothing I've seen on the river in the past twenty-five-plus years, infrequent though my visits have been, would disprove these numbers.

But the Firehole, as I've written elsewhere, is where Peter Syka and I first recognized the likelihood of catching trout in the park, pitching live grasshoppers into the river and, rodless, watching them disappear to obediently rising fish; and today the river remains as inviting to anglers as it has been since fly fishers first ventured into the Yellowstone caldera.

Still, Patrick could see, on approaching the river at the bottom end of Biscuit Basin, that this was the sort of place that could make for an uneventful session. Everywhere Brooks mentioned the Firehole in his writings, he pointed out the need for precise, careful fishing: "stalking," "subtlety," "stealth." We all know the game. For a thirteen-year-old, it can seem like a trip to the dentist.

An hour or so after Patrick gave up, I wandered back in the direction of the van, looking for the widely spaced rising fish I had seen scattered in a series of corners in the river on first entering the meadow. The trout hadn't moved to anything I had drifted past them, on or beneath the surface, the first time through; as usual, such refusals prompted me to try smaller and smaller flies. But the other half of this inexact strategy is the use of what Brooks called the "shocker"-type dry fly: "a big spider or variant, or a big Palmer-tied dry." The analogy he used was, "As the fellow said when he smote the mule between the eyes with a two-by-four,

'First you have to get their attention.'" No one believed in big flies—nymphs or dries—more than Charles Brooks. More than anyone before him, Brooks argued that big bugs move big fish. I'm very often reluctant to employ this approach; yet as often as not, it's precisely the trick that saves the day.

I began to make something happen with a yellow Humpy, size 10; there was absolutely nothing of the sort on the water. The fish were small, nine, ten inches, brown trout, but a couple I rose without hooking seemed a size larger. I looked through a shallow mayfly box I keep zipped inside my vest, a box with some of my very best dry flies, ones that usually seem too delicate, at whatever size, for the water I'm on. I chose a big quill-bodied parachute pattern—and with it I managed a drift that went from one chute all the way down to another, a forty-foot drift that you leave on the water only because the fly keeps doing exactly what it is supposed to do so why would you pick it up and cast again? As the fly entered the second chute—really, just a ribbony seam of current and foam—a fish rose and took with the authority of something bigger, that imprecise but unmistakable size that anglers everywhere recognize the instant they strike a fish.

Big? Hardly. But a foot-long brown trout in Biscuit Basin is a fish Charles Brooks described as "more difficult to catch than they are else-where," and I know from experience it's easy to do a lot worse. Guiding the trout to hand, I hollered up to Patrick in the van. He came running, camera ready.

The Gallatin

There's a prescription for fishing the Gallatin River in *Fishing Yellow-stone Waters* that has always seemed to me the quintessential account of fly fishing in the West. Brooks suggests that to fish the upper Gallatin, where it follows Highway 191 in the northwest corner of the park, you should

> *take along a big lunch, perhaps a pleasant libation, and park along any stretch that suits your mood for the day. . . . The trout are not many nor large but they are friendly and willing, and you will have a relaxing, pleasant day on one of the friendliest rivers in the West. Its open counte-nance is just as it seems, it holds no secrets from you. The fish are where*

you think they are and you fish it as you think you should. No stream can be more honest than that.

Of course, there's more to it than that. There's always more. But a stop along the Gallatin, either on entering or leaving the park, offers practically all of the basic ingredients that attract anglers in the West to the sport of fly fishing. I do so badly want to tell you about one more fish, a larger trout, one of several, that I found rising almost imperceptibly along a deeply undercut bank in a meadow where, later, we saw from a distance a small grizzly enter the stream. I want to tell you about this fish and the way it rose to the big Humpy, the way it raced off in heavy current, taking line as only truly good fish can. I want to tell all that, and maybe a little more—but, really, that would only be repeating everything Charles Brooks ever said, and which he told me again as we visited once more this summer on some of his favorite Yellowstone waters.

LESSON 15

BIG OLIVE BUGGER

I went an entire spring hearing about bass in the boat marina. When baseball rolled around again, I figured I should drive upriver and see what all the fuss was about. The guy telling me about the bass—smallmouths— coaches at the high school where I teach and played some ball himself, a small lefty who you're pretty sure drove hitters crazy with good control and a lot of junk, two skills I also connect with bass fishing. Of course, anymore, most everything in my life seems connected with some kind of fishing—although that may say more about what I don't have in my life rather than what I have.

Spring, anyway, offers its share of challenges—not the least of which include fickle weather and, frequently, high water. It's an especially tough time for steelhead, and trout, if they are rainbows, are often on or around their redds, not a time they need to be pestered. Shad haven't quite started up in fishable numbers. The surf is still too cold for much besides perch. Of course, you can fly to Cancun. But I can't—for reasons that also reflect a mismanaged adulthood that no one needs to hear another word about.

Bass, then, belong to that category of game fish that, in my mind, fill in the blanks, are second best. I know this is a narrow view. The lefty, the coach, thinks of smallmouth as the ultimate game fish—although I believe this opinion has to do with the fact that he lives in the town upriver near the dam, which doesn't enjoy the trout and steelhead water we have where I live—and which, by way of an obscure order to things, usually ends up fielding a much better high school baseball team, one that delivered two state championships while the lefty hurled junk from the mound. I don't want to raise the class issue too boldly here, but I think if you are an angler and you wish to make sense of the world, you must recognize that class, although rarely definitive, does point anglers, like athletes, in one direction or another, and different species of fish invite—by way of their "character" and, I would propose, surroundings—certain types of anglers as their devotees. As Tom McGuane once noted, "One hardly need mention that more lynching has been done by largemouth bass anglers than by the fanciers of any other species."

On the other hand, you fish for what you can, when you can. The bewitching proposition of casting flies in the surf was really, for me, a call to immerse myself in a five-hundred-year-old sporting tradition that cohered to the circumstances of a buzzed and wayward surfer. I would have liked to have fished in Key West, on the Gaspé Peninsula, or in British Columbia—but no one invited me. And I doubt I would have had the licks to make much happen even if I had been given the opportunity to tag along.

By the time the lefty was helping his high school secure state pennants, he was also a serious bass fisherman. Naturally, this created a conflict of interests—one that persists to this day. About the same time district playoffs approach, spring temperatures finally rise to the point that smallmouth—an innately warm-water species—grow active, moving into shallow or protected lies, first to feed and, eventually, to spawn. Hence, the boat basin. Games and practices crowd the lefty's schedule, yet he's still able find time for visiting the docks or similar in-town water, precisely the kind of spots that can appeal to certain anglers—especially those who enjoy hooking seventeen-, eighteen-, or twenty-inch smallmouth bass, not uncommon, reported the lefty, each time I asked.

Two things kept me from getting right after those fish. One of these issues resolved itself quickly enough: Sooner than he would have liked, the lefty was freed up to serve as a guide, following yet another sub-.500 season, a won-lost percentage that dashed his playoff hopes again. The other issue was a bit more subtle: Not only is the lefty a baseball-loving bass fisherman from up the river, but he pursues his prey with spinning gear, a breach of angling tradition I find as tiresome, if not also blasphemous, as designated hitters, aluminum bats, and failures to hit cut-off men by outfielders beyond the age of ten.

The creek mouth, not the boat basin, turned out to be the start. Mostly, I liked the idea of hooking "twenty or thirty bass, all about a foot long, in a couple of hours," as the lefty reported he had done one evening there earlier in the week. Lots of fish, he claimed—which is why he didn't see any point arriving too early on the Sunday morning I could get away.

He didn't, but I did. I figured a dozen or so bass before the lefty—and his spinning gear—showed up would do me about right. I parked soon after dawn in the veterinary parking lot, as I'd been directed, followed the asphalt bike trail along the reach of a new industrial park, hopped a waist-high chain link fence, and pushed through a stand of bushes just where the creek began to open up toward the river itself, somewhere off in the distance beyond a patchwork of lots and graded terraces.

Is this any place for a fifty-two-year-old man to go fishing? I asked myself, tying on a little Olive Bugger by way of response to this rhetorical question. The water was still, colorless, opaque—*a good place for carp, maybe,* I thought. *But a prized if only second-tier game fish?* I yanked line off my reel, and I sent the fly across the water toward a bank of bramble and soggy reeds.

An hour later, when the lefty arrived, I'd landed two bass—although neither of them could have been called anything close to a foot. The lefty pitched his own offering into the creek mouth—and within five minutes he had hooked and landed two bass, each one twice the size that I had managed in my hour of solitary sport.

"So what are using?" I asked, curious despite his unrefined ways.

"Four-inch Senko." The lefty held up a rubber lure that appeared something on the order of a link of breakfast sausage, a ring finger, or a length of fuel line. "I usually use the five-inch. But these are pretty small fish."

Mine would have needed to strike in tandem to handle the lefty's downsized offering. Yet even his two bass seemed like they should have been overmatched against such a formidable chunk of rubber. I looked at my fly. Tied on a size 10, 3X long streamer hook, it measured all of an inch, maybe an inch and a quarter, max—including the tail. Wet, my Little Olive Bugger had the bulk of a French-sliced green bean. The brass bead in front, tied there to help the fly "get deep," would have been about the right size for one of the eyeballs on the lefty's giant rubber worm.

"Maybe I need something a little more . . . substantial," I commented.

The lefty glanced over at my fly. His look suggested I had stepped to the plate to face him—and his off-speed junk—armed with a chopstick.

What we want to believe about all "second best" fish, of course, is that they will grab practically anything, that all we need to do is target them and we can pretty much count on ringing up fish by the dozen. That's the appeal. You don't have to get serious about it. Show up, unlimber that old odd-weight rod, cast a simple, easy-to-tie fly, stick a bunch of fish. What could be more fun than that?

Like most fantasies, this one rarely plays out on the ground—or on the water—as it does in the mind. You are, after all, fishing—not acquiring a commodity available online on the installment plan. Much if not most of what happens whenever we go fishing has never happened in quite the same way for us before. Every fish, every cast, every ever-changing piece of water offers the makings of a fresh experience or story, events that transpire while we can but speculate why. "These episodes," McGuane observed over thirty years ago, "are remembered as complete dramatic entities, whose real function, finally, is to be savored." Which is only to argue, as I have before, that it's what we don't know that makes fly fishing so consuming—even if some of us may have taken this idea to the extreme and kissed a few too many known quantities in our lives goodbye.

We were talking about bass, right?

Inside of a week, I met the lefty on the water again, this time, finally, at the boat basin. The name seemed vaguely misleading. Why not, simply, the boat docks? We were going to fish, it turns out, right where you picture a couple of towheads with upside-down Zebcos, stationed at the end of a planked and rubber-bumpered walkway, leaning over the water watching sunfish nibble their bait. Already suited up in vest and waders, I felt conspicuous as a drum major at a discotheque. The lefty directed me where to cast—*Okay, in the water, now what?*—while from under the dock something suddenly made his spinning rod look as though the tip of it were about to disappear down a hole beneath the spike of his taut line.

The lefty leaned over the edge of the dock, reached down and lipped the fish. He held it up for me to see. This was a real bass: fifteen, sixteen inches long, heavy bars running vertically up its broad, green and gold flanks, a fish that seemed somehow more oceanic than any sea run salmonid.

The association with saltwater prey was, to a large degree, based on the smallmouth's resemblance to calico bass—at least the manner they are so often taken: short lines, heavy lures, tight drags. Whether you fish with spinning gear, level-wind reel, or fly rod, it appeared you had best mimic the efficacy of poke poling: a stout line tied directly to the end of the pole, lower bait to bottom, wait for the take, strike—then lift that sucker to the surface, refusing to give an inch.

This would not be delicate sport, I concluded, tossing my fly from dock to rip-rap embankment that rose to the parking lot and created the impression that water and boat slips lay at the bottom of a declivitous basin. Naturally, the flies I had tied in response to my first outing with the lefty were on an order of magnitude, compared to earlier Olive Buggers, of zucchini left too long in a garden. I had also brought my 9-weight to propel these awful beasts. Weighted with 1/20-ounce plated dumbbell eyes, the fly hit the surface of the water like a stone and sank with appropriate haste.

When the fly found nothing but bottom, affixing itself to an immovable obstacle, I was forced to point my rod tip directly toward it and break the leader. Although this assured me that I had been "deep enough," clearly a matter of import, I was now temporarily out of the game while the lefty moved about the dock making crisp accurate casts, twice more finding fish that bent his rod double. I liked that he was catching fish: Soon I might, too—a thought I continued to have despite losing two more flies in quick succession to the bottom of the basin.

There seemed, finally, to be two choices I faced in my emphatic lack of success in this fishing. Either it was all beneath me—an unlikely conclusion—and I should return to more familiar sport and waters; or I could pay closer attention, figure out what the lefty was doing, and perhaps gain some insight into my own rootless self.

But it turned out there was only this: Over the course of the next few weeks, I married the right hook size and unweighted flies to a sinking shooting head and long, exploratory casts, coming up tight on the occasional bass without any clear indication why. I never discovered a pattern to any of it, a verifiable approach about which I could say, *That's it*. It was simply a matter of keeping the fly in the water, off the bottom, swimming around in dark places hiding God knows what but, now and then, another bass that tried to eat the fly. Come the start of summer—and the full swing of trout season—that was all I had learned.

As I told the lefty: "Maybe I'm outclassed."

We were up above the dam, at a spot where I never did catch a fish. "But wait until next year," I added.

Big Olive Bugger

Hook: Mustad 79580, size 2–6
Thread: Danville 6/0 Flymaster, olive
Tail: Marabou blood plumes, olive
Body: Antron dubbing, olive
Ribbing: Fine copper wire
Hackle: India Hen or similar large soft hackle, olive
Eyes (optional): Plated dumbbell eyes

Tying Notes

Step 1: Secure hook and start thread. The 79580 is an old, inexpensive hook that belongs in everyone's hook selection for tying offbeat flies for offbeat fish.

Step 2: Select an entire marabou feather with long straight blood plumes at the tip. Strip the webby quills from the base and sides of the feather. Tie in a tail anywhere from half to the entire length of the hook shank.

Step 3: Secure a length of copper wire at the root of the tail. This will be used later for ribbing atop the palmered hackle.

Step 4: Prepare two hackle feathers by holding each one tip down, glossy side toward you, and stripping the quills from the right side. Because you will be using two different feathers for a fly of this size, you can experiment with feathers of different size, shade, or even color to create the variegated tones of so many living things in nature. By the tip, secure one of the prepared hackle feathers at the root of the tail.

Step 5: Add dubbing material to your waxed thread and create the back half of the body. The trick here is to wrap just enough body that can be covered by the first hackle feather.

Step 6: Palmer the first hackle feather over the rear half of the body. Tie off and clip excess. Tie in the second prepared hackle feather by its tip, add more dubbing material to the thread, and create the front half of the body just as you did the back half.

Step 7: Wind the copper wire forward, being careful not to pin down the palmered hackle. Tie off the wire behind the eye of the hook and clip off excess.

Step 8: (optional): To create a heavier profile at the front of my biggest buggers, I will often prepare and tie in yet another hackle feather. I then make several tightly spaced wraps, one in front of the other, before tying off and clipping the excess. At this point, if I want, I can also tie on dumbbell eyes. Either way, whip finish and add head cement.

LESSON 16

NORTHWEST SHAD

Steeped in the traditions of California fly fishing, I had always assumed, on moving north, that I would take up shad fishing. The lineage runs back to the fabled masters, the legendary Bill Schaadt, the prodigal Russell Chatham, leaving us awash in misty tales of gargantuan runs and hundred-fish days. One look at the figures of fish moving over Bonneville Dam in June can make even the most profligate sport seem possible—if not altogether tasteful—again. The math alone affords obscene conjecture. When half a million fish pass a single counting station in a day, you are capable of imagining the kind of lurid fishing, finally, that you feel somehow owed to you—just this once—for having embraced the sport in these ever-leaner times.

Yet while shad fishing in California has traditionally occurred in the broad, streamy flows of the state's Central Valley, in rivers like the American, the Feather, the Yuba, and the Sacramento itself, shad fishing farther north appeared confined to the powerful, deepwater rivers of the region, most notably the Willamette and the Columbia. (Only recently did I learn of the shad fishing on the Umpqua, a budding sport which, like the smallmouth bass fishery, foretells even graver alterations to that great river's troubled ecology.) Though word of fly rodders targeting these big-water shad was not uncommon, the stories inevitably included mention of specialized gear—high-powered boats, gate-chain-like shooting heads, anchoring systems sufficient for bridling the Queen Mary—all of which seemed yet another example of overkill in the sport, especially on taking into account the nature of the prey itself, an introduced planktivore with bloodlines marking its kinship with the family of herrings.

Still, those dam counts do get your attention. Did I mention something on the order of all the steelhead swimming annually up the Columbia passing over The Dalles Dam in a single day? Okay, it is only a herring—but when's the last time you cast into a river that rose because of the water displaced by the sheer volume of migrating fish?

Or so it can seem with shad.

You're told to wait for forty thousand. Fewer fish, goes the logic, crossing a dam in a day, and you just can't be sure of finding them. I love that kind of logic. The other nice thing about this number of shad is that it begins to show up in some of the dam counts just about the time that school ends, a significant moment when you're both a teacher and a father of student-age sons.

One of mine is still young enough to accept the proposition of running down a bunch of fish for no earthly reason but to catch them. The other one has discovered cars, music, girls—and the connection between such diversions and money. I trust it's but a phase. In the meantime, his brother and I try to maintain the rigors of a well-rounded angling education, heading off any which way at the first mention of fish biting somebody's flies.

The John Day Dam, we finally heard, offers a semblance of genuine fly water. *Heard* may not be quite the right word; Fred Trujillo and I took off one evening during finals week after I kept pestering him with daily shad counts gleaned off the Internet. Fred also teaches at the local high school, the same school he attended as a teenager, so he's long past the point of a full-on shad jones. But enthusiasm proves infectious. Either that or I might have dragged him up there at knife point.

Still, that first outing possessed some of the awkwardness I generally associate with first stabs at a new fishery. I always get nervous, for instance, when the alleged hot spot sits right alongside a parking lot. Rigging up, I peered over the concrete curb and saw a half-dozen rods, short and stout as deep-sea gear, standing unattended along the steep sweep of granite boulders, rod tips flexing against the strain of the current. At the far end of the lot, a chain link gate kept vehicles from proceeding to the dam; clusters of fishermen monitored the rods below. Climbing down to the water, we watched a teenager fight and land a fish that turned out to be a salmon that looked close to twenty pounds—and suddenly I wondered why the place wasn't crawling with guys.

"Indians," answered Fred.

"That explains it," I nodded. "So what about us?"

We spread apart and stationed ourselves on boulders just above the surface of the water. Shad in the West don't belong to anyone's tribal ancestry. We might as well have been standing at the base of a tall jetty. Current swept by at a heavy, dangerous pace.

"They'll be right in close," directed Fred, upriver from me. "Just swing your fly tight to the rocks."

Fly? Fred had given me a handful of tiny jigs whose lead heads he had painted with green, yellow, or red epoxy. That's it.

"Let it swim in the current."

Fred did, and in a short while he stood with a fine arc in his rod, a fish taking line in short, frenetic bursts. I grabbed my camera and snapped off several shots, Fred poised with his 8-weight in June sunlight against a backdrop of blue skies and power lines and enough concrete to, well, block the biggest river in the West, the nation's twentieth-century answer to the question "What else are these mothers for?"

The shad itself was bright as a dime, with the profile and sharp lines of a propeller blade. It seemed far too small to have tugged so persistently, which I immediately understood as the species' most endearing trait. *Okay*, I thought. *Now my turn.*

But while Fred found fish, not many but some, I caught nothing. I switched flies, changed size, color, swings. I varied depths. I tried different currents. I moved from rock to rock.

"Just keep it in close," called Fred, releasing another fish. "You want it to be swinging but just barely."

Yeah, yeah, I thought. *How tough can it be?*

Then Fred hollered to me again.

"Look at that!"

Water poured from spillways running the length of the dam. The surface of the river began to churn, advancing on us as if untold acres of feeding fish. Or stampeding horses. In minutes the water at our feet started rising. We backed up onto higher rocks. The current slowly subsided. Then ceased.

Guys in both directions from us headed up the rocks. We heard truck engines start up. Water continued to pour from the spillways, filling the vast pool beneath the dam faster than the river could carry the water away.

"Guess that's it for today," concluded Fred.

But that wasn't at all the way it was supposed to be—certainly no way to get started ringing up a hundred fish in a day. I tried to question Fred's so-called "flies": Did I even want to catch fish on a pattern that belonged in a hardware store? Of course I did, if that's what it took. But I also figured I might adapt the concept of his painted jigs, creating something that required materials other than those you find in a body shop.

Actually, come to think of it, I ended up just filching another of Fred's shad patterns, one that at least required you tie it. I mean, the sport's called fly fishing for a reason.

I'll admit I experimented and came up with some patterns of my own, too. I've got a whole box of them, and I can tell you none of them made the shad roll over and beg. One pattern did end up catching a few steelhead in the fall and early winter, probably because it looks a lot like a salmon egg. Even the pattern I lifted from Fred demands little in the way of technical tying skills.

Like the sport in question, shad flies have a feel about them that points back to days when there were enough fish around, and few enough fishermen, that what you tied to the end of your leader was more or less a lure—in this case kind of a cross between a crappie jig and a steelhead fly from 1954. I'm going to have to bring him up sometime, so I might as well mention John McPhee right here and his riffs on sophisticated shad darts—their design, weight, color, the rest. He also makes the distinction between fly fishing for shad using shad flies, and shad fishing with a fly rod using shad darts. I'm not going to go too far with this argument, but this all smacks of the usual culture wars, the way that some of us still feel ambivalent about ruining our casting loops by affixing lead to our leaders, while others just get over it and let the son of a bitch fly.

Most of us fall somewhere in between. Yet the whole point of shad fishing, if I've got it right, is to leave pretention behind. In this case the old sixties adage still applies: "If it feels good, do it."

Which is also how my own children have come to accept the sport. I mean, now, fly fishing in general. There may very well be some higher good in suffering the moods of finicky trout, only to fool one cagey old codger in the twilight's last gleaming. But they don't buy it. A good tug on the line remains the source of their fishing pleasure, and the more tugs, and the harder they are, the better.

Shad fit a teenager's temperament. When I eventually got around to catching shad myself, not just watching Fred catch his, I had little trouble convincing my youngest son that a few hours of shad fishing would be a good way to start or end a long summer day. He showed some reluctance, however, when I explained to him that he would have to use one of my old surf rods, an 8- or 9-weight rather than his 4-weight he uses for trout. You don't really need quite that heavy a rod, I told him, but the fish do pull and the current is hell for strong. The only 7-weights we now own, I went on, are the cane rods that belonged to my father and his father, because I left that Sage leaning on a tree along that stream in—

"How big *are* these fish?" asked Patrick, politely cutting me short.

"Not big. But you don't want to spend forever landing them. You need a rod with some backbone."

"Sounds fun," agreed my son.

Fun? What a concept. A few of us have been known to elevate our sport just a wee bit now and then, but shad fishing keeps you right at ground level, your feet planted firmly on earth. Pound for pound a shad is still a shad. If there's something profound at stake, you've probably missed the whole point.

Patrick fished circles around me the first morning. I confess I grew antsy a couple times, watching him coolly apply a good deal of backbone to yet another fish churning off with the current. Maybe I had been a little too generous offering him what looked like the best water. *Maybe,* I thought, *he knows something I forgot.*

But over the course of a couple of weeks, things balanced out. That is to say, we both caught enough shad to satisfy a kind of hunger that exists in every one of us who has ever cast flies to fish. It never got out of hand, not by a long shot—not anywhere near as bad, anyway, as some fellows downstream from us one morning, guys with spinning gear who called out the number of each new shad caught, ringing up totals on the order of bowling pins.

We both agreed that morning that we had better things to do than stand in one place and catch a hundred fish. I'm pretty sure our reasoning was sound. Right now, however, I just can't remember what it was.

Fred's Shad Fly

Hook: TMC 5263, size 8–10
Thread: 6/0 Danville unwaxed, flourescent green
Tail: Olive Krystal Flash
Body: Floursecent green rayon chenille, medium
Head: 3/16" Hot Orange Cone Bead Head

Tying Notes

Step 1: Slide the cone bead head onto the hook and up to the hook eye. Of course, you can experiment with both size and color. Mount the hook and start your thread.

Step 2: Tie in a tail of six to twelve strands of Krystal Flash. Clip the Krystal Flash so it looks neat and tidy, leaving a tail that extends three-eighths to half an inch past the bend of the hook.

Step 3: Tie in the chenille. Advance the thread to the head of the fly. Wrap the chenille forward, ending with turns that force the cone head tight to the eye of the hook. Secure the chenille with the thread, clip the chenille, and tie off the thread behind the head.

That's it? Yep. Like I said, they're just shad.

LESSON 17

A FAIR SHARE
OF TROUT

Three days on a given stretch of river often proves long enough—long enough to get what you came for, or long enough to see you probably won't. Twenty-five years ago I was capable of waiting out phases of the moon on the off chance fishing would improve. And sometimes I still go through a dry spell with steelhead where I threaten, far from home, to "stay until I get one." Yet a string of good days can start you packing, as well. You probably won't go so far as to think there's more to life than catching fish. But you at least might figure it's time to move on and try to catch something new.

Still, the logic to a three-day trip—especially a visit to favorite water—is simple enough: Keep your fly in the water. You hear of guys who will fish only during hatches, over feeding fish, when the sun's off the water, when the sun's on the water, alone, with friends, when they feel like fishing, or other spuriously arbitrary imperatives. You even hear of guys who stop fishing so they can relax. I can go there myself—although rarely until I get my fill, a quantity of sport that seems dependent as much on time as it is on effort and results alike.

Which is not to suggest, even remotely, that the mere act of going fishing for three days is an end itself. Let's not mince words; I always want to stick some good fish. No doubt there lies a rich vein of enlightenment to be mined through acts of omission, frustration, and denial. But I feel it safe to contend that no one picks up a fly rod for long solely as an implement of self-degradation—or even simply to cast a pretty line. I *can* go fishing, get skunked, and still feel good about myself and my remedial citizenship. Yet eventually even our exemplary behaviors fail to temper the evidence posed by a waving, unfettered line.

Three days on a good piece of water, anyway, usually does feel about right—right, that is, if you employ a range of tactics broad enough to ensure your share of success. Given a robust trout fishery—say on the Deschutes, for example—the challenge is the opportunity to find fish all day. Great rivers make great anglers because they demand a complete game. I've never once claimed to be a hotshot—but if you keep at it long enough, you can't help but fashion a repertoire of tactics for fooling your fair share of trout.

#1 Dry Fly
Feeding Fish: Upstream

The fish was feeding beneath the dead limbs of a shrub hanging over the edge of a deep, narrow side channel of the river. The holding water was a dark eddy no bigger than the seat of a stool, and you could see the fish touch the surface of the water to sip in whatever invisible fare drifted into the safety of the shadows, the movement of the trout leaving those elegant bulges as if muscles flexing beneath oiled skin that pull at the heartstrings of anglers everywhere.

With a leader long and fine enough, I believe, you can get more than one shot at a fish like this. I'm not afraid to miscast to the river side of a tight spot in order to get an accurate feel for what, eventually, will need to be a cast that lands right on the money. I don't ever expect to pull off this kind of thing. But now and then we do. The take is inevitably as shocking as it is satisfying. *That was me.* Tight to the fish, I immediately began lunging upstream, trying to gain control as the big trout bore off up the channel, under a dead snag bisecting the current, taking to air as I attempted to feed my rod under the snag while line continued to empty off the reel.

How old is *that* story? But does the antiquity of the tale, no matter how recent one experiences it again, make it any less memorable? What impresses me more and more about this kind of fishing is how often you encounter it if only you slow down and look. Large trout often take up the prime feeding stations; because of their size, you can easily spot them—or at least the disturbance they create in the surface of the water as they feed. This is exquisite sport. No one has to remind any angler who has done it even once that a successful cast to a single feeding fish, a cast the fish accepts and eats with the same deliberate assuredness with which it has been previously feeding, is, as Tom McGuane once wrote, "the absolute champagne of the sport." What many anglers fail to recognize or remember, however, is that single feeding fish are frequently available and require only patience, stealth, and resolve to find and fool them. The purity of the encounter seems a distillation of everything the sport has to offer. You see the fish; you devise and execute a cast. The fish takes—or doesn't. Wasn't that why we got into this from the start?

#2 Dry Fly
Feeding Fish: Downstream

It was kind of a lucky shot. I admit it.

Swinging through camp to pick up lunch, I spotted the doctor and his wife on the prime water a half-mile upstream. These two catch more trout than any couple I know; after watching them through binoculars, I hustled down to the river and intercepted them working their way through the tail of the run. The doctor directed me to a stretch of quiet water, lined with reeds, with good trout moving just beyond a blanket of weeds.

The doctor fooled one fish and then set about guiding me into another. I couldn't get it quite right. A fidgety wind, the tall reeds at our back, treacherous wading through the bottomless muck, all conspired against my attempts to put the fly where it needed to be. Finally, the doctor gave up on me, heading to his car for lunch with his wife.

The solution, of course, was the right cast. Presentation, I believe, offers many more answers than the so-called Right Fly. I worked my way upstream of the fish, and I placed a cast so that the line itself landed directly on the surface weeds, the leader puddling in the open water just over the edge, the fly drifting unencumbered with the quiet current. Mind you, this didn't happen the first time. But when it did, the fish I had been fussing with for close to an hour rose straight up under the fly and inhaled it, its attitude reminiscent of a breaching gray whale.

This is the other half of the single feeding fish equation: There it is, a good trout plucking something from the surface, yet in such a position that you may well spook it if either line or leader pass over the trout's window of observation. The imperative, of course, is the execution of one of about a half-dozen different slack line casts. Learn them. Practice them. Open your loop. Bounce, shake, shimmy, or goose your rod. Sweep your arm left, right; stop high, stop low. Somehow you've got to get that fly to drift without a tug from your leader. One heartbeat longer is often enough. There's a fish watching, waiting. Most of them will say yes if you don't do something that tells them no.

#3 Dry Fly
Searching

The remains of a dead cottonwood lay parallel to the bank, its fan of weathered roots forming a dark depression in the shallows at the edge of the river. Twice I saw evidence of a fish feeding in the ribbon of current tracing the deeper water. But both times I put the fish down, failing to place the fly in the appropriate spot to gain a natural drift, mostly because of another tree, this one alive and well, with branches that seemed strategically positioned to interfere with every angle of my backcast.

Some spots are like that. The third time I approached the dead tree, wading toward it from deeper water, I had no intention of trying for the trout up near the roots, whether I saw one feeding there or not. I had given those fish my best shot. Or maybe not. But while contemplating the setup, this time from a new angle, it occurred to me that I might at least try a cast toward the good water at the downstream end of the tree, where the remaining branches created their own mix of structure, shadow, cover, and currents.

In other words, a likely looking spot: How often do we approach these lies with the care they deserve? This one required a longer cast, which I managed partly because of the room afforded by the broad river at my back. There was also this funny thing I hoped the leader would do so the fly sort of curled around the top of the tree. I think the breeze helped me out. And then, right when I was thinking *That's a good little drift*, a big dark fish eased into view, tilted up and ate my fly.

Sometimes it happens. Usually it doesn't. But the angler willing to slow down, move quietly, search for likely lies and attempt to cover them with accurately placed casts will be rewarded with surprising success. The biggest challenge I find to this type of fishing is maintaining both the faith and concentration it takes to keep making one's best casts without the obvious urgings of a sighted, feeding fish. Often, I make these casts while moving upstream, using a consistent and comfortable length of line that allows me the greatest control of my fly. Too often, I'm afraid, anglers simply ignore these shots, plunging ahead toward obvious holding water without considering a timely cast that could very well provide excitement of the most satisfying kind.

#4 Wet Fly
Swing

A shelf of boulders reached into the river, ending at an abrupt ledge from which, knee deep in current, you could run a nymph through dark, promising water. But first thing that morning I'd found nothing, adding lead to my leader until I hung up and lost flies at a depth more appropriate for crab pots than genuine fly fishing.

Late in the morning I returned to the spill of boulders. But rather than wade to the edge, nymphs at ready, I followed the bank, pushed through a stand of brush, and stepped into the river at the precise point where the smooth surface broke into roiled and riffly water, here and there laced with ribbony seams, narrow slots, and pinched, sharply defined currents.

I love this kind of water. What surprised me was that I hadn't actually seen it, not until now, so intent had I been earlier to pitch a nymph from the farthest edge. Now I tied on a light-wire Partridge and Green, and I quartered it downstream on a straight line, starting it on a swing through those twisted currents and provocative lies.

The take, when it came, spoke instantly of a big trout that had moved into one of the tight, funneled slots, a pragmatic, one-fish lie. And when the fish, hooked, panicked and blew out of there, it seemed fueled by the weight of the river and a current throttled to high.

So much has been made for the efficacy of the wet fly swing by soft-hackle aficionados like Sylvester Nemes and Dave Hughes that I'm surprised how infrequently I see other anglers employing this timeless and elegant technique. This is, I confess, my favorite way to explore broken, seamy, or riffled water. The mix of currents means your fly swims at different speeds, sometimes swinging, sometimes adrift on a slack line. Practiced wet fly advocates fiddle with the angle of their casts, the timing of mends, the choice of dressing and hooks, all of which affect the depth and speed of the swing, the manner in which the fly is presented through the likeliest holding water.

This is subtle to a point practically beyond words. The wet fly swing invites the shrewd manipulations of rod, line, and fly that mark the presentationist's game. He feels his way through a run, recognizing through rod and line—and a kind of muscle memory—those unmistakable lies that can hold trout, a tactile familiarity that grows more pronounced each time a trout grabs the swinging fly.

Nymphing

Then there was the nymphing.

Because nymphing has captured so much attention in recent decades, ever since the great Charles Brooks argued that here was the best way to hook "larger" trout, I hesitate to offer more than passing remarks. Which is not to imply I didn't do my fair share of nymph fishing during the three days in question. In fact, during any serious stretch of trout fishing, I will often exclaim, "When in doubt, get the lead out!"

My basic nymphing setup is made up of two flies, the top or "dropper" fly tied to one of the tag ends of the tippet blood knot. When necessary, I squeeze splitshot halfway down the tippet, between the dropper fly and the point or bottom fly. That's it. Of course, the amount of weight affixed to the tippet between the two flies is the significant variable in the system, mostly depending on the technique I'm using: shallow upstream nymphing, short-line nymphing, or deep nymphing.

I should also add, right here, that I rarely use a strike indicator. I understand the efficacy of the tool. But in an ongoing attempt to simplify matters streamside, I generally refrain from use of an indicator, relying instead on the visual clues afforded by a floating line. Too often, from what I see, a strike indicator, once affixed to a leader, remains there—often throughout the course of an entire session or even day. Rigged in this manner, the angler limits himself to specific tactics—the antithesis of what I would argue is the single most important attribute for finding fish throughout the day: a readiness to employ the full range of tactics available to the versatile trout angler.

#5 Nymphing
Shallow Upstream

The broken, seamy water that I like so much to cover with a swinging fly is also where I often begin shallow upstream nymphing. After fishing downstream, I move my soft hackle up to the dropper position, tie on a nymph at the point and, if the water is swift enough, pinch on a single BB-sized splitshot. Then I turn around and fish back through the water I just covered, probing slots and channels with upstream casts that fall much as they would if I were fishing a dry fly with only ten or twenty feet of fly line outside of my rod tip.

This is precise yet methodical fishing. You are covering likely water, maintaining control of both line and flies so that you are quick to respond to either fish or the touch of the bottom. Most of the fly line is rarely on the water; currents diminish line control while moving leader and flies in ways that negate the possibility of a natural, lifelike drift. Less line on the water also allows the junction between fly line and the butt of your leader to serve as a strike indicator. The sudden, upstream stab of the nail knot should be met with a swift but soft-handed lift of the rod.

Generally, when upstream nymphing, you pick up and cast again before the fly drifts back to where you are standing, just as you would while fishing a dry fly. Yet on a cast off to one side, you may allow the fly to drift past and downstream, a drift that segues into much the same path used in short-line nymphing.

#6 Nymphing
Short-line

Sometimes I refer to this technique as "vertical" nymphing: A cast made upstream but only slightly across the current allows the fly and weighted leader to cut vertically through the water column. Again, most of the fly line is lifted off the water; the goal is to come into contact with the fly without actually doing anything to inhibit its sink and natural drift. As the fly approaches the angler, he raises the rod tip higher, finally throwing an upstream mend in the line so that now the fly begins to lead the line downstream.

Think of the fly and leader as a pendulum dangling from the rod tip. You are fishing an all but taut line, connected to the fly without tugging on it. You should immediately feel the touch of either the bottom or a fish. The very best short-line nymphers seem capable of tightening up on fish in a manner that goes beyond quick reactions; what appears to be an almost intuitive response, however, is actually a nearly instantaneous sorting out of various clues that experience has taught is, quite simply, a fish intercepting the drift of the hidden fly.

#7 *Nymphing*
Deep

Unlike short-line or vertical nymphing, deep nymphing begins with a cast not only upstream but also across the current. Because depth is so difficult to obtain while line and leader drag horizontally with the current, deep nymphing requires serious weight—either built into the flies one chooses, or affixed to the leader. Or both. Repeated mends that create slack in the line allow flies and weight to gain depth, but as soon as one leaves the near vertical axis of short-line nymphing, current of any strength pulls at leader and line with forces difficult to overcome.

Are the rewards worth endangering, if only theoretically, both angler and rod? Of course. Whatever works. And the take to a deep-sunk fly just as it begins to swing across current, followed by the line shearing through water and, often, a trout taking to air a remarkable distance from where the line disappears, is heady stuff indeed. Less subtle than most other tactics, deep nymphing still offers a flavor of sport that a well-rounded angler accepts—given the alternative—with appropriate relish.

LESSON 18

SOFT HACKLES
REVISITED

I tried my hand at one of those elaborate hopper patterns: bright foam butts and finicky legs, teased from stems of dyed and stripped grizzly hackle, knotted and kinked to approximate the appropriate appendages. On the water these things produced astonishing rises—but only one per hole on the sparkling headwater creek high in the hallowest of old growths, as if even those lusty little rainbows and native cutts couldn't quite believe the good fortune of such wanton fare.

I switched back to my box of soft hackles. It's a cheap plastic affair, on the order of a container for assorted screws, with six deep wells that do nothing to prevent the propagation of six separate wads of flies. I don't mind. The flies themselves are sorted by color—Partridge and Green, Partridge and Orange, Partridge and Yellow, and so on—with each tangle containing sizes and hook styles ranging from light-wire steelhead hooks with upturned eyes to 18s and 20s with hackle so sparse it all but disappears at the first touch of water.

That is if I can find these smallest flies. Or any other particular size. Teasing single specimens out of a knot of hooks and feathers, I assume an attitude as if inspecting the contents of an owl pellet. What do we have here? Yet despite the bombast and fanfare, I've never once claimed I was organized in my pursuit of angling enlightenment. Opening my box of soft hackles is not so much a decision to look for a certain fly or even pattern as it is a kind of submission to a style of fishing as pragmatic as leavened bread. I turn to my soft hackles as a man looks to his religion: not in search of answers, but affirmations of faith.

I've written before about soft hackles. A Partridge and Green is often the first fly I swing through broken or seamy water, especially on big rivers like the Deschutes, where I'm confident in my knowledge of holding water and the willingness of trout to move from their lies. I know as well as anyone that we can't use terms like *thought* or *words* to describe what goes through a trout's picayune knot of nerve endings we call its brain—but when something suddenly grabs the slowly swinging P and G, often with such force that you feel the shock of the take in your knees, you can't help but conclude that the trout now in question spotted that sucker and thought *Hey, one of those! I want that for* me!

High in those cascading headwaters, however, things looked different. For one, time itself seemed altered, the summer a good month or two behind what had already transpired at elevations below. Late August and wildflowers stood bright along the stream and in patches of sunlight offered up by fallen fir or cedar. Knee-high grass melted into shade. The stream itself seemed to issue from a source untouched by season or sun, spilling through pool and pocket without absorbing a trace of the warm, sullen air.

And the bugs were yellow. There weren't many—certainly not enough of any one kind to qualify as a certified hatch. Yet beginning back at the edge of a small clear cut, carved out of the woods at the end of a narrow logging road I had used to find my way to the stream, bursts of yellow had accompanied me beyond where I'd parked the van, the rattling explosions of juvenile grasshoppers rising like dust at my feet. Hence, the initial offering. But hoppers were only the start. By now I had also seen the fluttering descent of the diminutive *Isoperla*, the little stonefly that few of us can resist calling by its common name, Yellow Sally, as well as several instances of that fast-water favorite, the *Epeorus* mayfly, or Little Yellow May. Plus, on rocks up and down the stream, often in clusters suggesting the oddest of unveilings, as if fabulous miniature prehistoric beasts had suddenly chosen to take up nude sunbathing, lay the shucks of golden stonefly nymphs, many of them fresh enough to suggest that certain stragglers had only recently grown convinced of the propriety to get naked with their less timid brethren.

Of course, I'm never a hundred percent sure about my entomology. Given the approximate size and color of any order of insect, be it stonefly, caddisfly, or mayfly, my response to details and Latinate nomenclature is often a disaffected *whatever*. I mean I like this shit as much as the next guy. But how much smarter than a trout can I ever hope to be?

Which is probably the reason why I reach so often for my box of soft hackles. Do I really need to get closer than that? Probing headwaters, for example, where trout must be willing to embrace a broad menu of moderate fare, your objective, it seems to me, is not so much a fly that trout will say yes to, but one that they won't refuse.

I opened my box of soft hackles and considered the lot. The question posed by the tangles of options, however, wasn't really a matter of which fly will work. I know they all do. Something yellow seemed in order—but experience has proven to me time and again that the soft hackle I fish is the one I catch fish on, and there's often little to show for the results of one pattern in favor of another.

Still: Color *is* part of the equation. A Partridge and Yellow it would be. But as I pulled apart flies, separating first one, then another, I remained a good distance from a final decision. For every fly I inspected was different than the others—either because of hook size, hook style, color or density of partridge hackle, or the makeup of the yellow body itself.

I would like to say I recall which fly I chose and tied on. I love it when I can relate the size of the hook and the manufacturer's name followed by a string of official numbers. I'm a professional fly fisher, for chrissakes. But the fact is I remember little but the pattern itself, that the fly was "a pretty big one," and for the rest of the day, and the two days that followed, I caught fish after fish on Partridge and Yellows, most of them much like the first one, but no two of them quite the same.

Dave Hughes and Sylvester Nemes have done much to standardize an approach to tying soft-hackled flies. Hughes especially helped popularize a method that calls for affixing your hackle feather so that it extends past the eye of the hook before starting in on the rest of the fly and then, later, winding the hackle back from the eye, finally securing it with the advancing or forward-moving thread. Both tyers also like working with Pearsall's silk thread, using the same material for the body as well as the tying thread itself as it comes straight from the bobbin.

None of this is new. In fact, tying soft hackles, in one form or another, dates back as far as the start of fly fishing itself. Another recommendation for learning to tie—and fish—this style of fly is the basic pattern's versatility. I tie soft hackles—or something quite like them—for flies that range in size from midges to small mammals, and I experiment with patterns that employ aspects of soft hackles for every species of fish I seek.

And not all of it is whim and fancy. Picking through my wad of Partridge and Yellows on that headwater stream, I was actually doing more than awaiting some sort of cosmic vibration to guide me through the fly selection process. Well, a little more, anyway. For despite all the juju and literary posturing, I do pay attention to details, some of them entirely pragmatic. When it comes to soft hackles, for instance, the detail I address most is the hook—not only the size, but the style of hook on which each fly is tied.

This is subtle but far from splitting hairs. I'm especially conscious of what can be done employing a broad range of hook styles for a single pattern as I try more and more to keep from affixing weight to my leader, probably the worst thing you can do to undermine the seductive swing of a soft hackle. Steelhead guru Bill McMillan championed the use of various hook types for fishing flies on the swing at various depths in various types of water, and it takes no great leap of logic to translate these ideas to trout fishing. For some of us, connections of this sort become the very stuff of our sport, offering yet further retreat toward simplicity in the face of ever-increasing argument for more complicated gamesmanship and gimmickry.

I use at least six different hooks for tying the Partridge and Yellow—or, for that matter, any of my soft hackles. Each hook gives a different look to the fly. Just as important is the kind of water each hook seems best suited for. There's a rich alchemy to all of this: Each fly reveals its own logic; it makes sense in the context of a given situation and how you wish to present the fly.

The list of hooks that follows is anything but exhaustive. Tyers favoring other brands will have no trouble finding a similar assortment to work with. My intent here is not to claim possession of definite answers, but merely to point out the versatility of a single soft-hackle pattern when coupled with an array of different hooks.

MUSTAD 94831, size 10–12: This long, fine, dry fly hook proves effective for larger surface soft hackles; lightly dressed, it will leave a wake on the swing, or fish just beneath the surface, without sinking, in the quietest water. I especially like this hook for swinging a fly over and around boulders and through seamy water: It offers a substantial profile without requiring depth, moving fish that have ventured into tight, shallow feeding lies.

TMC 5263, size 12–14: Slightly stouter than the 94831, this is another long hook, excellent for spent insects—especially smaller stoneflies and big mayflies—awash in current. But I expect this hook to swing the fly below the surface—not by much, but more in the manner, say, of a low-water steelhead pattern fished on a traditional greased-line swing.

MUSTAD 9671, size 14–16: This one feels a fraction stouter than the 5263—but not by much. It's also shorter—which makes for a smaller, heavier fly. Now I have a fly that can gain a little depth, especially if I start it farther upstream than usual and mend slack line into the cast before the fly begins to swing. With this hook I'm thinking more about insects coming to the surface—swimming mayfly nymphs and caddis pupae—or egg-laying caddis strong enough to make headway for the bottom, even in current.

MUSTAD 3906, size 12–14: Your classic wet fly hook: stout as a boot heel, stocky as a fire hydrant. I love this old-fashioned hook; it sinks fast and you can tie a "small" fly on larger sizes. Especially good for swinging deep in small streams, this is the fly you hang in riffles and swift water, getting those jolting grabs on a tight line that feel like the rod almost left your hand.

TMC 3761, size 14–16: I switch from the 3906 to this hook for small flies that I want to swing beneath the surface without gaining much depth. Also, something about the sweep of the sproat bend looks right to me, a more natural attitude than strictly straight-shanked hooks. This hook breaks through the surface film, but because I'm fishing a relatively small fly, I'm expecting fish to rise to it, even if I can't get them to take a fly I can actually see.

TMC 900BL, size 16–20: A true dry fly hook, the 900BL means I'm fishing a wet dry fly—or a wet fly on the surface. I crave this kind of fishing: Greased fly or not, you end up with just a little blemish drifting along—until it suddenly gets sucked into a ship-sinking whirlpool. Try a Partridge and Yellow like this during your next pale morning dun hatch; call it what you will—emerger, cripple, damaged dun, jettisoned cargo—a soft hackle fished exactly like a conventional dry fly drifts within that tough membrane between water and sky where so much foodstuff collects, asking a fish to come to the surface without expecting it to pass through into thin air.

Partridge and Yellow

Hook: See above
Thread: Yellow Pearsall's Gossamer silk or Light Cahill 6/0 UNI-Thread
Body: Yellow tying silk, yellow floss, or yellow dubbing
Ribbing (optional): Fine oval or flat gold tinsel
Thorax: Hare's mask fur
Hackle: Dark or light partridge

Tying Notes

Step 1: Secure the hook and start the thread.

Step 2: Prepare the hackle by holding it at the hook eye, stem toward the bend, concave side toward you. Strip the fibers off the top side, then tie in the feather by the stem, leaving it to be wrapped later. Wind the thread to the hook bend.

Step 3: If you intend to rib the fly, tie in a short length of tinsel. Then tie in a length of floss. (If tying with Pearsall's silk, simply build the body out of thread. Dubbing is also an option.) Wrap a slender body. Add ribbing.

Step 4: Wax the thread and twist on a pinch of hare's mask fur. Build a small, distinct thorax with two or three turns of dubbing, leaving plenty of room for the hackle.

Step 5: Hook your hackle pliers to the very tip of the partridge feather. Wrap the hackle, starting from the eyes of the hook and working your way back to the thorax. Two or three turns are enough. Then secure the hackle, winding the thread through it and up to the hook eye. Clip the excess hackle and tie off the thread.

LESSON 19

SPRING TRAINING

The problem with fishing year round, if you can call it a problem, is recognizing when the season actually begins. One moment you are deep in the miseries of winter steelheading, wondering if another fish will ever again show a hint of interest in the masochistic swing of your fly; the next thing you know you're up until midnight tying Blue-winged Olives, because someone reported a hatch described as absolutely sick, an explosion of bugs that came off in the teeth of a nasty low that spun in off the ocean and then just stopped and pissed while the trout cavorted like drunken leprechauns. Of course, it doesn't help that you chose a single-digit day in February to dead-drift egg patterns for whitefish, an outing that featured not only frozen guides but frozen reels as well, plus an onset of hypothermia that left your son momentarily seeing black before you got him into the van and wrapped in a pair of fleece blankets. Or that you've been on the water day after day now, trying to eradicate bad habits in your Spey casting, practice sessions you don't even count as fishing, although they somehow fall shy of genuine downtime, a spell or two at the drawing board to map out a season where you really get serious about fishing like a Real Guy.

But at some point it happens: There's a trip in the works that feels like the start of the new year. And because it's the first, and this year you hope to do a few more things right—elevate your game, if you will, to a more refined level—you make a decision to put your gear in order—right here, right now, from day one. The decision, however, is based more on necessity than a commitment to self-improvement. What option is there, anyway? An old saying says something about knowing where you start if you want to reach your goal—but I forget how it goes. All I know for sure is that you only get one chance a year. After that, you're too busy fishing. Or, like my son says, unpacking the van, "We might as well get ready to leave while we're cleaning up."

We're less than ten miles from home when I realize I forgot all of the maps. The fact that we've been on the road, more or less, since dawn, and it's now early afternoon, suggests any number of reasons why I don't immediately turn back and rectify my error. Let's see: two dentist appointments in the city, a trip to student housing to pick up my other son, a stop at the drugstore to refill prescriptions, another at a taco dive for burritos all around, each one the size of a low-top canvas sneaker. Dad and his checkbook. Finally, we drop off number one son back at the house, well stocked with groceries as incentive to hold down the fort a couple of days before returning to classes. His brother and I make half-hearted attempts to convince him to join us. Not a chance. The thing about college, I recall, is the freedom to choose. If my oldest son needs a reminder how to tie an Albright knot, or remedy a persistent tailing loop, he knows where to call.

Then I consider a choice of bridges ahead, discover we're mapless, and decide we'll wing it, come what may. *Maps*, I scrawl, the yellow note-pad on my lap. *Follow the signs, yo-yo*, I chide myself.

Three hours later, the tent pitched, rods strung, wading belts secured, I add *Swiss Army knife* to the list, immediately below *paper towels*. That night, after looking for channel locks to loosen the fuel cap on the Coleman lantern, I'm forced to add *flashlights, headlamps*, and *batteries*, the notepad illuminated by a tiny pulsar affixed to my keychain.

What's going on here? I want to blame the canoe. This is the first trip we've brought it along for the express purpose of carrying us to fish, rather than as a diversion to humor nonfishing parties. That's probably another story—but then again, maybe not. My ex-wife got the canoe and the house, a couple more things she relinquished about the same time she called to say she was not longer capable of caring for either of our sons. Eventually, a neighbor called, said he had the canoe in his shop and, though it wasn't any of his business, he could see where my sons and I might get on the water before my ex-wife did.

No doubt. Nevertheless, the canoe offers its own set of demands, creating in me the kind of low-grade anxiety that has moved me to keep my distance from boats all these years. Mostly, I recognize my aversion to complications that detract from the attention I want to pay to fish and fishing. I understand this is a contracted view. But we each come to the sport with our own peculiar set of needs and desires, and I make no apologies for urgings to simplify in the face of a sport that, in many ways, grows more and more complex the longer you pursue it.

All of which suggests to me—the first night on a river with my growing list of forgotten essentials—that I'm not just losing it. *This is precisely the point of the first trip of the season*, I remind myself. *Now is the perfect time to get . . . your . . . shit . . . together.*

Long, long ago, my mother prepared for trips to Baja with an exquisitely detailed list written in elite type on an Underwood Standard that suggested a vintage closer to Model A Fords than the recently launched Mercury space rockets. The list ran down the left margin of multiple sheets of onion skin paper. The remainder of each page was covered by a carefully drawn grid, with check marks in the columns beneath trip dates penciled in along the top of the page.

The list, however, never quite worked. Despite her efforts at organization, my mother seemed resigned to forgetting some essential ingredient for a well-ordered camp on a remote Baja beach. Even while planning and packing, she believed fatalism was the best attitude to adopt for the magnitude of the task at hand.

"Don't worry," she'd say, despite prospects of my father's reproach. "Whatever we forget, Clella will have."

Clella was Mrs. Snider, the mother of the family that usually accompanied ours to camps both in Baja and north of the border. Mind you, this was family tent camping of a style that has all but slipped from the page. My father had fashioned a station wagon roof carrier that, unloaded, could be turned over, bolted to legs, and seat a family of six. Food and utensils were stored in hinged and eye-hooked plywood boxes. Canvas tarps gave off musty odors from eight-hundred miles of coastline, desert, and Sierra forests. Camp fuel was white gas, and flannel-lined sleeping bags, spread without insulating pads directly onto tent floors, urged siblings, regardless of gender, into the spoon position to stay warm during long, dream-filled nights.

Both a schoolteacher and a Girl Scout leader, Clella ran a tight ship. Play was contingent on completion of chores, none more painful than the dishwashing assigned to two of us kids following every meal. Out of camp, the buddy system was strictly enforced, whether you were in the water, on the beach, or blowing off firecrackers in the dunes. And with her store of supplies, Clella seemed to all of us a kind of sorceress, able to produce the goods necessary to complete any recipe, nurse any wound, or patch a leaky inner tube, wetsuit, or even radiator.

My mother made little attempt to compete. Her list, though extensive, never quite seemed to match what we had with us in camp or what she was able to find. I now suspect her of a casual brand of subterfuge. The list may well have been like an outline a student creates after she has written her essay, because the teacher requires one, even though the student couldn't possibly have brought the appropriate form or coherence to the assignment without having composed the essay in the first place.

Today, my mother's attitude toward the details of camping seems reflected in my own shyness toward boats: Why jeopardize a perfectly good vacation, suggest her measured lapses, worrying about soy sauce, the cheese grater, or score pads for bridge? Early in my own camping career, initiated in the High Sierra and on those same Baja beaches, I also tried employing the all-encompassing list. Mind you, this was the same period in my life when I once embarked on a trout fishing trip, only to discover, five hundred miles from home, that the trout season hadn't yet opened. A list, anyway, felt to me like double duty: When you thought of something you needed, why not just grab it and toss it in the pile?

This style of preparation evolved into a method more suitable for my particular temperament. Rather than selecting what I thought I would need on a trip, I began taking everything I owned. This is not as outlandish as it may first sound. By this time in my life I had achieved that youthful, ephemeral state of grace when the things I needed to live were the exact same things I used in pursuit of sport—in this case, surfing and fishing. Because the other necessities of life—food, transportation, clothing, sleep—were the same whether at home or on the water, "packing" for a trip meant little more than the kind of repositioning of resources that one imagines, say, a call girl performing when she heads out on a date with her actual boyfriend.

Marriage, of course, changed all that. It's difficult to imagine how a leather sofa would fit into anyone's fish camp, although I often suspected my ex-wife of hankerings of just this sort. Instead of raiding the house-hold, however, we replicated the appropriate possessions, which were then assigned to plastic storage crates in the garage, where they often sat for seasons at a time, moldering like unhealed wounds.

Divorce left me in possession of the contents of the garage—minus the canoe—if not the garage itself. For a couple of years I hauled those same plastic crates to fishing camps—until I finally realized there were two of them, trip after trip, that I rarely opened. I sorted through the lot; I don't have the heart to report my findings. Suffice to say there was excess. I do not reprove the luxury of tablecloths in a fish camp. But four different ones, each with its own seasonal color scheme, crosses a threshold.

Finally, I refined the container system so that my camping equip-ment and three Rubbermaid crates filled with supplies were stored in a garden shed behind the house I rented. I'd drive across the lawn, pull up to the shed, toss everything in, and be set to skedaddle. The fact that this system also included a pair of cheap Sterilite drawer carts, chock-full with fly boxes, reels and lines, and tying supplies, and that these draw-ers were now part of the furniture of my living room tying station, says something as well about reestablished priorities.

It also matters that I drove a big van. I still do. With over 200,000 miles on it, however, its days, I understand, are numbered. And mine aren't? Meanwhile, my system seems to work—although it does require, each year, I take a designated shakedown trip to see what I've got, what I need, and deal with the shortages the first chance I get.

Hand soap. ChapStik. Big sponge. The list keeps growing, and by the end of our first full day on the river I'm all but convinced the canoe has some-thing to do with my sloppy preparations, disturbing my already blurry system as if communion served at a twelve-step meeting. Either that or it's a case of bad juju, I think, a notion not entirely farfetched when I take into account the spirit of intercourse that spawned the vessel's purchase and eventual return to my tarnished hands.

But we've done a half-dozen miles today, paddling back to camp and enjoying that exquisite sense of social harmony that comes from having a shuttle service, manned by strangers, deliver your rig to the appointed site by the appointed hour. Then again, we've touched only three fish. Throughout the day I watched the driftboat guys skirting the banks, upright casters pounding the edges of the river with Skwala Stones or little *Baetis* nymphs dangled under indicators. At one point, I considered trying the same thing ourselves—an idea that soon evaporated as I tried to imagine how I would manage the canoe in current while Patrick fought a fish.

The next morning, nothing new goes on the list. Okay. We head upriver and arrange our shuttle, and then we continue north another twenty miles to the nearest town. Inside the grocery store, I feel like a ship steward preparing for a six-month voyage—which is what we're looking at, more or less, if the season goes anywhere close to plan.

A half hour into the paddle, we ease past a slick tucked in along an abrupt bank of impenetrable brush and bramble—the exact kind of spot reached only by boat. Or a canoe. Dark water mirrors the low, windless sky—until a rise disturbs the surface, the rippled rings drifting alongside us while the river reabsorbs them.

Then there's another.

Downstream, we maneuver into the bank, find our footing, tie up, and start a careful, upstream wade. The fish are directly above us, feeding tight to the bank beneath the wall of tangled branches; deep current restricts us to the river's very edge. Only one of us will be able to fish at a time. I guide Patrick into position, standing at his left shoulder, rod under my arm, helping him plan his casts. I don't see any bugs yet, but by the time of day, the cloud cover, the season, and a little bit I know about this water, I'm all but certain we're at the start of a blue-winged olive hatch, a big reason we showed up on this river in the first place.

I raise a hand to my vest. Then both hands do a number as if trying to swat away a fleet-footed spider. Where is it? For a brief moment, I have the awful sensation that my box of little mayflies isn't where I always keep it, isn't where it belongs, isn't with me at all. Have I done it again? Has the canoe screwed up everything?

But I'm wrong. The flies are there all right, right where they're supposed to be. I take out a pair, identical size 20 duns, and my son and I tie them to our leaders.

The trout, it turns out, like just where we put them. The season has begun.

LESSON 20

BIG RED HUMPY

It seems fitting somehow that when I finally get around to needing it, my new ex-girlfriend calls to retrieve her backpack. Her son is headed off for a week of summer camp; of course, I concede, I can manage an alternative on my own. My son and I have been gearing up for a hike into wilderness trout waters deep in a remote canyon in the northeast corner of the state. This will be our very first backpacking trip together—yet another step in rectifying omissions of fatherhood scattered throughout the steep terrain of life: marriage, divorce, uprooted households, abandoned careers, and friendships with women who seem always to reclaim their wares shy of the point I no longer need them.

I phone a friend and fellow teacher, the Argentine mountaineer, Oriol Sole-Costa. He has the extra pack—plus, it turns out, a break in his summer schedule. I'm glad to accept another member into the party; nearly two decades without camping in the backcountry have left me oddly tentative about planning the details. Oriol has little angling experience—years back, while guiding climbers in the southern Sierra, he outfitted himself with a secondhand Pflueger and fiberglass Fenwick, equipment as dated as my Svea stove—and he's quick to remind me that he has never actually caught a fish on a fly. In the past, I've given him a casting lesson and twice taken him to rivers where his streak of futility remained intact. Yet Oriol's real interest in venturing into the backcountry with us lies not so much in fishing, but in further pursuit of the kind of private eccentricity common among a certain breed of alpinist—in his case, a midlife obsession with the spartan minimalism of the ancient Scottish Highlanders.

"If you don't mind, I'd like to wear my kilt—my *plaidie*."

I consider the possible rattlesnakes, the poison oak, the . . . "Whatever," I say.

"I've been experimenting the past month, sleeping out on my deck. I'm fine down to nearly fifty degrees. My goal is to not carry a sleeping bag or a tent."

"You gonna fish in it?" I ask, only half in jest.

"Why not? Those guys used theirs for everything."

I'm not exactly sure a full-on kilt fetish is something I want to deal with on a fishing trip. Yet after thinking it over some, I realize that part of my own motivation for carrying a backpack into a wilderness river is also a longing for simplification—a desire to reclaim a spirit of fly fishing that seems increasingly foreign to the sport my son and I often pursue.

Or that I drag Patrick into. A week earlier, we returned from several days of casting to persnickety tailwater trout—fishing that, quite literally, separated the men from the boys. Patrick got skunked. Yet I didn't exactly light up the river, either—and on return home I went straight to the vise, determined to create the Right Fly, the one I hadn't had to fool those rising, broad-shouldered browns by the dozen. I pored over the contents of my vest, pawed through the Sterilite drawers I transport to fish camps in my oversized Dodge van—and in the process I found more good flies, perfectly viable pattterns, the right sizes, the right colors, the right profiles—than all of the flies I had tried on the water.

The problem? Sitting at my tying bench—located directly in the living room, a prominent feature in the household of many single anglers—I opened no less than eighteen different boxes of flies. Eighteen. Mind you, some of these were Altoids tins, some were diminutive "special occasion" boxes with patterns specific to this hatch or that. But, come on: *Eighteen*. No wonder I can't keep track of all my flies.

It's a sickness, I decided, a thought I return to during the week as I sort through flies, creating a tidy collection of traditional attractor patterns—Stimulators, Humpys, Muddler Minnows, Royal Trudes—for fooling unsophisticated rainbows in a wilderness stream. Makes a kilt fetish seem tame as corns.

But a trip to the backcountry is about to cure all that. Rod, reel, wading boots. Vest. Tippet material. A couple of boxes of flies.

A couple of boxes . . . each?

Besides his kilt, the Highlander, according to Oriol, depended on one other essential ingredient to carry him, unencumbered, through the wilds: oats.

"Oatmeal?"

"Steel-cut oats. Scotch oats. Pinhead oats. Boiled. Simmered. Guys went forever on the stuff."

"Oatmeal," I conclude.

"Impressive, isn't it. Funny thing is, my buddy Stewart in Scotland says that no one there even eats porridge anymore."

It appears we will. Following a trip together to Safeway to stock up on nuts, dried fruit, yogurt, pasta, jerky—all supplements for the staple of our backcountry diet—Oriol has produced a plastic container, the size of a cookie jar, filled with the all-important grain. On my living room carpet we divvy up shared supplies—food, stoves, fuel, cooking utensils, first aid—aiming for an even distribution of weight. Patrick gets the oats—on their own, equal to the weight of the other thirds.

"There's a cup a day for each of us," explains Oriol. "We cook all three cups in the morning, eat half of it warm for breakfast and the other half cold for lunch."

"Good thing none of us is Scots," I observe.

"They're all into continental breakfasts, hamburgers and French fries for lunch. Highlanders got caught out in the mountains without fire—or if their enemies were chasing them—they'd put the oats in their mouths and soak it in their own saliva before eating it. Tough guys."

"You'd have to be."

"You know the phrase 'to cinch up your belt'? That's a Highlander trick. Run out of food and he'd tighten the belt on his *plaidie*, squeeze away the hunger pains."

"Good thing we've got plenty of oats," I say, nodding in the direction of my son.

We reach the trailhead at the wilderness boundary midday under low, drizzly skies. Gray clouds drape the canyon walls, sheer in both directions of the river, two thousand feet below. Oriol claims the mists and tattered clouds, snagged by the rimrock, remind him of Scotland—even though he's never been there.

The wet weather keeps us close to the van. No one is eager to plunge over the lip of the canyon, and we eat lunch and mill about like a road crew, staying dry under the firs and Ponderosa pines. After eating—sandwiches from home for Patrick and me, Oriol his oats leftover from breakfast—Oriol produces another Scottish tradition—this in the form of "a wee dram," the first single malt, he says, he's ever found for less than fifty dollars. One sip of it—smooth as the moist air—and I'm ready to hike, rain or no rain. Either that or start thinking about my ex-girlfriend.

I defer to Oriol's hiking experience and invite him to lead us down to the river. In his kilt, beret, and tall, single-compartment alpine pack, an aluminum rod tube positioned as if to receive radio signals from above, walking poles in each hand, he looks the part of a special agent in a James Bond movie—although no goofier, I decide, than a fly fisher in a vest, floppy hat, waders, rod in hand. Packs creak as the trail falls away into a series of long traverses and steep switchbacks, often covered by lush undergrowth bent beneath the weight of the rain. I check in with Patrick a few times early on—and then I settle into the rhythm of a long descent, more concerned with the mettle of my legs than with anyone's getup, garb, or anachronic finery.

We are all wet to the thighs by the time we reach a campsite at the edge of the river. Oriol's tartan hangs like a dish towel around his knees. But the clouds have lifted, revealing patches of blue above the distant canyon rim, and it appears we have at least this stretch of the river to ourselves. We build a fire, Patrick and I pitch our two-man tent, and Oriol smooths out a spot in the dirt and unrolls a tattered rectangle of Thinsulate, alongside which he spreads a bivy sack, his concession to safety should his *plaidie*—five yards of wool in all—prove inadequate against a night of wind and rain.

"I've read that when it really got cold," he says, drying his kilt, front and back, at the fire, "during a serious frost or even a snowstorm, Highlanders would soak their kilts in a stream. When the wool swelled and froze it acted as a layer of insulation, protecting them from the worst of the cold."

Sipping his *mate*, Oriol looks as incongruous in a western fish camp as a Tibetan monk at a rodeo.

"I'm not there yet," he adds, gesturing toward the bivy sack. "But imagine the look on the faces of a bunch of climbers if they woke up and found me snoring inside this thing"—here he touches his kilt's hem—"covered in snow."

We fish that evening, failing to make much happen in the falling light. The river seems high, swift, and I can see we'll have to choose our crossings carefully. Committed to levity, we wear wading boots and synthetic tights, although Oriol, kilted, soon discovers he needs both of his walking poles to manage through deep water over the slick rocks. Swinging a Muddler, I get two small fish—little rainbows that reveal virtually nothing, beyond assuring us that we are, in fact, on a trout stream.

Come night I fall into an uneven sleep. Outside the tent, Oriol rustles about like a nocturnal rodent. I also grow increasingly anxious about our selection of flies. What if we can't move fish to the surface? Besides the Muddlers and a small stash of soft hackles, I've left wet flies and nymphs at home. I recall, sharply, the moment, while struggling to squeeze my undersized steelhead vest into my pack, when I removed yet another fly box from the pockets, setting aside my favorite selection of Hare's Ears, Sparkle Pupas, Diving and Spent Caddis—flies I rely on, near home, like tortillas and cheese. Instead, I packed mostly big, bushy, hairwing dries—the kind of flies we would all like to fish, if only they would move trout as they once did in all but forgotten times.

Yet this is precisely the plan: Like Oriol, I've bound myself to a restricted range of options, a sharp reduction in gear, choosing this time to "tighten my belt" in order to—what?—see what I'm made of? How good a fly fisher I am? How simple I can make this silly, fascinating game?

Come morning, my anxiety dissolves. I don't think it's the oats. Nor sight of Oriol, huddled close to the fire, half his kilt draped over his shoulders, a pose as old as stories themselves. Without debate, I tie on a big red Humpy, size 10, plump as a marble, confident—in that way anglers must be first thing each day—that even in the short stretch of river we saw the evening before, there are trout holding where trout ought to be, and that some of them—if only the young and foolish—will rise to such a fly.

Confirmation comes in sharp, animated waves. Just above camp, in a deep seam where the river rejoins after splitting around an island, a good trout rushes up to the Humpy and takes it down, starting a ruckus that brings Patrick and Oriol out of camp and to the edge of the water, rods at ready, as though they, not the fish, have been drawn to the fly.

The river, it turns out, belongs to that delightful, in-between size on which pools and productive runs seem always "up ahead" or "just around the bend," inviting rapid progress along the banks and short, energetic fords, all of this movement punctuated by the careful fishing and slow sorting out of details that goes into the discovery of sweet spots and best lies.

By noon I feel I've seen fish as good as I can hope to find on the river. Bright, wild, fourteen- to sixteen-inch rainbows, they rise, here and there, out of the void of clarity that threatens, just as often, to reduce my confidence in the big Humpy when it fails to attract fish. At the same time, I struggle with impatience—a failure in character as both a father and a friend—making sure Patrick and Oriol keep flies in the water. It's a responsibility, anyway, I can't quite bring myself to fully embrace—until a trout opens a hole in a pool and porpoises down with the Humpy, beginning an encounter that eventually ends, a long while later, with a fish in hand that shatters my recent opinion about how big a good trout on this river can be.

That afternoon, Oriol gets his first fish—a grab, like they so often come for beginners, with the fly sunk, swinging downstream. The next day, as I again stand at his side, I get him to understand a paradox of dry fly fishing—"shorter casts, longer drifts"—when a bright rainbow rises elegantly to his own red Humpy a rod's length upstream. The good dry fly fishing lures Patrick into stories of his own: I get treated to the last one when he moves a big fish at twilight from under a fallen tree, upstream from where I sit on a log watching him fish the pool alone.

In fading light I check the end of my leader. I still have on the same red Humpy I started with the previous morning—the fly now tattered, frayed, the deer hair along the back broken and splayed into the tail. The hackle looks as if it had been wound inside a blender. Countless times in the past two days I've been forced to clip off the fly and replace my tippet or rebuild my leader, twisted into knots from the Humpy helicoptering during casts, always an issue with oversized dry flies, more so when the fly looks as if it has collided with a school bus. Once I actually broke off the fly, dragging it out of a back eddy where I was dapping tight to the bank, only to find it snagged on a stick of driftwood hanging over the water. This was the same spot, I recall, where I hooked a fish that blew out of the pool, forcing me to cross the river, rod held high, at a run—a performance, Oriol conceded, a Highlander in a kilt would have been hard-pressed to match.

The next morning, following Oriol out of the canyon, I remember a question I've been meaning to ask: Since these guys wore kilts, what the hell did the women wear? But the long climb does funny things to my thinking—and I find myself hatching a new scheme: I'll attach the battered Humpy to a gold necklace and present it as a gift to my ex-girlfriend.

But I doubt I can get her to rise.

BIG RED HUMPY

Hook: Standard dry fly, size 8–12
Thread: Danville Unwaxed 6/0 Flymaster, brown
Tail: Moose body hair
Body: Deer or elk hair over red silk or rayon floss
Wing: Tips of deer or elk hair used for body
Hackle: Grizzly and brown mixed

Tying Notes

Step 1: Secure the hook and start the thread. Humpy tyers in the past often used 3/0 Monocord, which offers added strength for cinching down on deer and elk hair. Danville 140 Denier Flymaster has all but replaced Monocord. I find the unwaxed 6/0 Flymaster perfectly adequate for my Humpys in all sizes.

Step 2: Clip, clean, stack, and secure a tail of moose body hair. The tail should be equal to the length of the hook shank.

Step 3: Secure a length of floss at the root of the tail. This will be used later to wind the underbody.

Step 4: Advance the thread to the midpoint of the hook. Clip, clean, and stack the deer or elk hair for the overbody and wing. In the thumb and forefinger of your right hand, hold the stacked hair directly above the tie-in point so that the tips of the hair extend slightly past the end of the tail. Transfer the stacked hair to the fingers of your left hand and clip the butts. Lower the butts to the tie-in point and begin securing the stacked hair, starting with loose wraps that grow increasingly tighter.

Step 5: With your thread, completely cover the hair lying along the hook shank. Return the thread to the midpoint of the hook. Wind the floss forward, creating a smooth underbody. Tie off the floss and clip excess.

Step 6: Pull forward the tips of hair extending past the tail. Give the tips a slight twist as you lay them over the floss body. Secure the tips at the midpoint of the hook.

Step 7: Stand the hair tips and hold them upright with wraps of thread. Using a figure-eight or crisscross wrap, create a divided wing.

Step 8: Secure the butts of your two hackle feathers behind the wing. Advance the thread to the eye of the hook. Wind hackle one feather at a time, using the quills to keep the wing upright or cocked slightly forward. Hackle the fly heavily. Tie off the hackle feather, clip excess, whip finish, and add head cement.

LESSON 21

BY ANY NAME

Vises stood at opposite ends of the table. Details of the upcoming annual whitefish outing crisscrossed the room, while club members gathered around, looking for tips on how to tie the appropriate flies. The president mounted a large curved-back scud hook into one set of jaws. Across from him, hands jittery as dice, the club hotshot did the same.

"Glad I'm not performing brain surgery."

"Don't worry," I offered, setting a hand on his shoulder. "We wouldn't want you to, either."

The president let on that they would each be demonstrating a version of the Glo-Bug. I tried to recall particulars. Unaware of the subtleties of the pattern, I watched the president lash on a wad of yarn and, with a crisp stab of his scissors—*voila!*—execute the necessary gesture to produce a round ball of orange fuzz. I waited for more. *Glo-Bug, huh? Maybe like those ones that time with that girl in Kansas City.*

"Now the way I do it—" Beside me, the hotshot's fingers approached his vise like staggering sailors. His yarn glowed pink. He affixed a wad of it to the hook as if chopping scallions. The tip of his scissors, aimed at the budding fly, trembled like a tuning fork.

Do what? I thought. *That?*

Wind swept out of the east, ruffling the surface of the casting pond. Students, sixteen in all, rallied themselves against this sudden affront to their newfound skills. Loops of all shapes and sizes tussled with the gusts of chill February air, the tragedy of lifelong bad habits already beginning to congeal.

I made my way from one student to the next, never free of the irony that I would be in charge of teaching anyone to cast. *Those who can, do*, I reminded myself, watching another one of my tailing loops collapse into the pond. I like to point out that students can always gain by watching the mistakes of others. For the price of a parks and recreation class they should be happy I don't demonstrate my double-haul as well.

By the end of class I no longer feel shortchanged for having had to miss the whitefish outing. Moments before regathering students and rods, a burst of sunshine sliced through the opaque skies, showering light across the waving multicolored lines. *A casting carnival*, I think, not exactly sure what that makes me. But this time it seems like a legitimate image, not a literary device pressed into service in hopes of spiriting a response from the crowd.

Like a Glo-Bug. The thought pops into my head the way the sound of geese at dusk is simply, suddenly there. *Like a Glo-Bug.* I'm not sure what this thought means, either, and I refuse to take it upon myself to consider whether or not I would introduce my sixteen initiates to a fly and tactics that seem, on the surface, as appropriate to the sport as firearms. "Cheap back-alley tactics" my surf pal Peter and I used to call them, often in our own employ. Which begins to point out my own ambivalence in such matters, and why, in the late stages of winter, an angler may press these fuzzy edges of his or her own game.

The argument, if you care to go there, is whether or not a fly "tied" to represent a salmon egg has any business in the ethereal realm of the sport of fly fishing. The pro Glo-Bug camp will contend that where those eggs occur naturally in a river, they provide feed for fish that know better than to turn their noses up at such nutritious fare. Trout and steelhead, especially, are known to key into a salmon egg "hatch," those times of year when spawning salmon are on their redds and misplaced or dislodged eggs tumble willy-nilly down the river. Given the paucity of insect activity throughout much of winter, it's only natural, say the Glo-Buggers, to fish with flies that look like something fish want to eat.

The other side of the argument goes something like this: *Give me a break. You're fishing with something that looks like bait! Why not just use a damn salmon egg. Tie it to your hook. Call* that *a fly!*

Like most arguments, this one quickly descends into rhetoric, his-trionics, and not-so-vague intimations regarding one's upbringing and social standing. No one has a problem with the use of such techniques in Alaska because, well, it's Alaska. What else would you expect from Alaskans? See how it works?

Which, again, is not to deny my own queasy feelings about the use of such a blatantly down and dirty fly as the Glo-Bug. I like to think of myself as a sporting fellow, cultivating refined ethics despite a history of slipping, now and then, between the cracks. Let's just say I've attempted, throughout it all, to keep to the spirit of the game. What you tie on the end of your line is not what makes you a sportsman. Then again, you can't keep putting that lightshade on your head and expect another string of invitations to the governor's summer parties.

Whitefish, however, provide opportunity to sidestep the issue. Nobody will fight you on this one. I don't know of a river in the West with a limit on whitefish. This will tell you something about status. Most regulations list whitefish under a special category called "Other" or "Nongame Fish," which puts them right in there with suckers, carp, shad, and the northern pikeminnow. This means you've got to have a license and a fishing pole, but that's about it. If there's a whitefish season, I've never heard of it. Most anglers consider whitefish "better than nothing," but only if they're on the water catching nothing else. Very few anglers head to the river stirred by visions of whitefish.

Nevertheless, whitefish are often found in the exact same rivers trout are found, although usually in reaches that are slower, warmer, or less desirable—from a trout's point of view. This means that if you fish for whitefish, or at least act like you are, you can pretty much fish anywhere in the West all year long. The fact that whitefish are known to feed on the same foods as trout makes it probable, as well, that when you are fishing for whitefish you can easily hook a trout. Or two. Given that you're fish-ing for sport in the first place, you can slip anything off your hook and call the catch an accident. You may know better, but. . . .

At least that's the pitch. Frankly, I don't buy it. Ethics, someone once said, are what you do when no one else is around. I've muddled through enough dumb things without compounding my mistakes by trying to outwit my capacity for self-deceit. I like to stand by the river and hol-ler, "Who loves you, baby!" And like a lot of other anglers, I don't mind tying on a kooky fly if it means mixing it up with whatever's in season that swims.

It was still dark when I left the freeway, and only barely light as I descended into the canyon and began following the river by gravel road. Nearly all the campsites were empty. Those that weren't looked still as doom, so that anyone stirring would have questioned his or her own reasons for rising.

February is an odd month on a river. The days have lengthened, but little else gives evidence of impending spring. The oaks and cottonwoods stand bare. Willows bend in the breeze, stripped of shadows and leaves. For once the sage seems almost scentless, the smell of it more a memory than fact, as if opening a dresser drawer in which your ex used to keep her under things. The great blue heron moves off as if disdainful of your presence. Mergansers paddle furiously upstream, opening a crease in the river, yet reluctant to take to air.

I had no trouble deciding what to do. The man said Glo-Bugs. Interestingly enough, I had some from a trip my father had taken to Alaska, plus a few I kept in my steelhead wallet ever since fishing with a guy who was convinced—as many fly fishers are—that you should use flies that represent effective bait. I had never really understood the connection between egg flies and the fact that fish actually do feed on salmon eggs. I thought it was more along the lines of that *Cheet-o Fly* I kept threatening to tie ever since seeing these huge rainbows gather for snacks every time bathers crossed a footbridge to a hot springs I once visited in New Zealand. And, anyway, I was fishing for whitefish, although I do need to clarify right now that I was on a sixty-mile stretch of river open year round for flies and lures—to both trout and steelhead fishing.

Which was why I didn't descend into a moral tizzy when, a few casts into the very first slot, I hooked a fish that couldn't have been mistaken for a whitefish any more than a tire iron. The fly? Glo-Bug tied beneath a Pheasant Tail dropper. And not a small trout, either, although I did notice a certain darkening at the margins, as if in response to spawning transfigurations. Mostly, however, I found myself thinking that this was an awfully good fish for the middle of winter, and if this was any indication of what I was in for, this might turn out to be a pretty darn good day.

In its own strange way, it was. I waded up into the riffle and, casting directly upstream, moved fish from behind rocks and down in tight, shadowy slots. Some of the fish were whitefish. Three out of four were not. I passed up and down the river, driving a few miles this way and that, and in each spot, whether in seams along eddies or in the fast water in riffles and runs, I plucked out fish after fish, never tiring of it despite the regularity and sameness of one and the next.

I don't do this very often. I quit for lunch and then kept right on fishing. I ended up in a long, thigh-deep run not at all different than the one above the slot where I started, only now things went absolutely bonkers. Even the whitefish were big, for whitefish, two of them reaching past the top of the diamond wrap, on this rod exactly sixteen inches from the butt. The trout were just too good for words—nothing larger than the whitefish, but hitting the Glo-Bug with a frequency I personally don't associate with much of my trout fishing, and taking the fight to midair despite those tiny splitshot—one for each foot of depth—affixed to the leader between the two flies.

All of which should teach me something. But I failed to come away from it feeling smarter at all. I went out and caught a bunch of fish by a method that, though not particularly savory, proved effective given the circumstances. *Is there something else I'm missing?* I asked myself, peeling off my waders. The sun dropped behind the profiled ridge; I knew if I hurried I could catch it a second time from the road up through the ranches and sage. The point of that sort of effort escaped me, too. *Fifty fish or one,* I thought, *it's all the same,* not believing a word of it but glad for another chance to consider the angles, the rhymes, and the game.

MY COMET

I once wrote a story about steelhead in which I claimed, upon killing said animal, that I would never kill a steelhead again. This past year my son and I ate freshly dressed steelhead on several occasions—he likes it baked beneath a thick coating of freshly grated parmesan cheese; I prefer mine grilled—a fairly typical year, if there is such a thing, since I began fly fishing for steelhead in earnest.

After the first steelhead I caught on a Spey rod, I announced—to anyone who would listen—that I'd never again fish for steelhead with a single-hand rod. Last fall, when I sheared off the tip of Gary Bulla's fifteen-foot Winston, on loan to me *ad infinitum*, I fished six weeks with an old Sage nine-foot 9-weight I originally built for my father, and I liked nothing better than wading deep and firing a long line, double-hauling a fatty old double taper over long forgotten lies.

And sometimes I swear off nymphing for steelhead, too.

Because I'm committed, anyway, to certain vague traditions that make up an imprecise and evolving sporting ethic, I know better than to trust most of my contentions and prophecies. I suppose, like most of us, I kind of make things up as I go along. You could argue it's much like the lowest permutations of love: You fall for a fashion or style of sport, and then one day you discover you've changed; what mattered then doesn't seem to matter anymore.

The truth, however, is I don't like nymphing for steelhead. Weighted flies, strike indicators, splitshot, and egg patterns all inspire in me a kind of benumbed lethargy that brings to mind studying for a class in which the only thing you are expected to learn are facts. You know you can get an A. But so what? Twenty years ago, steelhead guru Bill McMillan presaged my own feelings when he wrote in his seminal work, *Dry Line Steelhead,* about success with his Stone Nymph: "The Nymph hooked a remarkable number of steelhead for me in the early years of usage . . . but I could never develop a fondness for the method—despite its effectiveness."

Fished deep on a natural drift, the Stone Nymph served McMillan well. In less than three years he once caught over a hundred steelhead on the pattern. Yet McMillan described the fly, over time, as one he used "when all else fails," "a last resort," a pattern whose "monotonous effectiveness is sometimes maddening." Still, at almost this same time in his career, McMillan also developed his Paint Brush, a smallish, red-orange fly he fished with a floating line—precisely as one sees egg patterns fished under indicators today.

All of which begs the question: If McMillan, like so many of us, claimed he was dissatisfied nymphing for steelhead, why did he do so much of it? Or, conversely, if we know nymphing for steelhead is effective, why do we rail against these tactics so plaintively?

The answer to the first question should be obvious: Nymphing for steelhead works. The method proves especially effective in tight, deep, pocket water, so prevalent on both coastal rivers and tributaries from California to the Canadian border—the same water favored, traditionally, by guys with conventional gear. Without intent to pass moral judgment on any of this, let me just say that what passes for fly fishing is often, when it comes to nymphing for steelhead, a close imitation of the methods employed by these same gear guys with their drift rods, level-wind reels, slinkies, yarn, and corkies. The main difference, of course, is that fly fishers use fly rods—to which they affix the reels, lines, flies, and other accoutrements that give the sport its name.

The second question—why do fly fishers complain about the efficacy of nymphing for steelhead?—requires a more subtle treatment. I'm reminded of a recent breakup with the sexiest woman I've ever known. For awhile you're certain there's no one out there who can take her place; everyone else looks like she was fabricated out of Portland cement. You'll be damned if you'll settle for something less. But eventually you come around. There really are other women worth considering—nice women, friendly women, fine, upright, independent women who can offer both intellectual and emotional captivation—even if you are still pretty sure it won't be anywhere near as exciting, down the road, should things play out like they sometimes can.

Nymphing for steelhead feels a little like that, too. Once you've moved steelhead to swinging flies, especially flies swung on or near the surface, affording you a clear view of the fish's heart-wrenching takes, you grow reluctant to settle for anything else. Even one fish—even one grab or mere rise—can leave you committed to the traditional swing long after all evidence cries for a change of tactics. Some get over this faster than others. But get over it you will if your dry spell extends long enough while high-stick nymphers tussle with steelhead right under your nose.

Or, to put it another way: Nymphing is the least interesting way to catch a steelhead. But all steelhead are interesting.

Everyone, it seems, has a go-to steelhead nymph. Mostly, I think, this favorite nymph reflects one's personal history more than it does any sophistication of insight or reasoning. This might be true, to some degree, of all steelheading. Faith in one's fly, coupled with effective presentation, yields far more in terms of fish than any amount of fussing over the particulars of different patterns.

Patterns per se seem especially insignificant when one decides to fish down and dirty. Delivering the fly to the fish rather than moving the fish to the fly becomes a mechanical problem that is usually solved simply by adding weight to the fly or the leader. This delivery system can be enhanced, of course, by hook size, fly design, or the myriad of line options marketed as tools for taking the fly to the fish. But all of these subtleties seem inconsequential when placed on a scale alongside the oldest piece of nymphing advice: "When in doubt, get the lead out."

I make these assertions based on the singular success of one of the oldest, most popular, deep-drifting flies in the history of California steelheading: the Comet. The Comet goes back to the state's first great wave of technical innovations, made famous by pioneers like Myron Gregory, Jon Tarantino, and the legendary Bill Schaadt. (An account of Schaadt's version of the Comet's origins can be found in *Steelhead Fly Fishing*, Trey Combs's monumental paean to the sport.) Shooting heads and lead core lines, coupled with the Comet and its next of kin, the Boss, made possible a solution to the difficult challenge of taking the fly to the fish in high-water or winter conditions. No more a true nymph than McMillan's Paint Brush, the Comet—and its untold variations—became, over time, less a fly to swing deep than a simple, expendable pattern fished as a nymph—that is, a small heavy fly cast upstream and allowed to sink on a slack, well-mended line.

Of course, there's more to nymphing for steelhead than this. Yet it's surprising to read McMillan's descriptions—some of them thirty years old—of fishing the dead-drifted Paint Brush on a long leader affixed to a floating line, a method with uncanny similarities to today's Glo-Bug and indicator rage. Despite his ambivalence toward nymphing, McMillan took full advantage of the efficacy of a deep-running fly for the same reason it's used today: No other method proves more effective for hooking fish made reluctant by falling water temperatures to move from deep winter lies.

The Comet, anyway, remains a venerable favorite of many anglers who resort to nymphing, especially in winter, but who do so without choosing to restrict themselves to the most obvious winter pattern of all—the yarn egg. While nearly all winter steelheading requires rejection of anything that hints at the sublime, the use of yarn eggs—or even plastic beads—marks fuzzy territory that many anglers simply refuse to enter. I question all such cowardice. Yet I would almost always rather tie a fly to my line that traces the history and lore of the sport—rather than something that attempts to mimic what gear guys, God bless them, do so effectively with tools of their own trade.

My Comet won't inspire any songs of praise. I like the high-end, hoochie-coochie hooks for steelhead flies as much as the next guy, but when it comes to My Comet, I use whatever I have lying around—from old size 2 Mustad Limericks to Partridge single salmons to the short and heavy Tiemco 2457, size 6, which compresses the body down to the profile of a dainty sand shrimp. These are the same hooks, mind you, that I often cut off at the bend to use as the front half of articulated Bunny Leeches. The point of My Comet is that they're cheap and easy to tie—sound criteria for a fly fished on or near the bottom. At the vise, churning through a dozen of My Comets at a time, I often recall Trey Combs's description of Schaadt's small, nondescript nymphs or "Feeler Flies": "He ties the flies roughly, can complete one in a couple of minutes, and loses them *by the gross* (italics mine)."

I like that picture. I especially like how it helps free me from fussing over flies that I ask little more of than that they sink fast and look alive—or at least offer movement on their deep ride through tenebrous currents. What I don't like, of course, is fishing these damn things, a dislike I'm sure I'll keep suffering as long as steelhead seek cold winter lies.

My Comet

Hook: Size 2–6
Thread: Danville Flymaster Plus, fluorescent pink
Tail: Marabou blood plumes, pink
Body: Cactus chenille, pink
Rib: Flat silver tinsel, small
Hackle: Pink schlappen
Head: Dumbbell eyes

Tying Notes

Step 1: Secure the hook and start the thread. I use the heavy Danville Flymaster Plus (or the older 3/0 Monocord) so that later I can lash down the dumbbell eyes without thought of breaking my thread.

Step 2: For the tail, choose a marabou feather with long, slender blood plumes at the tip. Cut these from the stem and tie in a tail about one and a half times the length of the hook.

Step 3: At the root of the tail tie in the tinsel ribbing material. Then secure the cactus chenille. Advance your thread to the front of the hook, leaving plenty of room behind the eye for both the hackle and dumbbell eyes. Wind the cactus chenille body; tie off and clip excess. Rib the body with the tinsel; tie and clip excess.

Step 4: Hold a schlappen feather, glossy side toward you, tip pointing up. Strip the hackle from the left side. Tie in the feather by the tip so that the remaining hackle points toward the back of the fly. Wind the hackle forward, adjusting the stem so that the hackle fibers lay back along the body. Make three or four complete turns. Tie off and trim excess.

Step 5: Tie in the dumbbell eyes directly behind the eye of the hook. Once you get the eyes in place, take several turns of thread at one angle and then the other, crisscrossing the tie-in point. Build up a thick layer of thread. Don't worry—it's not a beauty contest. Whip finish and apply a big dollop of head cement to the heavy buildup of thread.

LESSON 23

WHAT IS A FLY?

A fellow fly fisher at the school where I teach stopped me in the hall the other day to share his solution to the problem of losing innumerable deep-drifting flies during winter steelheading. New to the sport by way of conventional gear, he had settled on egg patterns, tied beneath robust bunny leeches, as his favorite combination for moving fish made sluggish by cold. Yet he found the depletion rate—and replacement costs—of even the lowly Glo-Bug to be excessive.

"So I went to Wal-Mart and bought a bunch of small hooks," he explained. "Now I just put a little ball of Power Bait on the hook, and it looks just like a fly. The stuff falls off after a dozen casts or so, or else I hang up and lose the whole thing, hook and all. But it beats spending a buck twenty-five a fly."

Such effects, though startling, are not as egregious as they may first seem. Another fly fisher I know claims that when he visits Alaska with buddies of his who don't tie flies, he knots yarn to their leaders and simply slides it down onto the hook, a "pattern" as effective as he finds necessary for fresh run silvers. And my pal Fred, a professional tyer of local repute, sees nothing unusual about threading a preformed Krystal Egg onto a hook, hitting it with a little Zap-A-Gap, and calling it good.

Or this. In *Greased Line Fishing for Salmon*, a text as influential as any in the sport's broad breadth of literature, no less a fly fishing luminary than the legendary A.H.E. Wood is reported to have fished with "flies" that were no more than painted hooks. Though Wood considered the

Blueshank and Redshank mere "toys," they were the logical conclusion of his experience fishing for Atlantic salmon and the importance, he argued, of "cutting down the dressing of flies for use in low water and beneath a strong sun."

All of which begs the question: What is a fly? The argument seems more to me than mere hypothetical debate, as an answer, if one can devise it, might help in the arrival at a coherent definition of fly fishing itself. Or, perhaps as important, what *isn't* fly fishing, a question I ask myself often of late, especially as I watch—and sometimes employ—such cutting-edge techniques as upstream nymphing with a fifteen-foot Spey rod, a form of prodigious dapping that may be just as well suited to a cane pole, lead-head jig, and red and white plastic bobber.

Yet it is not my intent here to cast disparaging remarks on an outgrowth of the sport that seems as natural as the webbed pocket of a baseball glove. That certain techniques make catching fish "easier" would seem the whole impetus behind discovery and invention. Still, carried to its logical end, such reasoning leads to seining, dynamite, or, analogously, as alluded to by both Robert Frost and Thomas McGuane, tennis without the net.

Voices ring out from all sides of the question.

What is fair? shouts the ethicist.

Fair to whom? replies the moralist.

What's this got to do with me? asks the narcissist.

I just want to have fun! claims the hedonist. *And the more fish you catch, the more fun!*

It's all about being in the moment, offers the Zennist. *The here and now.*

Try paying attention, solving the problem, states the pragmatist.

More like let 'em go so you can catch 'em again, chimes in the most cyn-ical—and perhaps forthright—of them all.

You can see I've thought a lot about this—ever since I first tied wads of mussels to a hook while surf-fishing, wrapping black thread over the slimy bait to keep it in place. A traditional fly is also made from parts of dead animals. How long must the animal be dead before its flesh no lon-ger qualifies as bait? Or are we talking specific parts of the body, an ana-tomical dialectic such that the outside layer of an animal is okay, but the inside is not? Yet what about traditional silk lines? I seem to remember an internal source of that material upon glimpsing a Discovery Channel documentary, just before covering my eyes.

And then, of course, you arrive at the question of synthetic versus natural products, which at this point in the history of the sport seems as inappropriate to raise as concerns about the worldwide distribution of trout, that skewed reflection of colonial impurities and centuries of imperial abuse.

Whoa, doctor! I just want to go fishing. Leave the sticky issues for the advanced placement class. A fly by any name would still smell as sweet, said Shakespeare, or someone who chose to go by the same name.

Yet is it so simple as that, a fly being whatever we call a fly. Are there no restrictions, no parameters, no rules?

Now we approach dangerous territory. For rules, we know, are anathema to invention, while at the same time they provide the very definitions that make the sport what it is. I would like to introduce the notion of the "spirit" versus the "letter" of the law, but at that point I feel I've already sucked the magic from the act, reducing the question to a debate about operating procedures.

But where do we draw the line? Or is there a line at all? And why are we possessed of this need to call one thing fly fishing and another thing not?

I recall an evening's fishing last summer with a woman I wanted to impress. Not for any romantic reasons, mind you, although naturally there's always a different sort of buzz when you fish with a woman—even one who is happily married—than when you head out with another guy. But the real reason I hoped to make a good impression was because to do so would mean we would catch fish, on a stretch of river that is anything but easy, and despite all the baggage I can bring to any day on the water, catching fish is still pretty much the name of the game.

She arrived an hour late. Actually, half an hour, but since I had shown up a half hour early, I ended up waiting twice as long in the lot near the campground, fiddling with gear in the lengthening shade alongside my van, while my younger son Patrick hammered away on his Game Boy inside.

She apologized profusely. But she'd been lucky to get away at all, what with the usual unexpected this and unforeseen that. Life. Five minutes down the trail, she gestured away from the river and said, "That's quite a spring."

"That's the biffy," I said, nodding toward an old wood-sided outhouse fifty yards off the trail.

"No. That."

She pointed toward a deep crease high in the canyon wall, where a miniature oasis hung beneath the rim as if fresh grass clippings pitched from above. Ten years down this trail and I had never noticed this patch of green, brilliant as ripe fruit against the hardscrabble and sun-drenched sage. Patrick and I had been on the water four days now; my evening mojo was just starting to rise. Yet when your fishing guest points out a piece of natural beauty that you mistake for a toilet, you've got your first clue you might be a little too keen on the end, not the way.

At the first riffle, where I hoped to get everyone into a couple of quick fish on swinging Hare's Ears and soft hackles, I discovered I'd left my pliers for pinching on splitshot back at the van. Nor did I have them for crimping the barb on the barbed fly I had carelessly tied on my guest's leader. Or for removing the fly from the eight-inch trout my guest immediately hooked and landed, a fish so small for the river that I treated it as a nuisance as I forced the hook out of its lip.

"Be careful!" said my guest.

Grousing about my forgetfulness, I hardly noticed when my guest began talking about how nice it felt to be simply standing in the river. She got Patrick interested in the tiny ranch on the far side, where dogs barked and horses whinnied in the falling light. She noted how the first refrains of the chorus of crickets rose and fell on a light, fitful breeze. Her gaze followed a trio of mergansers as they shot by.

"It's nice just to stop, isn't it," she said.

Well it will be, I thought, after we get a couple real fish. Close to the magic hour, I made everyone move to a broad quiet eddy, where big trout were already on the feed. In fading daylight I re-rigged everyone with Diving Caddis, adding an emerger to the tag end of the bloodknot above my own tippet as well. We spread out along the eddy—although by this time Patrick had pretty much lost interest in the deal, a response I intended to rectify soon with the wail of fly line peeling off my reel.

But I didn't move a fish. Not a single one mistook my fly for the real thing. I went through the usual panic, this fly and that, finally succumbing, quite suddenly, to the certainty that I had gone about things all wrong but it was now too late to change, and then I just gave up and kept casting, determinedly but with little or no hope.

Well into dark, my guest and Patrick sat waiting patiently in the grass alongside the tall reeds somewhere below the line of my futile backcasts. Bats and nighthawks danced overhead. A night heron squawked. Cool air settled to the surface of the river as the last blush of day faded above the ridgeline far to the east. I reeled in my line, found the leader by feel, secured the fly in the keeper. Patrick asked if we were going now.

"God, what an evening," said my guest as I approached. I shouldered my daypack, and the three of us moved up onto the trail, climbing just high enough to return to the warm daytime air. Together, we turned and took in the river, the dark eddy, the last breath of light over the horizon. "It's just so nice to be here."

True, I thought, wondering how it was I just got skunked. Not even close. As if I'd never played the game before. Reluctant to put a damper on my guest's spirits, I said, "That's fly fishing."

And for the first time that evening, I got it right.

LESSON 24

NOVEMBER STEELHEAD

First off, these are summer fish. They arrive in freshwater during the hottest, driest days of the year, a time that will feel utterly remote when you finally encounter them, hundreds of miles from sea, in the low, hard light of fall. By then, the banks of the rivers will have been visited by frosts, the press of autumn freshets, the walleyed gaze of deer weary of flight, the taint of rotting salmon. The steelhead, as well, will seem colored by the new season. No longer the polished alloy of sun and high seas, these are shadowy inland creatures that settle into secure, pragmatic lies, still forging upstream, but more slowly now, climbing natal rivers although not yet that final creek—some faint conduit, falling along a mountain flank, hardly large enough to contain, however briefly, a fish over ten, fifteen, even twenty pounds.

These are steelhead, anyway, a long way from sea, yet still months from spawning. They move quietly across the Northwest landscape no more conspicuous than the stories told about them, swimming one by one against the tide of the year's ebbing light. To find them proves nothing other than that you know they are there. Yet to bring them to the fly means also that your belief proves stronger than your inevitable doubts, a conviction often tested, hour after hour, by the pull of nothing more than steelhead memories and a river drawn restlessly back to sea.

It's nearly Halloween by the time I get back my two-handed rod. I would like to ignore my part in its absence, but it seems unlikely I'll be able to cover my tracks. The posse out at Twin Bridges has fashioned a reasonable replacement for the protracted taper in the top section of a rod slower than any you can buy today. But I remain haunted by the sound of a collision between this elegant fishing tool and the accelerating flight of a fly with dumbbell eyes large enough to rival a 1960s-style hood ornament. *You can break a rod that way,* I'd said to myself, as the shock waves subsided. The next morning, tugging on a fly hung up at the end of a swing, I discovered that's exactly what I had done.

Worse is the question I've been forced to ask myself these past six weeks: What was I doing fishing a fly like that in the middle of September? The easy answer is always the same: Whatever it takes. While a part of me also suspects that I've visited, once again, the dark side—and paid the price for my transgressions if not actual sins.

Faith in steelheading, of course, reveals itself in matters of depth. The true believer refuses to question the efficacy—as well as the propriety—of the swinging fly. No one who has ever witnessed the take of a steelhead to a fly swinging on, in, or near the surface will deny himself the possibility of such pleasures again. Tradition also allows for sink-tip lines and heavy flies as water temperatures drop or for fish reluctant to rise. Less orthodox anglers, however, are known to give up on traditional tactics without undue hesitation—in my case, about fifteen minutes after my buddy, Fred Trujillo, hooked his second fish of the afternoon using a pendant of splitshot to bounce an egg pattern and an Egg-Sucking Leech down the throat of a favorite run.

"Great minds think alike," offered Fred, suggesting an affinity between him and a chrome-bright hen, glistening in the shallows, positioned for the customary snapshot and release.

So where am I in this keen-witted coupling? I asked myself. A dozen casts later, I clipped a Spey Car from my tippet and affixed the articulated Bunny Leech, complete with muscle-car eyes, that soon sent shock waves through my rod as if, midstroke, I had tripped a rat trap.

"You hear something?" hollered Fred, thirty yards downstream, looking this way and that. "Gunfire? A car door slam?"

The long rod crippled, packaged, and shipped to the House of Winston, I felt suddenly exempt from the restraints of tradition. For the next month I fished a fast, one-handed 9-weight, brandished with the delicacy of a nightstick. Pretense and posturing aside, I settled into the pragmatic indecency of the surest way I know to find fish with a fly rod: short-line, high-stick nymphing.

It's never pretty. I'm not always sure it's fun. Use two flies, one of which should be short, stout, and a shade of red. (Whether or not you call it an "egg" is up to you.) Add a couple of hefty splitshot in between. Wade deep. Get tight to the slot. Lob your cast upstream. Lift your line off the water. Lead with your rod tip. You want to be snug to your flies without inhibiting their drift. Strike indicator? Forget it. You need to feel as close to the business end of your work as you do in a bar fight.

Whether or not this qualifies as genuine fly fishing remains a matter of debate. You use a fly rod, a fly reel, a fly line, and those are "flies" affixed to your leader. Mostly, however, it seems a matter of looking the other way. I would like to claim I don't know what came over me this fall, when I force-fed a handful of hatchery steelhead in neighborhood rivers while awaiting the return of my hand-me-down Spey rod and the big November natives that often prove willing to move to the swinging fly. The rationale, of course, was simple: All steelhead are interesting. Dead-drifted nymph and egg pattern techniques are undoubtedly the least interesting way to hook steelhead with a fly rod—but it takes little subtlety in the way of logic to conclude that any steelhead is more interesting than none.

I am loosed from this perverse, spiraling logic just in the nick of time. A week before the Winston arrives I get into three exquisite natives, one of which leaves the water on nine separate occasions in the course of the sort of otherworldly aerial elastomania that sends even seasoned steelheaders to their knees. But in my heart of hearts I know this isn't right. They outlawed this shit on the North Umpqua, I remind myself. What would Bill McMillan think? Yet another part of me can't get enough— not until the big rod shows up on the porch, leaning neatly packaged against the windowsill, an attitude reminiscent of a friend come by to collect on an old debt.

It sounds silly but there you have it. I feel I've let someone down. The rod's on loan to me from Gary Bulla, who sent it my way five years ago when I finally escaped from a life that had all but severed my sporting ties to water. Before Gary, the rod belonged to Yvon Chouinard, who has tried throughout the course of his remarkable life to help all of us become better practitioners of the sporting arts, as well as superior stewards of this fragile planet. What I have done, of course, is succumb to the profound temptation of catching steelhead at any cost, a deleterious prescription for a kind of defeat in its own right, regardless that it says as much about the fish themselves as it does about my personally slippery ethics.

Suddenly I see the error of my ways. Late October and I've failed to move a single steelhead to the swinging fly. This seems more foolish than tragic. Come December, the opportunity to take steelhead will fall off drastically, despite the arrival of true winter run fish, targeted by bait and hardware anglers eager to fill the pot. Crowds, cold temperatures, and high water, plus a range restricted to rivers west of the Cascades, all conspire to make winter steelhead an entirely different enterprise for the fly fisher. You might find takers for claims that one is better or worse. But no one will argue the two fisheries are the same.

What I'm left with, finally, is a narrow window of opportunity to salvage the end of the summer steelhead season—a chance that gradually shrinks and threatens to fall shut as five inches of rain accumulate over the course of a week. Everyone agrees we need the rain; every angler you talk to postulates a sudden increase in fish, that rain offers exactly what we've been lacking for the fish to move into better lies. No one says much, however, about what a tough year it's been all around. Four years ago we were counting our fish by the dozen. This year double digits to date means you've been at it long and hard.

And not a few of us have all but given up swinging the fly.

Every river within a hundred miles blows out. By the time local haunts drop back into shape, frozen turkeys are on sale for less than a buck a pound. Driving to the river Saturday before dawn, I resolve to make a stand: no nymphs, no weight on the line. Either that, I think, or I'm stuffed and trussed and served up on a platter. Or we're all back to tennis without the net.

I leave the big rod in its heavy tube for the bike ride up the river. Despite the pavement, I proceed cautiously, shying away from shadows and roadside boulders. Deer I can dodge, I think; but I doubt I can really fend off a cougar or startled beer, despite the good Winston name. Stars hang overhead, fading into a pale chevron of light rising between foothills along a branch of the river. Beside me, the water's dark movement seems linked somehow to the speed of the coming day.

I'm warm inside waders and fleece as I reach the lower runs of the canyon. Ice lies in little puddles alongside the high-water logjam where I set my pack. By the time I put up my rod, just enough light has risen that I'm able to tie on a fly, a 1/0 Green Butt Spey held at arms' length against the eastern sky.

Then it's into the river and a series of lengthening overhead casts, putting enough line on the water to begin actual Spey casting. Upstream from the start of the run, I still allow each cast to swing through the riffle, reminding myself of an old Haig-Brown adage: "Always start in higher than you think you should." Without moving, I begin to reach across the river, and I settle into the easy pleasure of two-hand casting and the long rod delivering a big fly to a spot where it can initiate its elegant work.

All of this, I recognize, is timeless sport. The practiced steelheader advances on the river a cast at a time, attempting to replicate an ideal presentation from his first cast to the last. In the top third of the run I picture the precise location of a half-dozen takes in this and seasons past, including the glamorous fish of nine successive jumps just two weeks before. Overhead, a sudden rush of wind transforms itself into a flight of turkeys crossing the river in a single, descending pass. Low in the run, I let the big fly swing far into the shallows, bumping and sometimes hanging up on rocks from behind which, in the past, fish have grabbed, though none this year or even the last.

Two runs later, my convictions start to waver. *I had a fish here once*, I think. *I had a fish there.* I've crossed the river, fording a tailout to reach water opposite the road, a strategy I readily employ—and now I'm fifty yards through the best water, approaching that palpable spot that tells you, somewhere in the swing, that you're too low in the run, you're below the holding water.

Maybe I just need to run a nymph through the top of the slot.

Then I have a touch. The moment is so brief, the sensation so subtle, that I'm willing to accept I might have only imagined something nipping the fly. But the debate plays out on the side of what experience alone confirms is real, a conclusion that inspires its own small despair: The fish that has just moved to the fly may now well be one that is gone.

On the other hand, even a single touch keeps you casting. Late in the morning, with sunlight sweeping the orange oaks framed by Ponderosa pines, I work my way toward the same spot of the single trace of evidence I've had of a fish in the river. The fly swings through the fan of soft water inside the heavy current, and I feel what seems like a replica of that touch hours before. Cued by the earlier fish, perhaps the same one, I let the fly continue to swing, leading it with the rod tip. Then there's a second touch, and a third, until at last I see the line begin to drag against the current and, sweeping the rod toward the bank, I hear the fish begin to run against the reel.

There, I think.

I can tell from the start it's a big fish. It presses deliberately for the deep channel that runs beneath the tangled remains of a cottonwood hanging from the bank. Dreading what could be there, I wade in up to my belt and force the issue, using the long rod to direct the pressure of the line out toward the center of the river. The fish stops, then suddenly breaks the surface in a violent burst of spray. Then it's off again, this time riding the current, so that all that remains is the question of whether or not I gave the fish time to turn with the fly at the take, the moment steelhead, in most cases, are either well hooked or hooked and later lost.

Which is all there is to this, I tell myself, some while later, measuring the fish against the bottom length of the rod. A wild male, rosy as cold flesh along its cheeks and broad flanks, an arc of piney green along its spotted dark back, it reaches just short of the Winston decal, thirty-six inches from the well-worn butt cap. That's all there is to it. By the end of the month, I've measured three more fish taken on the swing from the exact same lie, the last one stretching longer than the first. A hatchery fish, I kill it—a decision that requires I ride with the fish pried upward from the handlebars on a stick of driftwood running through its gills, so that its broad, spotted tail swings free of the shaded pavement.

And once more, November steelheading is over.

GREEN BUTT SPEY

Hook: Partridge CS10/1 Standard Bartleet, size 1/0
Thread: Danville 6/0 Flymaster, black
Tag: Small oval tinsel, silver
Tail: Black schlappen fibers
Body: Half light green silk or UNI-Floss; half medium chenille, black
Ribbing: Small oval tinsel, silver
Hackle: Black schlappen
Wing: Black marabou blood plumes

Tying Notes

Step 1: Secure the hook and start the thread. Wind the thread toward the bend of the hook, stopping directly above the point. Secure a five-inch length of oval tinsel. Wind the thread forward, leaving just enough room to take three turns of tinsel to form the tag. Secure the tinsel with the thread.

Step 2: Clip ten to twelve hackle fibers from the schlappen feather you will use later. Make sure you cut fibers from the left side of the feather as you look at its convex side, tip pointed up. (Eventually, you will strip all of the fibers from this side of the feather.) Tie in the tail, securing the fibers directly in front of the tag so that the tail "stands proud." Clip the butts of the tail fibers.

Step 3: Secure a foot-long length of floss at the root of the tail. Advance the thread to the midway point of the hook shank. Take a turn of floss behind the loose length of tinsel, then pass forward of the tinsel and cover the back half of the hook shank with an even double layer of floss. Tie off the floss with the thread and clip off the excess floss.

Step 4: Strip the remaining fibers from the appropriate side of the schlappen feather. Tie in the feather by the tip, convex side facing you. The position of the feather at this point is important. When you hold the feather away from you, perpendicular from the hook shank (as if starting to wind the hackle), the fibers should point toward the rear of the hook, parallel with the shank.

Step 5: After securing the hackle feather by its tip, tie in a three-inch length of chenille. Advance the thread to within about an eighth of an inch of the hook eye. Wind the chenille forward, forming the front half of the body. Tie off the chenille and clip the excess.

Step 6: Wind the schlappen feather forward, forming a palmered hackle over the chenille body. The goal is to have the hackle fibers lay back along the hook shank, an effect easier to describe than execute. Pay attention to the orientation of the center quill of the hackle feather as you wind the feather forward; you're trying to wrap the feather flat around the hook shank rather than twist it. Tie off the butt of the hackle and clip the excess.

Step 7: Rib the fly with the length of tinsel left dangling at the tail. Make the wraps approximately one-sixteenth of an inch to one-eighth of an inch apart. While winding the tinsel through the palmered hackle, use a needle or bodkin to keep the hackle fibers from getting pinned beneath the wraps of ribbing. Secure the ribbing in front of the body and clip the excess.

Step 8: For the wing select a complete marabou feather with straight, evenly tipped blood plumes. Strip the raggedy lower fibers. Tie in the wing directly in front of the body, securing it all but on top of the final turn of hackle. I like the wing to extend to the root of the tail. Clip the butts of the marabou plumes and form an evenly tapered head over the butts. Whip finish and cement.

LESSON 25

WAKING
MUDDLER

Little remains from that era. The Volkswagen van, pressed patiently the length of the state, vanished through the hands of a family addict, victim of a payment plan doomed to collapse beneath the weight of love. The Oregon in-laws, who seemed so much a part of my earliest steelhead dreams, exchanged small-town life for the suburbs, an escape that foretold my ex-wife's own need to remove herself, once the shit hit the fan, from anyone associated with her past. The rods were one-handed, the waders rubber, the flies themselves fashioned out of a faith too simple to last beyond those first fishless trips. The house, the garden, the chickens, the cats—all of it gone, a sober reminder that when the dust settles, all you're left with, say what you will, is the source of more dust, a recycling scheme that seems poised to embrace us, once and for all, in all its infinite glory.

Still, loss comes freighted with its blessings, too. What you find, over time, are the promises you keep—and the stories you still believe. I can remember purchasing Bill McMillan's seminal text, *Dry Line Steelhead and Other Subjects*, on the strength of a sales clerk's emphatic recommendation: "*This* is what we're all trying to do." At that moment, it appeared I might leave southern California for good; fly fishing had begun to fire my imagination in ways that surfing no longer could—at least not with the heat and frequency of my misspent youth. All I knew about steelhead was they were big trout that returned from the sea—that, and the fabulous whispers of bands of elite fly fishers who targeted these great fish along rivers of the West, the coastal West, and whose mist-shrouded lives seemed to rival the mysteries and allure of steelhead themselves.

Twenty years later, *Dry Line Steelhead* still speaks to me in a voice as wise, if not prophetic, as it sounded the first time I pored through its pages of guileless, high-minded prose. In the wake of fly fishing's first great slide into technical gimmickry, McMillan offered the temperate thesis that all of our steelheading could be accomplished with a floating line and the versatile methods developed over the five-hundred-year history of the sport. West Coast steelheading remained young enough that it had spawned its own fresh brood of evolving methods, fly patterns, and theories. But McMillan argued that all such innovation, and more to come, could be embraced within the legacy of ethics and traditional tools of presentation that defined the spirit if not the essence of fly fishing.

Yet there was more than old-school elegance to McMillan's claims. Much more. Beyond the appeal of his call to skillful angling technique rather than a growing dependence on mechanical inventions lay McMillan's bold assertions lauding the efficacy of the timeless, double-taper floating line. This graceful yet versatile tool, argued McMillan, offered not only the most attractive methods for hooking steelhead on a fly, but also, under certain conditions, the most productive.

No words from the literature have stayed with me more firmly over the years than these: "In water flows of 48 °F and above, I'm now convinced that surface fishing methods will move more steelhead per hour of casting time than any other single level of presentation." In chapter after chapter, McMillan repeated this claim—a contention so radical it seems, now, the cant of some distant era, issued from a remote corner of the world. Surface presentations? For steelhead? Travel West Coast rivers today and more steelhead anglers than not will have strike indicators affixed to their leaders, a telltale sign that they are nymphing, probably with some sort of egg pattern or rubber-appendaged concoction. The minority who favor the traditional swing will often rely on sink-tip lines; or, when you do encounter the single hue of a full floating line, the fly of choice will likely range from an elegant Spey fly to the coarse but effective leech patterns, some long enough to appear more like eels as they slither and writhe through their slow, seductive, subsurface swing.

But an actual surface pattern?

Who believes in that?

Bill McMillan did. And like all true believers, he found evidence, time and again, that confirmed his beliefs, persistent testimony from steelhead themselves. Armed with thermometer, notebook, and a scientist's will and discipline, McMillan recorded the results of untold numbers of days on the water, and his firsthand experience proved—to him at least—that in water temperatures from 48–58 °F, flies swinging on or in the surface moved more steelhead than flies presented at any other level in the water column.

There was one snag, however, in McMillan's methodology—the age-old conundrum in all theories about fishing success. Granted, McMillan showed, with carefully plotted graphs, that his catch rate, when fishing surface presentations, increased dramatically as water temperatures approached and then entered the 48–58 °F range. But did that prove surface methods worked better than other methods? Or was it simply evidence that in this temperature range the fishing was better, that steelhead moved more readily to any lure or fly?

But what did I know? Here I was, straight off the beach, where, without examples in front of me, no one else to show the way, fish had come roaring through the surf to grab my crudely constructed streamers—and now some guy was telling me, if I understood him right, that I could get steelhead, in certain conditions, to rise to the fly, opening the surface of the river as if a breach of consciousness itself, a five- or ten- or fifteen-pound fish eating the fly like a goddamn feeding trout?

It sounded good to me. For beyond the talk of "catch rates" and "fishing success," beyond even the proof of hundreds and hundreds of steelhead raised to surface flies, I fell under the spell of the spirit of McMillan's sport. In a late chapter of his book, from the portion titled "Other Subjects," McMillan told how his father, an experienced bait and spinner angler, found success fly fishing for Deschutes trout only after heeding the advice of "Old Slim, the tall railroad man," who convinced McMillan's father to "leave the meat stick"—his bait casting gear—"at home." McMillan himself came to realize the import of Old Slim's advice during his own adolescent struggles to catch his first steelhead on a fly: As a sixteen-year-old, when he finally left a meat stick of his own at home, he promptly moved his first summer run to the fly.

Framing these anecdotes was McMillan's fundamental belief in the efficacy, the versatility, and, as important, the pleasures of fishing with the floating line. We even suspect him of intimating the moral superiority of dry line aficionados. In his preface, he mentions how he "weaned" himself from the use of sinking lines. Throughout the rest of the book, the floating line is a given, the appropriate tool for all steelhead fly fishing. McMillan recounts his development of deepwater presentations and nymphing techniques using long leaders and heavy flies, as well as his persistent explorations into the limits of surface presentations to move steelhead in all temperatures and all seasons of the year—so that, come book's end, we can hardly disagree with the argument that the floating line works just fine, thank you, a case built on the evidence of over two thousand steelhead caught in a career spanning approximately twenty years leading up to the publication of *Dry Line Steelhead*.

All of which I understood—and believed—at a level that had little to do with success, nor the versitality or even consecration of the floating line. Reading *Dry Line Steelhead*, I recognized the tenor of sport that had compelled me to wade into surf with a fly rod. I recalled that moment in my surf fishing career when I realized, almost childishly, that if you fish with flies, you'll catch fish on flies. Beyond the data and the graphs, the proofs and articulate reasoning, McMillan offered incentive and inspiration to attempt methods of presentation that invited one to learn more about steelhead—and, in the process, one's capacity for growth as an angler—than any other fly fishing methods. The fact that McMillan employed surface presentations whenever water temperatures approached the optimal range, and he often experimented, regardless of temperatures, with these same methods, meant that, over time, he could attribute much of his success to surface methods. In other words, McMillan caught fish by the methods he fished, and liked to fish, the most—one of the great axioms of the sport.

But first you must believe.

I wish I could say I always do. Yet belief in steelheading—if not all fishing—is a most fragile substance, and only the purest of heart will maintain faith in surface presentations should other anglers, using other methods, produce fish on the ends of their lines. You ask yourself, "Why should *I* go without?" And thus begins the cycle of temptation that undermines belief, such that the surface fly is abandoned, making it impossible for one to develop the skills—and faith—required to make those startling discoveries about steelhead and, at times, their remarkable responses to presentations of the surface fly.

Of course, some will argue, "All I care about is catching fish."

To which McMillan responded, "Given the right water temperature, surface presentations work best."

My own lack of faith is immeasurable. I remember the afternoon last year, sometime in late September, when I finally decided, *This is it. If I don't start fishing the* Waking Muddler *now, the season for surface flies will pass.* The day was warm, the sun behind the hillside, the oak trees the color of olives in the deep shade spread across the water. A hundred yards of textbook steelhead run stretched between me and a broad tailout where the river split in two, spilling off into heavy riffle that chafed the flanks of a narrow island, trimmed in sunlight at its lower end. I'd been on the run once before, a quick pass with a sink tip and Green Butt Spey, a routine I had settled on, with some success, since the season began in earnest in late August. Following that brief attempt, however, I'd met a guy coming down from the road who informed me, after I said I hadn't touched anything, that he had taken two fish there the evening before.

So it was holding water—the very first thing you must believe before you begin etching the surface with a swinging fly. McMillan mastered and honed his dry line skills on waters he knew as intimately as his own family. For some of us, that might not be well enough. The corollary to any theory about steelhead, of course, is that presentation is meaningless if the water you're fishing doesn't hold fish. Yet how do you know for sure? Experience, coupled with the act of fishing itself, provide, at best, an approximate answer—such that, at some point, the whole subject must be treated as a kind of abstraction. You don't know if a steelhead is there, and you won't know unless a steelhead grabs your fly—or reveals itself in some other definitive way. By a profound leap of logic, one can eventually reduce all of these questions to truisms so simple that they, too, take on an abstract quality, the consideration of which, once you enter the river, will do nothing to improve your chances of catching a fish. To wit, (a) you won't move steelhead to the surface if you don't fish with a surface fly, and (b) you don't catch fish without your fly in the water.

Now where was I?

As I left the swift water at the top of the run, I could finally see the muddler's provocative wake, drawn against the current as if by a finger trailed along the face of a wave. At the right pace, there's a look to the wake, coupled with a tension running through the rod, that makes the hair on the back of my neck quiver, a kind of muscle memory that is based on genuine, empirical evidence, no matter the thousands of casts I've watched the same presentation, in the same water, do nothing but swing to the bank. You know, if steelhead hold in the run, this is where they'll be, and if they are, you know they can see that wake, spreading from the swinging fly as if a conflagration painted across a nighttime sky.

Eat it, you think—and if you are a better angler than I am, you can repeat that thought cast after cast, through the entire run, run after run, hour after hour, day after day.

I was still a believer, sometime later, when Jeff Cottrell arrived, snaking his two-hander through the streamside brush. Jeff, a shop owner, had phoned the evening before and said he'd look for my van; now, nodding, he held up his hands, spread apart the length of a steelhead. Got one? I shook my head. But as soon as he was close, I let him in on my game.

"How 'bout this water?" I gestured to include the weather, the shadows, the quiet air—the possibilities of the moment. "I'm gonna make one come up."

Jeff nodded again. *Why not?*

But a half hour later I was deep in the run, the muddler swinging through the broad, slow tailout. By now, the timeless anxiety of steelheading had begun to creep up on me: *You mean I'm not going to get one?* The loop, stretching off the tip of my rod, still held its shape; the line, on the swing, looked true as the path of a pendulum. Near the end of the swing, the fly settled into the surface, all but hanging in the soft current. Narrow slots traced the uneven basalt bottom, limned in lime-colored weed that had snagged the low-water Spey fly I had tried to swing, last visit, through these same shallow lies.

Eat it.

I didn't see the take. Perhaps, barely swinging, the trim little muddler had fallen just beneath the surface, so that, when the steelhead grabbed, gentle as a nudge, the surface remained undisturbed—at least until the fish had turned, and the pull of the line set the hook in place.

Later, when the water grew quiet again, I slid the fish back into the river, and Jeff clapped me on the back. "He ate it," he said—the same thing he repeated, later still, after another steelhead had grabbed the muddler from nearly the exact same lie.

Such is the source of belief. In the next three weeks, the muddler rose over a dozen fish, more than half of which came to hand. Slow water, fast water, shallow and deep, runs narrow and wide, it all seemed to hold fish not only willing to rise, but compelled to the surface by the sparse muddler's faint, seductive wake. The weather turned cold and I went right on swinging the surface fly—until, after two fishless outings, I switched to a sink tip and a 1/0 Spey Car, and steelhead responded to the traditional, subsurface swing.

Once again, I had quit believing.

STEELHEAD CADDIS

(by Bill McMillan, from *Dry Line Steelhead*)
Thread: Brown 6/0 prewax
Body: Spun hare's mask using orange-toned fur at base of ear,
or Australian opposum using orange/rust tones, or any dubbing that
matches prevalent insect activity (black, yellow, olive, etc.)
Wing: Mottled turkey wing rolled and cupped tent fashion
Head (collar): Sparse deer hair trimmed with a few strands
straying back
Hook: Wilson dry fly, size 6–12

Tying Notes

In Trey Combs's *Steelhead Fly Fishing*, McMillan describes his Steelhead Caddis as "essentially a sparse, low-water variation on the Muddler Minnow that is meant to ride on the surface with a trailing wake when fished against the current, or to float in the surface film when greased and fished on a dry-fly natural float." In his own book, McMillan states that after developing the fly and learning the methods to fish it, he came to rely on Steelhead Caddis for "the majority of his steelhead fishing from May through October." At times he favored fishing the Steelhead Caddis with a riffle hitch, a method anyone interested in surface presentations will want to experiment with, especially as a means to keep sparsely dressed flies waking on the swing.

Waking Muddler

Hook: Wilson dry fly, size 4–10
Thread: Black 6/0 Flymaster, unwaxed
Butt: Silk floss, red, red and orange, or yellow
Body: Black silk floss
Ribbing: Small flat tinsel, silver
Wing/collar: Soft-spun deer hair, sparse, trimmed, with a few strands
straying black—as per McMillan's Steelhead Caddis

Tying Notes

The Waking Muddler follows the Steelhead Caddis in a direction McMillan took in "undressing" and simplifying the original Muddler Minnow. After the usual unscientific experimentation that most of us perform, I decided the Steelhead Caddis's standard Muddler turkey wing didn't move any more fish for me. Likewise, the Waking Muddler's floss, ribbed body is as sparse as you can get and still have color and contrast. Clearly, this is a pattern for low, clear water—conditions so common to steelheading in late summer and early fall. At times I wonder if the Waking Muddler might not really be a kind of surface soft hackle, a notion that should help any angler think about how to present a waking fly. When I use a riffling hitch, I tighten the tippet material just behind the eye of the hook, never behind the trimmed muddler "head" or collar. Over certain lies, fishing the Waking Muddler hitched is the only way to get the fly to wake—yet as often as not, it seems that the fly moving up and down through the surface film is what triggers a grab. But do we ever know?

LESSON 26

STROKE AND
TIMING

The guide says switch tips. Steelhead hold, he believes, in the narrow slot tight to the far bank, and though clients have never taken fish out of the run, he feels certain this is only because none of them have been capable of throwing a long enough line. Flattered, I swap my Type VI for an intermediate tip, one I've never used before. I build a leader, tie on the guide's four-inch, black and blue String Leech, and I begin working line out into a sweep of slow current punctuated by isolated basalt boulders, the reason the guide doesn't want me swinging a fast-sinking tip.

Long before the fly is close to reaching the targeted slot, it begins collapsing on top of the leader. Flustered, I run through the litany of errors that plague my Spey casting, bad habits ingrained by years of unsupervised practice and reckless self-analysis. Nothing helps. From the bank, the guide asks if I mixed up tips, if I somehow looped on a 6-weight, say, instead of a 9-weight.

"It's like your rod's not loading," he says.

I assure him I have but one wallet with me—and the tips that came with my line.

"Try stopping the rod higher," he suggests.

I do. And we both watch, again, as fly and leader settle to the water as if a kite on a broken string.

"Or not," he adds.

I attempt a fresh series of minor alterations, making adjustments at specific junctures in my stroke that result, over and over, in the feeblest of fluttering presentations. By now, I'm pressing, rushing my casts, the very worst thing one can do in Spey casting, if not fly casting as a whole. I pause a moment, take a break, try to settle down. *It's good to be alive and fishing,* I remind myself—while across the river, that narrow strip of holding water slides just beyond my reach, undisturbed by fly, leader, line—or the frothy gale of a hooked and panicked steelhead.

Casting has often humiliated me. In this I feel certain I'm not alone. Although we've all been told that casting is only one aspect of the sport, and very many of us know successful fly fishers who prove only mediocre casters, we understand, most of us, that if we could deliver the fly more accurately, over greater distances, and in all manner of wind, weather, and perverse alignment of obstacles that haunt even our deepest sleep, we would nearly always improve our chances of catching fish.

And have more fun, too. For the truth is, good fly casting does offer its own discrete pleasures, even if the point of it remains, as it should, inextricably linked with attempts to catch fish. Good casts are, by definition, more effective casts—whether any one of them actually ends up moving a fish or not. Arguments weighing the relative merits of form and function find their advocates in nearly all other sports; but in fly fishing form wins hands down. A good cast is a pretty cast. Recognizing, creating, and repeatedly replicating an elegant, aerodynamic loop remains, for most of us, the salient challenge across the breadth of our various fly fishing experiences.

It's the guide's idea I check for ice—or a buildup of ice sufficient to prevent my line from sailing on its merry way. December, there's ice everywhere, from rod guides to rocks at river's edge, from the plywood floor of our pontoon raft to the canyon walls rising through a low ceiling of gray, merciless clouds. Have I mentioned the cold? My partner, Jeff Cottrell, and I resemble a new order of reprobate, the Fleeced Bandit, only our eyes visible through layers as complex as the skin of a turtle. Two runs back, after the first fish of the morning, Jeff and our guide, Marty Sheppard, had me expose my face for a round of photos, the usual assortment of grip-and-grin shots that Marty interrupted, midfocus, to comment on the brightness and exquisite contours of my catch—but would I please do something about that "two-inch-long thing" hanging from the tip of my nose?

This was the steelhead, anyway, that has prompted Marty to position me at the top of a promising run where clients have failed to take a fish. If only I can deliver another decent cast. That the run holds steelhead seems to me an all but verified fact. Moments before I hooked that first steelhead, Marty had pulled one of those guide stunts that make guys like me spend the rest of the day panting over suggested lies. Just as I cast, I had heard him tell Jeff, still at the raft, that I was at the spot in the run where he likes to turn his back, maybe for good luck, because when he does, he so often ends up hearing a voice, behind him, announce a hookup. While I had tried to sort out just exactly what Marty was saying to Jeff, my fly stopped midswing, and the line grew taut.

"Look at that," I offered, swinging the rod against the weight of a running steelhead.

All of which conspires, now, to nudge me toward the edge. The cold, the promise of another steelhead, a new tip I'm unable to cast, my own limitations with a two-handed rod—all of it compounds my timeless sense of having failed, despite the years, to master my craft. What have I been doing with my life if, suddenly, I can't even punch a four-inch fly across a timid reach of water where steelhead, I'm now convinced, await, jaws snapping, a decent presentation? Can I possibly convince myself, at this bleak moment, that the circuitous routes, the abandoned hopes, the messy wakes have been worth it?

I back out of the run. Cold air, gripping my waders, begins encrusting my legs in ice. If nothing else, I decide, I can restring a Type III tip, downsize the fly so it stays up in the swing, and at least put a cast into the holding water. This is the same argument, unfortunately, I've been known to use in the face of a bunch of unresponsive feeding trout: If I can't get them to eat my flies, I'll just annoy them until they quit eating or go away.

End of problem.

It's while swapping out tips again, however, that I notice two things that deliver me from the worst of my self-incrimination. First, my intermediate tip—a clear monofilament material—has taken on the pliancy of speaker wire. In comparison to the relative suppleness of traditional woven-core line, either floating or sinking, this transparent material, in the cold, feels like it should be attached to a kitchen appliance. *How are you supposed to cast this stuff?* I wonder.

Maybe I'm not a complete loser after all.

The other thing I notice is Marty, our guide, knee deep in the top of the run, launching a textbook cast toward the far bank with his own two-handed rod.

This isn't quite what it seems. Marty, as I understand it, is on limited duty; he's struck a bargain with Jeff, who owns a fly shop and can direct customers Marty's way. (My own role in this deal remains vague: "Just cover the tip," advised Jeff.) This good-ole-boy deal is part of the reason, of course, we're out here freezing our fannies off at the cusp of the season—and why Marty feels perfectly justified stringing up a rod and wading into action, especially when he still hasn't seen a cast good enough to test his theory that steelhead, if they're here, will hold in the sliver of current tight to the far bank.

Which, two graceful casts later, he discovers they do.

Fly casting *is* a beauty contest. And no form of fly casting reaches a higher level of aesthetics than the various forms of Spey casting with double-handed or sometimes even single-handed rods. Spey casting is to fly casting what snooker is to pool. The tools used in all of fly fishing are essentially the same. Yet Spey casting offers the widest range of solutions to the problem of delivering the fly across moving water, and when used properly, Spey casting presents the fly over greater distances, and with less effort, than any other means of casting the fly.

All of this is common knowledge. Attend a Spey casting clinic, watch a Real Guy perform his magic, and your perception of the efficacy and versatility of a fly rod will change forever. Less widely known, however, is the enigmatic truth that Spey casting reflects the same principles that govern all fly casting, and if anglers understand these principles, they can unravel the mysteries that haunt the various schools and styles and Spey casting dialects, if not also improve their casting regardless of the kinds of fly rods, lines, and reels they carry to water's edge.

Not everyone, of course, will buy this argument. At my very first Spey casting lesson, the instructor, a shop owner, told me that a beginner needs to "forget everything he knows about one-hand fly casting." In this fellow's defense, I should report that he made no pretense of being a genuine Spey casting teacher, and he gave me a lesson only because I begged him to let me hire him for an hour to show me how to get started after good fortune delivered the necessary equipment that I had been staring at, scratching my head, for six months. Now, a zillion or two casts later, I can still recall those first tentative moments trying to sort out how I was supposed to wield that long, powerful rod.

As for what the guy told me about "forgetting everything," I can only add this comment: *Horseshit.*

In two excellent books about fly casting, Ed Jaworowski describes four *principles* that hold true—and don't change—no matter what kind of casting you do. Jaworowski's contention, which I agree with, is that if you understand these principles and how they apply to what you are trying to do with a fly rod, you are well on your way to mastering any cast. Better still, an understanding and application of these principles allow you to critique and address problems in your casting, especially as flaws and errors are revealed in a careful reading of the line and casting loop.

My intention here is not to dilute Ed Jaworowski's ideas in any way. Read him yourself. Better yet, buy one of his books. But right now, before you pick up a fly rod of any kind again, you should begin committing his four principles to memory, begin thinking about them in terms of your own casting, and how is it, when things go wrong, you are violating one or—as is often the case—more of these four principles that are common to all fly casting.

Principle One: Before you can load the rod, you must eliminate slack, creating line tension against the tip of the rod.

Principle Two: To load the rod, move it with increasing speed throughout the stroke; stop the rod abruptly when you have the load you require for the cast you want to make.

Principle Three: The line goes in the direction the tip is traveling when the rod straightens.

Principle Four: The longer the casting stroke, the less effort required on your part to make the cast.

These principles describe what happens in every fly cast, both the good and the bad, and regardless of whether the cast is made with one hand or two hands, backhand, or, as the Brits say, cackhand. I especially like thinking about these principles in terms of Spey casting, which seems, more and more, to elicit a bewildering mishmash of contrasting opinions, styles, strokes, and even equipment. But at some level, everyone's doing the exact same thing. Or trying to.

Consider, in the end, your stroke and timing. Apply Jaworowski's principles to every cast you want to make, every one you want to learn, every casting problem you encounter. Those sexy loops that Real Guys throw reflect a precise application of Jaworowski's principles—and the elimination of the multifarious ways the most of us habitually violate one or all of them. Take the time to improve, because good casting is more fun than lousy casting. Believe me, I know—and I'm not just talking about a cold day in December, faced with a faultless steelhead run, a frozen tip, and a hungry guide breathing down my neck.

THE RAINY SHAME
OF WINTER

The Rain

In the Rockies it's snow. In the Northwest, it's rain.

When it all breaks loose, as it did last week, I like to check the river levels online, scoping out the magnitude of the hydrological giddy-up that makes the region the special place it is. Example: Between the second and sixth of November, flows on the Queets River, on the West End of the Olympic Peninsula, increased from 600 to 115,000 cfs, the river rising, in the process, twenty vertical feet. These are not typos—but, instead, the stuff of wild rivers, a shot of genuine Northwest weather, and, perhaps most important, the raw material of healthy, anadromous fisheries.

Still, the point is to avoid these epic spates—despite the allure of their Biblical dimensions. Oddly, the majority of photographs I bring home from winter visits to the West End are garlanded with low, clear water and sparkling blue skies—evidence I head that direction only when a strong high pressure stations a protective shield across the region. This strategy probably costs me dearly in numbers of fish. But in this case I feel prudence takes precedence over my tendency toward the long shot. A serious storm or soggy front can break one's spirit in a way that fish-less days rarely discourage the ardent steelheader. In the right light, he can conceive of fish in every shadowy lie, no matter the number of empty casts he strokes over the lively water—while casting, chilled to his Capilene in the gloom of dirty skies and high water, even the most sanguine stoic feels the limits of his resolve. Only a fish itself can oblige the sodden angler's hope, compromised, hour by hour, by thoughts of dry fleece, warm food, camaraderie, and renewed interest in the plausible benefits of distilled fare.

The Nights

Nights, for some of us, prove tougher still.

Consider: 4:30 p.m. and you're already pressed by darkness off the water, stumbling back to your vehicle, fish or no fish, in a mildly hypothermic daze. Adorned in headlamp you change attire, making absolutely certain you isolate boots and waders and rain gear—which will not dry one iota by morning. On the drive back to camp you consider your options: No, for some reason, dining out in Forks, the sole hamlet of consequence en route, seems contrary to the demands of the sport, a descent into comfort you feel might undermine your chances the next day. Instead, back in camp, you build a fire, seeded by dry kindling stored, like water in Baja, in the safest confines of the van—and you set about fashioning dinner, seeking to strike that perfect balance between expedience, efficiency, fuel intake, and flavor in a form other than yet another Wrangler or quesadilla.

All of this presupposes, of course, a dry evening—unlikely unless that high pressure you bet on really does hold firm. Even then, it is entirely possible for rain—or something quite like it—to fall on the peninsula from beneath star-studded skies. Don't ask me how. But whatever the form, should precipitation arrive, you unfold a camp chair in the back of the van, bring the Coleman lantern inside, and while condensation begins to drip from above, you finish your meal, imbibe if you're so inclined, gaze out at the dwindling fire, and try everything in your power to stay up past nine before bedding down for a night you won't soon forget.

Dawn, you understand, doesn't arrive until sometime near seven. That's a long night—unless, of course, you're fortunate to have the company of the appropriate partner. But let's get real about this. The few people you can drag, midwinter, to the West End of the Olympic Peninsula are mostly sickos just like you—wrinkled, newt-faced anglers hoping to hold it together long enough for another shot at a chrome-bright missile willing to grab a swinging fly.

The Rivers

I like the Queets. I like the Bogachiel. I like the Sol Duc. I like the Cala-wah. I'd probably like all of the West End rivers, but I'm just a visitor, and when I show up in winter I tend to return to what little water I've come to know.

The good news is there are so many West End rivers that, despite the rain, you can generally find water that's in shape. The sad news is, unless you live on the peninsula, or hire a guide, you're going to often feel like you're taking shots in the dark.

As in all steelheading, West End knowledge is precious and hard-won: You touch a fish one run, you remember that spot for life. The dilemma, then, is this: Do you return next time to water you know or do you venture somewhere new?

In his exemplary reference, *Steelhead Fly Fishing on the Olympic Pen-insula*, Doug Rose talks about his willingness to walk "an hour or more to fish a drift the size of an Airstream trailer." That's how it is. In much the same way that surf fish will gather in only a few select spots along a given beach, a winter steelhead river is, by and large, empty.

The old steelhead adage states, not insensibly, that "steelhead are where you find them." The practiced hand understands this to mean that the fish in question are unpredictable, highly individualistic, and that they must be hunted before any attempts to fool them with a fly. At the same time, the successful steelheader—especially winter steelheader—harbors a list of precise lies, or holding water, where he has found fish before, and where he knows steelhead will hold again. A knowledge of holding water is the reason a select few West End steelheaders expect to catch a steelhead, even in winter, any time they venture to the water—and why visitors will generally feel they are shooting blindly into the forest in all but those few places where they have moved fish to the fly before.

In a larger view "where you find them" speaks to a quality of envi-ronmental integrity that lies at the heart of what both the steelhead and steelhead fly fisher seek in their private, contrasting desires. Today, the West End rivers of the Olympic Peninsula share the largest runs of wild winter steelhead in the Pacific Northwest. By way of contrast, in Califor-nia, steelhead have been eliminated from ninety percent of their historic range.

The difference? In a word, habitat. Not only are West End rivers free of dams, but the upper reaches of each watershed lie beneath what Rose calls "the umbrella of protection" of Olympic National Park. For nearly a hundred years now, while habitat degradation has eroded the health of anadromous fisheries up and down the Pacific coast, spawning and fish-rearing habitat in the park has remained virtually undisturbed. Old-growth forests, tragic victims throughout the rest of the region, continue to supply the big trees crucial to the integrity of rivers, which, in their lower reaches, receive as much pressure, from sportsmen and native fishers alike, as other Northwest fisheries. Scramble into the catch-and-release "fly-only" water on the upper Hoh, however, and you'll find springs and tributaries, scrubbed and silt-free gravel beds, spongy side channels, and enormous logjams—all surrounded by canopies of dark, fecund, moss-laden forest—and you'll see what healthy habitat really looks like and how it plays into a genuine narrative of exuberant salmonid nurseries.

The Fish

Emerging from a tangle of riparian hardwoods, I recognized the sort of steelhead run that recurs in fly rodders' dreams: broad, deep, evenly paced, embellished with hidden boulders revealed as seams and ribbons of current woven into the restless texture of the river's blue-black face.

It helped that I was miles upriver, far from the hatchery and requisite gear anglers crowding the banks, above the highest drift boat put-in, an hour's walk through the dripping hemlock, alders, and fir, beyond the end of an abandoned logging road, washed out by recent high waters. Steelhead, we sense, seek something similar that stirs within ourselves. Or at least we are happier fishing for them where we feel they lie resting undisturbed, momentarily more vulnerable than pressured fish to the lure of the swinging fly.

I started high in the run. Of the bits and pieces of advice I shuffle through each time I step into the river, a cautionary note from an old Haig-Brown story has stayed with me as if a line of sacred text: to wit, start high, higher than you think you should start. In time, experience teaches the seasoned steelheader that fish can hold in the upstream extremes of a run, holding water that is often neglected by anglers eager to wade deep and throw a long line. I'm not always as methodical as I intend to be. But as hours if not days of casting go unrewarded and confidence wanes, the ardent steelheader recalls the few absolutes he's come to trust, a litany of beliefs as much folk knowledge as actual wisdom.

The fish took during the long moment when, as the fly hung directly downstream, I wondered if it was time to pick up and cast again. The most profound truth in all of fly fishing, of course, is that you don't catch fish without your fly in the water. And in fishing for winter steelhead, perhaps more than in any other type of fly fishing, keeping the fly in the water is an act of faith that separates, figuratively, the men from the boys. More than success, the serious winter steelheader seeks absolution for the hours and days spent—or wasted—in empty-handed belief. With the fish on the reel, boring off in current, I felt not so much elation, nor even relief, but a grave sense of foreboding that now, finally, something could really go wrong.

This time it didn't. The fish, bright and wild, with the small head and sweeping configuration of a hen fresh from the sea, seemed almost translucent in the dark-shaded water, and when I slid it into the shallows, I could imagine it, months later, high in the watershed, combing its redd in the profuse healthy habitat of the park. Of course, I knew nothing about this particular fish—its origins, its history, its fate—beyond the simple fact that on the first day of winter on a river on the Olympic Peninsula it grabbed a fly I presented on the end of a swinging line.

The Flies

Along with the rain, the big rivers, and the wild winter fish, the West End of the Olympic Peninsula is known in fly fishing circles as the home of Syd Glasso, whose steelhead Spey flies changed the face of the sport forever.

Little has been written about Glasso's life. Yet his famous flies, inspired by somber, utilitarian Atlantic salmon dresssings from Scotland's Spey River, captured the imagination of Northwest steelheaders and, half a century later, now seem as much a part of regional traditions as catch-and-release ethics and double-handed rods. There's not a serious steelheader who doesn't tie some sort of "Spey pattern"—even if the designation today means little more than a fly with oversized hackle palmered around at least the front half of a long, sweeping hook.

Although linked to centuries-old patterns, Glasso's flies were a radical departure from the popular West Coast steelhead flies of the 1950s and 1960s, bringing an aesthetic elegance to the practical demands of swinging flies deep in big water. Prior to Syd Glasso, steelhead flies were short, bright, and stocky, suggesting as much a painted lure as they did a fly fashioned out of feather and fur. Glasso's flies were, by contrast, subtle, seductive, even sensuous—depending more on the lifelike movement of materials undulating under tension in current rather than on color, shape, or size.

Do steelhead care? No doubt Spey patterns have proven remarkably effective for West End steelhead, and their popularity throughout the range of the sport recommends them to anglers who need the assurance of time-tested flies. Then again, I am willing to bet that the Glo-Bug—or any other "fly" that imitates a single, drifting, salmon egg—fools as many winter steelhead for countless fly rodders as all of their other flies combined. I would like to offer that observation as evidence of some profound truth, a conclusive remark about flies, fly fishers, and steelhead, and the terrible inutility of venturing forth in winter to cast a long line into unknown waters under dark, uncertain skies. There are, I suspect, better ways to catch winter steelhead—and, probably, better ways to spend your time.

I just don't know what they are.

LESSON 28

OLD FRIENDS

Jeff Cottrell is the real deal. Raised in Whittier, he got his first guiding job in 1982 on the Owens River at the old Arcularius Ranch. He spent seventeen seasons in Tierra del Fuego along the Rio Grande, chasing sea run brown trout for a cadre of well-heeled luminaries that might include, in any year, the likes of Tom McGuane, Yvon Chouinard, Jimmy Carter, or—before he bought a local *estancia* of his own—the Salmo Scrooge himself, Ted Turner. During our own hemisphere's half of the trout season, Jeff worked out of Fort Collins, Colorado, guiding on the Rio Dolores, the North Platte, the Laramie, the Green, and the Wind. Over the years he also did a little Las Roques, Venezuela. He did some Iceland, some Russia. Guiding, exploring, instructing new guides, setting up camps in remote corners of the sanctified salmonid circuit, Jeff Cottrell got around the way that Real Guys do—not the rest of us who long for mere driblets of glory, unable to escape the quotidian undertow holding us to our humble lives.

So it came as some surprise to Jeff when, upon moving back to the coast and starting to fish a river we all know and love, he couldn't catch a fish—not a single trout.

He tried. Oh, he tried. "It was weird," Jeff says now, tugging at the bill of a ball cap advertising high-end rods. Tall and broad-shouldered, he carries himself with the good-ole-boy slouch of a guy who has spent a lot of time kicking dirt in Nowhere, Wyoming, talking to ranchers with access to private water. "I did what everyone told me. I did *whatever* they told me. And day after day I got nothing. I *sucked.*"

Come on, you think, listening to a Real Guy share this sorry tale. *Nothing? Not even a—*

"Not a one," claims Cottrell, shaking his head as if still in the throes of disbelief.

On the other hand, this show of angling futility all took place shortly after Jeff had opened up a fly shop, from the porch of which he now relates his spell of woe. A breeze carries his cigarette smoke away from the building, a century-old Victorian he remodeled in a downtown historic district just beyond the glow of gentrification. A fly shop? Real Guy though he may be, Cottrell had, apparently, gone through a period when he was all but out of his mind.

Finally, however, he showed up one day prepared to fish not like others on the river, but exactly as he would have fished on any thousand different days on rivers in the Rockies. Strike indicator. A little lead. A pair of Flashback Pheasant Tail Nymphs.

"I thought, *Wait a minute. I know how to do this.*"

And?

"Confidence factor."

Suddenly Jeff sounds like a Real Guy again. Lifting his cap, he reveals enough blond hair that you realize he never quite escaped the look of an LA surfer—and the attitude that goes with it when a break comes his way.

"Fish what you believe in. Fish what you *know.*"

And?

"I *whacked*'em."

Jeff lets loose a laugh, his voice a blend of booming surf and far too many cigarettes since he last paddled into the lineup.

"It's my new favorite river. Those fish *tug.*"

Smoothness, according to Tom McGuane, high deacon of the fraternity, is the one trait, above any other, we should all strive for in our fishing.

By "smoothness" McGuane means keeping the fly fishing effectively. What made Bill Schaadt such a great angler, claims McGuane, is that Schaadt "kept the fly in the water longer than anyone, ever." When I teach beginning fly fishers, I invariably share this glib advice: "You don't catch fish without your fly in the water."

You can spin such comments into profound dimensions. "Fly in the water" means, of course, that you get to the water at all; and herein lies the first obstacle most of us face to angling up our fair share of fish. At the other end of the scale, your fly remains off or out of the water whenever you false cast, whenever you snag a bush or tree, whenever you lose a fly, or—worst of all—whenever you stop fishing to change flies, no matter how sure you are this change need be.

Great anglers, McGuane has often told us, fish without doubt. Once a decision has been reached, the fly affixed to the leader, the smooth angler attends to the business of presentation. For the moment, at least, his mind runs free of debate regarding his choice of flies. This kind of undisturbed focus seems especially true of successful steelheaders and, we read, accomplished pursuers of other anadromous species.

The confidence factor begins with those choice few flies, our old friends, that we fish without question in circumstances we've encountered before. And sometimes in situations entirely new. Every experienced angler has suffered the humility of doing exactly what someone else says, fishing the exact same can't-miss flies, and failing—as Jeff Cottrell did—to touch a fish. At that point, smart anglers will back up, assess the situation, and turn to a game plan—a method and flies—they already know. It may not be the *best* approach. But if it's worked before, chances are it will work again—which is how certain flies became friends in the first place.

Now, I'm hardly a great angler. Recently, it appeared I might not even be a mediocre one: Four days on the northern coast, my youngest son and I failed to touch a fish. Or maybe, the second day, I *touched* one. Yet any evidence but a fish itself soon evaporates into phantasma when cast after cast swings hour after hour, day after day, undisturbed across misty, vanishing waters.

Did we change our flies? Reject old friends? Of course we did. Did I fish free of doubt? Well, let's just say I was only convinced that once—and even then for but the briefest of spells—that a fish even looked at my fly—and such conviction dissipates quickly, as stated, in the fury of unrelenting snake eyes.

Doubt?

I breathe the shit.

Yet I'm sure you're better than that.

For example: I have never caught a trout on a Pheasant Tail Nymph, flashback or any other kind. Not one. How can that possibly be? One of the great flies of all time, a classic on the order of a Hare's Ear, an Adams, an Elk Hair Caddis—not to mention Jeff Cottrell's breakthrough fly here on the coast, the old friend he turned to when it seemed, maybe, that he had *lost it* once and for all.

But for me? *Nada.* Zip. El Skunkeroo. And I can tell you why right now. I don't tie on a Pheasant Tail Nymph if I think there are fish to be caught. I understand completely that a little Pheasant Tail offers an adequate if not sometimes excellent imitation of a mayfly nymph. But if I really think mayflies are around, if I believe they make up a significant food source or a mayfly hatch is imminent, I use a Wild Hare, a Wyoming Mayfly Nymph, a WD-40, or even some kind of sparse soft hackle, a Partridge and Green, say, or Little Olive Soft Hackle. It's not that I have anything against a Pheasant Tail Nymph. We just haven't been properly introduced. We just haven't become . . . friends.

Or another way to look at it is this: When I do tie on a Pheasant Tail Nymph, I'm already pretty well convinced that things aren't happening, that the trout, for whatever reason, aren't actively feeding. I know this is a weak argument. A trout is always willing to feed; our job is to turn that willingness into action. A fly, we hope, delivers a message: Eat me! But I trust my old friends first; they're as reliable, as forthright, as friends can be. And if they haven't done the trick, I don't expect others will, either.

You see how it goes.

Here's another pronouncement I make to beginning fly fishers: "You catch fish on the flies you fish with." This is right up there with what I used to tell myself as I grew more and more committed to the challenge of fly fishing in the surf: "If you fish with flies, you'll catch fish on flies." I'm sorry if this all sounds obvious. That's kind of the point.

Still, a career without a single trout taken on a PT Nymph—or any other well-known, proven fly, as far as that goes—borders on the ridiculous. At some point, such negligence approaches affectation, a claim to delinquency not unlike, say, the kid who proudly announces he made it through high school without ever reading a book. You ask yourself: "So when did idiocy become a badge of honor?" I mean, what's it take to generate a little warmth toward a fly? Tie it on and fish it.

Which I decided to do on a recent visit with Jeff Cottrell to that same favorite river where the trout are known to *tug*. Under bright, mid-morning skies, I followed Jeff's lead and rigged up with a pair of Pheasant Tail Nymphs, two BB-sized splitshot, even a foam indicator, a device I generally disdain. The point of the exercise, however, seemed to me to be to reach a new level of understanding. For once, I thought, I'll try to keep my opinions to myself.

And I worked at it. Of course I did. But then, wading deep, inching into swift current in an attempt to gain room beyond the reach of over-hanging oaks, I ran the nymphs through a narrow slot—only to witness, an instant later, a fish of outlandish proportions porpoise in and out of view.

You ask yourself, "Was that me who made that happen?"

My answer, more and more, is yes, that behavior like this is nearly always in response to something the angler has done.

Still, another dozen drifts failed to move the fish again. Fish? A monster, I reminded myself, backing out of the river to consider the angles again.

At which point my resolve weakened. Don't get me wrong: I've hooked plenty of big fish in my life. What's one more in the face of an opportunity to begin a new friendship, the chance to reach out, extend myself, grow as both an angler and a human being? Yet perhaps "weakened" fails to capture the precise vacillations my intention to stick with a Pheasant Tail Nymph suffered as I reconsidered the image of a fish the size of a young spaniel slipping in and out of view. How about, instead, my resolve collapsed? Crumbled? Dissolved and turned to mush?

Who you going to turn to at a time like this?

I don't fish big Stone Nymphs like I used to. Over the years they've come to seem crude, awkward, inelegant—despite their effectiveness on swift Western rivers where stoneflies—especially *Pteronarcys californica*, the giant salmonfly—predominate. Across the reach of my career I like to think I've advanced to more refined flies and techniques.

But I know perfectly well why my Stone Nymph has long been a great friend.

Later, when Jeff showed up—in response, I suppose, to my antics and hollering downstream—he pointed out where he had seen two steelhead on his way upriver.

"Two?" I asked, tightening the knot on another Stone Nymph.

"They were holding right together, the exact same lie. Out there where the sun was."

A good guide and, I think, on his way to becoming a good friend, Jeff aimed his rod tip toward the slot of heavy water where I had last seen the earlier Stone Nymph, from which I'd eventually become separated a hundred yards downstream.

"Two steelhead?" I repeated, slipping into the current. In up to my waist, I felt no indication that if the Stone Nymph worked again, I could possibly control a fish like the one I had just hooked. Too much fish. Too much current.

But what are old friends for? I thought, pitching one upstream.

JEFF'S FLASHBACK PHEASANT TAIL NYMPH

Hook: Daiichi 1130, size 14–20
Thread: Brown
Tail: Pheasant tail fibers
Rib: Copper wire
Abdomen: Pheasant tail fibers
Wingcase: Holographic tinsel
Legs: Pheasant tail fibers
Thorax: Peacock herl

Tying Notes

Step 1: Secure the hook and start the thread. Tie in five to ten pheasant tail fibers for the tail. Leave the butt ends for wrapping the abdomen. Tie in a length of copper wire at the root of the tail.

Step 2: Advance the thread to the front third of the hook. Create the abdomen by wrapping the butt ends from the tail to the thread. Tie off and clip excess. Rib the abdomen with wraps of copper wire. Tie off and trim.

Step 3: Advance the thread to just behind the eye of the hook. Tie in eight to ten pheasant tail fibers with the tips extending past the hook eye. Trim the butts and wind the thread back to the front of the abdomen.

Step 4: Tie in the tinsel. Tie in the peacock herl. Wind the peacock forward to create the thorax. Don't crowd the eye of the hook. Tie off the peacock herl and clip excess.

Step 5: Pull the tinsel forward to create the wingcase. Tie it off and then pull back the tinsel and make a few turns of thread in front of it. Clip excess.

Step 6: Separate the pheasant tail fibers extending past the eye of the hook into two equal bunches. Pull the bunches back along the sides of the fly and secure them with the thread. This forms the nymph's legs. Make several wraps of thread over the front of the folded pheasant tail fibers to create the head of the nymph. Whip finish and add head cement.

Stone Nymph

Hook: Mustad 79580, TMC 5263, or TMC 200R, size 4–8
Thread: Black
Underbody: .030 lead wire, 10–15 wraps at front half of hook
Tail: Black marabou blood plumes
Abdomen: Black dubbing
Ribbing: Medium copper wire
Wingcase: Pheasant tail
Legs: English grouse hackle
Gills: Black ostrich herl
Thorax: Hare's Ear Plus dubbing, black or gold

Tying Notes

Step 1: Secure the hook; start the thread. Wrap lead wire around the front half of the hook and secure it with thread wraps front and back. Wind thread back to the bend of the hook.

Step 2: Secure a tuft of marabou blood plumes for the tail. Make the length of the tail about twice the hook gap. Tie in a length of copper wire at the root of the tail.

Step 3: Wax your thread and fingertips and dub in a thick, tapered abdomen that extends forward over the back two-thirds of the hook. On a size 4 hook, that's a lot of dubbing material—which is why some tyers use chenille. Rib the abdomen with five or six turns of copper wire.

Step 4: Tie in materials for the wingcase, legs, and gills—in that order, which is the *opposite* order you will actually use them as you build the front third of the fly. Use enough pheasant tail fibers to eventually form a wide wingcase. Tie in the grouse feather by the tip, upside down, stem toward the tail of the fly. Tie in two ostrich herl. Leave all of this material loose for now over the rear of the fly.

Step 5: Build a thick thorax out of dubbing. Although black is typical, I often find traces of yellow in the thorax area of various live stonefly specimens, which is how the old Montana Stone was tied when flies were a lot more impressionistic than they are usually tied today.

Step 6: Make three wraps of the already-secured ostrich herl around the thorax. Tie off and clip excess at the head of the fly.

Step 7: Pull the grouse feather forward to form legs off both sides of the thorax. Secure the feather at the head and clip excess.

Step 8: Create the wingcase by pulling forward the pheasant tail fibers over the legs and thorax. Tie off at the head and clip excess. Build a neat head out of thread. Whip finish and add head cement.

LESSON 29

HUEVOS TRUJILLOS

In "Small Streams in Michigan," an early piece from his original collection of sporting essays, *An Outside Chance*, Tom McGuane affords us a generous snapshot of his first wife's grandfather, a Michigan trout fisherman called Pomp, an angler McGuane admired for all the right reasons, not the least of which was that Pomp "belonged to that category of sportsman who will stop at nothing."

No matter that Pomp was a bait fisherman. To illustrate the breadth of Pomp's angling prowess, McGuane recounts the time Pomp stalked and hooked an exceptionally large brown trout, only to face losing it as the fish fought its way down an oversized corrugated culvert where the creek in which it lived passed beneath a country road. Certain to lose the fish if it reached the far end of the culvert, Pomp devised a simple yet brilliant solution: He had his wife lie across the far end of the culvert—and inside the pipe Pomp fought the fish to a standstill and eventually landed it.

Considering the challenges many of us have been known to face simply to go fishing, much less get our spouses to buy into our sport, Pomp's feat seems as remarkable as any described in the literature. Certainly McGuane was impressed. In the early stages of an inevitable, unstated rivalry between bait and fly fisher, he recognized, on hearing this story, what he was up against—an assessment that proved prophetic, as he was consistently outfished by Pomp, right up until the year of Pomp's death. More significantly, it's clear from McGuane's account that Pomp's unmatched success had little to do with any perceived superior fish-catching properties of bait in comparison to flies, but instead was based on that original appraisal of Pomp himself—a sportsman who will *stop at nothing.*

Guys like that, of course, are tough to beat. I ought to know. I fish with one all steelhead season long.

No doubt, the single most significant trend in modern steelheading has been the advent and advocacy of nymphing techniques. Spey casters may find such assertions blasphemous, but the truth is, there's very little that's new about presenting a fly with a two-handed rod beyond the usual subtle vagaries of the traditional, downstream swing. Besides the fact that you can cover more water with a Spey rod, and cover it more efficiently, you are still fishing the fly more or less as described nearly eighty years ago in Jock Scott's *Greased Line Fishing for Salmon*, and certainly pretty much like wet fly aficionados have been doing for the entirety of the sport's five hundred years of recorded existence.

But serious, concerted nymphing for steelhead reaches back only three or four decades—and there are still fly fishers who bristle at the idea of nymphing techniques as part of the lexicon of the sport at all. Older steelhead "nymphs" are on record, but it was only when anglers such as Bill McMillan, with his Paint Brush in Washington, and Brad Jackson, with his Ugly Bug in California and Oregon, began dead-drifting flies beneath mended slack lines that nymphing as we know it today became another of the remarkably few standard methods for catching steelhead on flies.

Two refinements—strike indicators and egg patterns—have made nymphing the most popular and oftentimes effective method for catching steelhead on many West Coast rivers. Indicators, egg patterns, and lead on the leader. At this point, of course, the strategy and technique is virtually a replica of what anglers with conventional and spinning gear and monofilament line are doing—and most of us know serious fly fishers who will, at times, concede the point and go ahead and fish with conventional gear, since that's how they would be trying to fish with their fly fishing equipment anyway. Most of us, however, fly fish for steelhead no matter what because we consider ourselves genuine fly fishers. After all, we fish with a fly rod, a fly reel, a fly line, and flies—regardless if the method we employ seems better suited to a completely different type of fishing equipment.

It is the matter of flies, however, that brings into question the margins of the sport—at least if you worry about such things. If you do, you'll find that attempts to arrive at clear definitions for what does or doesn't constitute a genuine fly generate sharp debates that usually fail to reach satisfactory conclusions. Arguing such fine points, you do little more than identify yourself as an angler who refrains, for whatever reasons, from employing certain materials you feel don't belong as part of a fly. We're not talking here about bait. Nor can you rely on legal definitions, which merely obfuscate the matter along the lines of descriptive prejudices that remain, like language, in constant flux. The typical fly fisher, instead, acknowledges a difference, without clear definition, between flies and lures, jigs, plugs, or other unacceptable artificial baits. I'm reminded, probably inappropriately, of the old court case in which someone concluded that it may be difficult to define pornography, but most of us recognize it when we see it. Most fly fishers also recognize, when we see it, something we find difficult—if not impossible—to call a fly. Most of us, that is, who can't quite bring ourselves to join that category of sportsman who will *stop at nothing*.

That wouldn't be Fred Trujillo.

Born in Long Beach, Fred had the good fortune of a move to steelhead country when his father considered the prospects for a teenage son in the glower of LA lights. In his own heyday, Fred's dad had chosen a stint in the military rather than time in jail, a decision made while standing in front of a compassionate judge. Today, the loss of uncles on Fred's mother's side to the perils of hard living make Fred's father seem prophetic—and maybe all of this has helped shape Fred's own thinking to the point where his flies, at least, seem at times as pragmatic as the nightstick.

Fred also coaches high school wrestling, another venue where nononsense efficacy matters. And Fred Trujillo, as many of us know, ties flies professionally, a vocation that accounts for all sorts of dour dispositions, not to mention the need to trim away all superfluities and affectations and tie flies that simply work.

Yet for all Fred's sober, matter-of-fact ways, I wonder sometimes about his business acumen. Fred, you see, often fishes with flies he doesn't sell. That seems odd; you would think a tyer would nearly always fish his own patterns, both to research and demonstrate their effectiveness. Which is exactly what Fred does—he *fishes* his own patterns. And because I fish with Fred, and fish often with him, I can attest to the success of his flies—especially during steelhead season, when I've made the wise decision not to keep track anymore of how many fish either of us catch, so lopsided would the score sometimes run.

But—and here's the point—Fred rarely sells the steelhead flies he fishes so effectively.

How can that be? you ask. His flies are simple, pragmatic, proven to catch steelhead and lots of them. Weren't we all raised under the dictate that claims our fortune is made if we but build a better mouse trap? And these are steelhead, by God, no lowly rodent.

Plus, we all know how much money we've been willing to invest at our shots at sea run trout.

Yet Fred Trujillo sells relatively few of his own favorite steelhead flies for the simple reason that his flies are tied to catch *steelhead*, not steelhead fly fishers—and Fred knows, like most steelheaders know, that nine fish out of ten will settle for an egg pattern, regardless of the day, the water temperature, the river height, the alignment of the cosmos, the frequency of your flossing, or how you've been treating your spouse and kids.

But who wants to buy a lowly egg fly?

The question Fred asks, on the other hand, is *Why fish anything else?* And if you're going to fish egg patterns, he's concluded, why not, as a tyer, aim for the best egg flies around. That may seem like a tall order. But Fred's a clever tyer, a skilled craftsman, an inventor, an experimenter, a problem-solver plus a great angler—and he just so happens to belong, as well, to that category of sportsman *who will stop at nothing*.

Or, as Fred told me once early last fall, when his eggs were touching fish and my Waking Muddler might as well have been swinging through midair, "You fish for aesthetics. I fish for meat."

Over the years, I've watched Fred Trujillo's egg patterns evolve from the traditional Glo-Bug to dressings that seem, at last, to negate all vestiges of the sublime. One of the early steps he took was to devise a method in which, ingeniously, he threaded lengths of Glo-Bug yarn through plastic mini-straws or the tubing inside ball point pens and then tied off and cut the protruding yarn, a method that allowed him to create small, perfectly shaped Glo-Bugs, thereby replicating the actual size of the salmon eggs on which most steelhead feed.

At about the same time Fred was refining his Glo-Bugs, he began experimenting with preformed Krystal Eggs skewered and glued directly to the hook. Later, like others, he went through his plastic bead stage. But it wasn't until Fred got out the glue gun and hot glue sticks that he really forwent all sense of decency.

This last phase has propelled Fred Trujillo into the outer limits of egg fly design. Single eggs, egg clusters, even egg tube flies. Is this fair, you think, fingering a tangle of Fred's most recent orange and red gummy patterns, each with a sparse beard of white egg yarn, a concession, perhaps, to actually tying something on the hook. Clearly, these are flies designed to catch fish. Clearly, this is the work of an angler who will stop at nothing.

But are they flies? I don't see why not. They might not be the last word in elegance, but they are just as much flies as foam-bodied poppers—and they are definitely an effective alternative for fooling steelhead. The real problem, as I see it, is that when you do tie on one of Fred Trujillo's egg flies, you'll think you should automatically catch a steelhead—which means you've fallen, again, for the oldest fallacy in the sport, that the Right Fly is all you need.

Even the guy who stops at nothing will tell you, it's never as easy as that.

Huevos Trujillos Single Glo-Bug

Hook: Gamakatsu Octopus (red), size 1–10
Thread: 6/0 orange or white UNI-Thread for smaller (size 8–10) egg patterns or 3/0 UNI-Thread for larger (size 1–6) egg patterns
Tools: 2–3 plastic coffee swizzle sticks
Materials: Two tubes of full Glo-Bug yarn strands (pink or orange) with an optional third quarter strand (cerise or red) of the Glo-Bug dot color

Tying Notes

Step 1: Thread the yarn through the tubes with a monofilament loop and set aside.

Step 2: Attach the tying thread and run it from just behind the eye to half the shank length and back toward the eye to the quarter mark.

Step 3: Lay the tubes with a small amount of yarn sticking out of one end parallel to the hook shank.

Step 4: Loosely loop the tying thread once completely around the yarn sticking out of the ends of the tube and then again a second time, but pulling down tightly this time. This will make the yarn flare. Loop the thread once more following the last two turns.

Step 5: Pull the yarn back toward the bend of the hook and loop the thread five to eight turns just behind the eye. Half hitch the thread and cut.

Step 6: Place a drop of head cement on the exposed threads.

Step 7: Pull up on the yarn near the eye and cut to shape.

Step 8: Pull the tubes back and pull up on the yarn. Cut to shape.

Step 9: Pull down on any of the yarn below the hook shank and cut to shape.

SINGLE GG EGG (GLUE GUN EGG)

Hook: Gamakatsu Octopus Hook (red), size 6–10
Thread: 6/0 orange, red, or white UNI-Thread
Tools: Glue gun, a cup of water with some ice cubes
Veil: White Glo-Bug yarn (optional)
Body: Glue stick (salmon, orange roe, etc.)

Tying Notes

If you decide not to use the Glo-Bug yarn then begin with step 4.

Step 1: Attach a small amount of the egg yarn to the hook shank with the thread (usually an eighth of a strand).

Step 2: Tie the thread to just behind the eye of the hook with only one-quarter to three-quarters of an inch of the egg yarn sticking out of the front (or out of the back). Only a quarter of the hook shank should be covered with thread.

Step 3: Tie off the thread and cut. Take the hook out of the vise.

Step 4: If you didn't use the yarn, wrap half of the hook shank with thread and then take it out of the vise. This helps to secure the glue to the hook.

Step 5: Pull the yarn forward (if you attached it) and squeeze a bead of the heated glue stick on the hook shank so that it covers only the thread wraps all the way around the shank of the hook (but don't cover the loose yarn in front of the hook eye or on the yarn that's sticking out of the back).

Step 6: While the glue is still hot turn upside down to get the glue to form into a round egg shape. If you don't turn the hook upside down it will cover the hook gape and make hooking a fish difficult.

Step 7: When you get the glue into the position you want, put the egg in the cup of cold water to get the glue to maintain its shape.

LESSON 30

SEARCHING FOR MR. CHIRONOMID

This is during one of those phone calls you make to a distant state where someone you know knows someone you need to talk to about fish you're aimed to fish for.

Or, more accurately, about the river where you intend to catch those fish.

Or, better still, about the flies you'll need to catch those fish from that river faraway.

Flies are nearly always the point of these discussions—at least if you've already decided to make the trip and you've reached the stage in planning and preparations beyond which, barring catastrophe, there's no turning back. And even that might not stop you. You cross a certain threshold and any updates or new information about the fish, the fishing, the river conditions or even the weather itself are, in a sense, irrelevant. There's nothing you can do about any of that now. You're going to show up and you're going to fish—come what may.

Flies, on the other hand, can—until departure—still be tied, reorganized, reconsidered, renounced. Or, at the very least, discussed over airwaves sweeping distances you'd now be hard-pressed not to cross for anything shy of Armageddon itself. You're going fishing, for Christ's sake. And though it's clearly a little late to put together that one perfect travel box you've often read about and swore, time and again, to create, you can still get a local on the line who will tell you which flies he uses, the bugs he uses those flies for and, hopefully, a couple of secret weapons that qualify for that most revered fly category of all: inside dope.

My source this time proves more expansive than most.

"You'll get a lot of 'em on chromoids," he says.

"Chromoids?" I ask, unfamiliar with the name.

"Chromoids," he repeats—this time a trace slower, a hint of impatience carried by the sweeping airwaves.

Nevertheless, I haven't heard the term before. You ask yourself: *Is he talking about an insect or a fly?* Neither answer speaks well of your recent efforts to pass for a Real Guy. Chromoids. CRO-moids. What's it like? What's it got to be? Androids? Hemorrhoids? Altoids?

"You know—like midges," offers My Source.

"Midges? You mean—"

"Chromoids," he says again.

But he should have said chironomids.

Chironomids. *Chironomids.* He's talking about chironomids, I realize.

Yet I don't say anything. More telling still, I feel no impulse to correct My Source's mistake. This isn't, after all, sophomore English—and, anyway, here is yet another example of that particular brand of barbarism McGuane once described as "the great Western tradition of corrupting language into the grunting of the midland yokel." When I grew up, no one thought to call the water near Long Beach anything but San PEE-dro, and by the time one reached the top of the state, both the county and town of Del Norte had been deflated into two syllables, as terse as the word *report*. Chironomid. Chromoid. So what? Debates over names will always fall to claims that fish don't speak Latin, an argument hard to refute when the real purpose of these calls is to fuel your stoke, the voice on the other end of the line conjuring spirits that promise to twist your mojo tighter than a bloodknot as you imagine heavy trout eating your garbled flies.

The lake rests in a shallow fold of tilted, windswept land. In the distance, jack pines stand conspicuously removed from the shoreline, evidence of the unnatural configuration of impoundments throughout the West. This one offers its own blend of peculiar ironies: Down the center of the lake the rancher has left a row of telephone poles wading toward the horizon, where a lone volcanic peak thrusts its snowy gable into a sky as blue as a tall blond's eyes.

The appeal of these places, however, is rarely scenic. Instead, someone has a key or combination that affords access to private water. The long-range forecast, of course, inevitably looks grim—yet another pay-to-play operation, that upgrade from the old Ma & Pa U Ketch 'Um trout pond that makes many of us a little uneasy about the future of the sport.

In this case, though, things remain in the R&D stage. The rancher isn't sure what he's got. All that's certain is a few years back he dumped in a thousand Kamloop trout—and the ones he has seen lately are, as he puts it, "big as catfish."

The lake, in other words, might not be the prettiest body of water around—but fly fishers can be a forgiving lot, generally willing to over-look any number of surface imperfections for a chance to hang a few hogs.

How these newer impoundments differ from the old-fashioned road-side trout ponds, of course, is that the fish in them are expected to act like real fish, not domestic animals that gather around the trough as soon as someone rings the dinner bell, rattling the feed pail. Not that fish are ever that dumb. Or maybe they're not that smart. What's certain is that after a couple of years of surviving—and, if the rancher is right, thriving—in a windswept rangeland lake, trout have assumed aspects of predator fish everywhere, feeding on the myriad insects that inevitably include, and are sometimes dominated by, the ubiquitous, aforementioned chironomid.

This is news to no one. "It can be said with confidence," wrote Mr. Hughes and Hafele, as far back as anyone should be able to remember, "that any water holding trout will also have chironomids." The trouble with chironomids—or midges—is they can be so small that they are next to impossible to imitate with flies that can be fished effectively. The good news is that midge patterns are generally fairly simple and easy to tie—as long as your thread is fine enough and your eyesight—or glasses—good enough.

Still, when fly fishers sit around and talk about chironomids (okay, I know it sounds weird, but it happens) they rarely mean midges—even though both names refer to bugs that are, scientifically, one and the same. When anglers mention midges, they generally mean the tiny guys. But chironomids—My Source's *Chro*-moids—are the big fellows, the big midges, ones that can suggest mosquito larvae on steroids and evoke images of adults large enough to bully the lowlife on an Alaskan marsh.

Trout, of course, like chironomids of all sizes. All else being equal, however, anglers believe that trout will inevitably favor big chironomids—just as much as they believe in the logical appeal of big mayflies, stoneflies, or caddisflies. My pal Fred Trujillo gets special orders for tens of dozens of those big Ice Cream Cone Bombers used by anglers traveling to the famous Kamloops lakes of British Columbia, and one look at a pile of chironomids large enough to hang my keys from inspires in me the kind of lurid phantasmagoria I know must somehow reflect the response of trout when untold numbers of chironomid larvae transform into pupae and color the trouts' world like song notes rising to heaven.

Jeff Cottrell—my host, R&D partner, and keeper of the combination to the ranch gate lock—discovers the first fish. That is, he hooks a trout that strips line from his reel in astonishing rushes, in quantities that seem preposterous in a stillwater fishery. Perched atop a rock at water level in the lake's shallow earthen dam, Jeff leans against the fish as if fighting a bonita from a harbor jetty. His rod, bent to the cork, bucks against the backdrop of blue sky as if lashed to the wind itself.

Yet this isn't Jeff's first research session on the lake. And so maybe he's not quite as impressed as I am when he eventually brings to hand a fish as long, and taller through the shoulders, than many a steelhead. Or maybe he's as impressed, but he just doesn't show it as much, I think, wiping saliva from my lips and muffling my barking.

"What it take?" I ask finally, an afterimage of the oversized trout dissolving into the water.

"Chromoid," says Jeff, no more capable than I am to drop the name since I first told him the story. He holds up his leader for me to see. "The top one."

Fished in tandem, Jeff's chironomids reflect the increasing attention paid by fly tyers to this once all but neglected order of insects. A fly shop owner, Jeff gets an early look at the latest production models that follow on the heels of new patterns by guys like Brian Chan, Skip Morris, and Philip Rowley, all of which seem to rely more and more on the latest and greatest synthetic materials. It's not all hoopla and stagy pretense. In his worthwhile online articles about chironomids, Rowley suggests focusing on bright synthetic body materials like Frostbite, Flashabou, Krystal Flash, V-Rib, and the like to imitate the trapped air and gases pupae use to aid their slow ascent to the surface. On first glance, Jeff's two flies seem fashioned out of materials better suited for the inside of a cell phone—the kind of stuff that makes an old traditionalist like me a little queasy—at least until he opens his box and lets me paw through it like a kid looking for the M&Ms in the trail mix.

"Try what you like," says Jeff.

But as is often the case, the so-called Right Fly doesn't seem to make any difference. I try this one and that, each of them all but irresistible in Jeff's fly box, patterns that command attention like the covers of Harlequin novels. Yet to the fish these brilliant miniatures of technological wizardry prove as seductive as marbles. I can't find a trout. Of course, I understand I need to fish these flies, that the Right Fly matters far, far less than the right presentation. Especially in the case of chironomids. These active, awkward bugs, frenetic in their perilous ascent as pupa toward the surface of a lake, writhe and squirm and jerk and squiggle against the calm of stillwater habitats, devoid of currents to carry them upward. It's a crude, bitter stroke chironomids practice, the infernal spastic arrhythmia of miniature Disney inchworms struggling heavenward through fermented, fish-haunted cider.

In other words, you must animate your fly. Much is made of various chironomid presentation techniques, and the serious lake angler will do well to study, practice, and experiment with them all. The difference between the clever manipulations of the seasoned chironomid aficionado and the typical cast-and-retrieve routine of the occasional stillwater fly fisher is the difference between choosing a target and aiming at it or shooting blindly into the forest, hoping to hit anything at all. Animate your fly, I remind myself, with a specific plan and purpose, the precise action of the insect—and the stage of that insect's life—it attempts to replicate. Otherwise you might as well be fishing with a yo-yo.

It works for Jeff.

He gets a second fish while I wade around as if clamming, imagining my pair of chironomids rising through the water column with the precision of drunken scuba divers.

"What about a bobbing strike indicator?" I holler, remembering something I read in one of those magazine articles where guys never get skunked.

"It works," answers Jeff. "But I can't do it. It's like watching paint dry."

And what I'm doing feels like . . . painting the outside fifty feet of the lake with a two-inch brush.

Suddenly it all feels wrong. The wind stiffens, ankle-high chop lapping against the dam. The telephone poles, quaint as windmills on our arrival, now look like fencing strung across an alpine meadow. What the hell kind of lake is this anyway? I ask myself—while the bend in Jeff's rod tightens against the pull of an angry Kamloop shattering the surface of the lake like an osprey.

"Chromoid?" I ask, when Jeff finally corrals the trout at his feet.

He shakes his head.

"Big black Bugger."

The fly he holds up approximates the size and attitude of a drowned mouse.

"Figured it was time to try the Big Mac. We should be getting more of these guys."

When I swap flies and finally hook one, I couldn't agree more.

CHROMOID

Hook: TMC 2457, size 10–18
Head (bead): Pearl/white metal bead, size 1/8 or 3/32
Thread: 8/0 black
Gills: White antron yarn
Abdomen: Black holographic tinsel
Thorax: Peacock herl
Rib: Red copper wire

Tying Notes

Step 1: Slip the bead onto the hook. Secure the hook in the vise. Start your thread just behind the eye of the hook and ahead of the bead.

Step 2: For the gills, secure a small tuft of white antron yarn so that it extends past the eye of the hook. Lift the front of the tuft and whip finish behind the hook eye as if finishing a fly.

Step 3: Cut your thread at the finish knot. Trim the butts of the antron tuft. Slide the bead over the butts and tight to the eye of the hook. Trim the tips of the antron so the gills protrude about one-eighth of an inch beyond the bead.

Step 4: Restart your thread directly behind the bead. Cover the hook with thread, winding toward the bend. Just short of the bend, secure the copper wire. Continue back onto the bend of the hook. Secure the holographic wire at the back end of the fly.

Step 5: Wind the thread back to the bead, creating an even taper from the bend of the hook forward. Wrap the holographic tinsel forward, continuing to refine the taper to make it as gradual and even as possible. Tie off the tinsel directly behind the bead and clip the excess.

Step 6: Rib the body with four to six even wraps of copper wire. Tie off behind the bead and clip excess.

Step 7: Strip the tip of a single length of peacock herl. Secure directly behind the bead. Make one wrap only. Secure and clip excess. Whip finish directly behind the bead.

LESSON 31

500 GRAINS
OF LOVE

Somewhere deep in the skipjack's first sounding, I experience the sensation of fractals shifting, gravity coming unhinged. Inside me, days of clams and ceviche, sashimi and wasabi, conch and fish head soup suddenly stir, welling up toward the surface as the tuna hits warp speed, plunging for some godforsaken depth where no fish affixed to a fly rod belongs.

Okay, so maybe there's some tequila in the mix, too. But I swear . . . I swear . . . intemperance aside, I've struggled faithfully throughout my life to fly fish with grace, to become what I call a Real Guy—not some fool on a kayak, his gorge rising, attempting to stop inverting dimensions with a lightning-quick 12-weight bent now in the configuration of a fully drawn longbow.

Then, by way of things going bad to worse, I notice my vaunted Swedish reel, its handle a blur, relieved of most of its backing, the machined alloy arbor spinning all but naked.

I recall, at this moment, the words of another recent skipjack victim, the stuff of angling legends: "This one's going to leave a scar."

To which I reply with my own brand of despair: "*All* my line?" I groan, palming the reel to the breaking point.

Rhetoric notwithstanding, the point is already moot. I'm spooled.

Now, when faced with this sort of failure in fishing, as well as the rest of my life, my immediate reaction is often to ask, "Who can I blame for this?"

In this case, I'm free of doubt.

For years Gary Bulla urged me to join him and an expanding cadre of angling *rancheros* for one of the week-long kayak trips he frequently hosts to islands off La Paz in the Sea of Cortez. The appeal of these trips for the adventurous fly rodder is simple—the opportunity to encounter an untold variety of both inshore and bluewater gamefish while skirting wilderness shorelines from the insular tranquility of the seat of one's pants. The challenge, of course, is the same. The seagoing fly fishing kayaker readily escapes the confines of traditional sport, while at the same time accepting the limitations of his aim, a modest approach with as much rigor and uncertainty as that faced by anglers on foot along Baja's endless miles of remote beaches.

Bulla has done as much as anyone to develop and simplify this spirited pursuit. Trips consist of inclusive arrangements that rival any sort of package the do-it-yourselfer might try to create. Boat transports, kayaks, camping equipment, and experienced cooks and captains eliminate logistics down to the essentials of the game: Show up with your gear and fish. After fifteen years probing the southern reaches of the Sea of Cortez, Bulla has pieced together a well-contrived assortment of kayak fly fishing locations that covers the vagaries of weather, seasons, and the experience and aims of his guests, from the inshore reefs surrounding Isla Espíritu Santo to the bluewater depths around Isla Cerralvo and the impressive mangrove lagoon at the south end of Isla San Francisco. Primitive tent camps are pitched just above tideline on narrow beaches lapped by gentle, transparent seas, the bare bones of desert islands rising abruptly from the plain of blue water. Anglers take meals and siestas in the shade of a simple tarp, beside which stands the screened kitchen and its steady supply of hearty camp fare, refreshments, and bold cocktails come nightfall. I might as well also mention, right here, that these trips carry with them the heady glow of the host himself, an unrestrained rake of the first order. Next time I fish with him, I intend to deliver a T-shirt that reads *Gary Bulla: Fun Magnet*.

But I'm the last one who can blame anyone for that.

Still, it seems someone could have at least warned me. Despite the humble profile of Baja kayak fishing, this is anything but playful sport, the feckless jollies of the light tackle enthusiast. *Fricking fish has all my line!* I observe succinctly, spinning the reel handle while the last loop formed by the arbor knot slips freely around the empty, rotating spool.

It's at this point, however, that I discover one of kayak fishing's odd little secrets: Faced with the prospects of attempting to subdue a projectile-mimicking pelagic fish, you can—like whalers of yore and Hollywood shark hunters and old men at sea—tether your line and hold on tight, using the floating device now affixed to the fish (in this case, you) as an instrument of drag to wear down your prey. It's not a particularly sophisticated system—certainly a far cry from the mechanics of the last reel that put yet another dent in your offspring's education fund. You may also quickly lose sight of your angling companions, who will then miss out on the opportunity to hear your continued exclamations of despair, as well as the chance, perhaps, to capture the moment of success—or failure—in digitized splendor. But by holding tight, and riding this thing out, you may in fact eventually see, seize, and claim for posterity the fish in question, and in the process free and regain your fly.

Isn't that what this is all about?

Skimming across the tops of a light chop scuffed up by the thermal breeze, I'm finally able to manipulate the tail end of the backing so that, like a first turn of thread when tying a fly, it rides over the top of itself, catches, holds, and I can begin retrieving line. I consider the excitement of this small show of success, only to recall how long it took me to unload and rewind the reel after discovering the guy at the fly shop had thought that by "right-hand reel" I meant a reel you wind with your left hand. For awhile I try to do the math to calculate how many inches of line I regain with each turn of the reel, and how many turns of the reel it might take to retrieve, say, 150 yards of backing. But I'm repeatedly distracted by an assortment of sharp pains in my lower back, another quietly kept secret about kayak fishing that may come into play if you've ever fallen from a two-story building and, later, you find yourself fighting a fish intent on punishing you for your angling hubris.

At least a fish like this, I tell myself, regaining line, *makes you forget all about the sun on your blemished flesh, the sweat that turns your tropical trousers the texture of a used dish rag—even if your stomach still feels like you're about to lose your lunch overboard.*

Big fish and epic battles, however, are hardly the only invitation for the likes of Gary Bulla's *rancheros* and other kayaking fly anglers exploring the Baja peninsula. What seems most provocative, instead, is the style of fishing, an unobtrusive, low-tech sporting adventure that offers an intimate look at elegant waters and the all but endless variety of gamefish that inhabits them.

Which isn't to suggest that the fishing is somehow easier or less demanding than the typical boat and open water caper. For pure numbers or tonnage of fish, in fact, Baja fly fishers are often better off working the *panga* scene—as long as they can find captains with fly fishing experience, fairly rare in a region with a long history serving the needs of anglers employing baits and conventional gear.

Rather than a numbers game, anyway, or some sort of pared down version of quality sport, Baja kayakers embrace that singular aspect of fly fishing that grows more and more difficult to obtain the farther one travels from home waters: They are—almost by definition—on their own. Seated atop their plastic vessels, each of them armed with paddle and rod and satchel of essential supplies, fly casting kayakers resemble solitary trout or steelhead anglers along river or stream. They rely on experience, cunning, and resolve, plus the hunter's keen sense of clues for the whereabouts of prey. The resemblance to trout or steelhead anglers seems especially appropriate when kayakers are faced with hooked fish. Whatever else such moments suggest, they present kayakers with no other option but to deal—by themselves—with whatever's on the end of their lines.

Discovering what eats the fly remains one of the fundamental pleasures of Baja kayak fishing. You just never know. During the week I spent with Bulla, I landed—besides tuna—roosterfish and jacks, cabrilla and ladyfish, the elegant gaftopsail pompano, triggerfish and needlefish and at least three different kinds of snapper. Who knows what broke me off, on several occasions, around rock and reef? The fact that most fish of these species range in size from a pound or two upwards to a dozen pounds—and some much more than that—means rod weights should be considered carefully. Granted, as in more fishing than most of us care to admit, the ten-pound fish is relatively rare. But remember: Ocean fish will inevitably transform a fly rodder's notions about the strength of fish if past experience has included only freshwater species, even salmon or steelhead. A week before my flight to La Paz, I stood outside Jeff Cottrell's fly shop in The Dalles and made jokes about the powerful 12-weight Jay Johnson from Echo had dropped off—along with two other rods— for me to use. One small skipjack into the trip, however—my first tuna besides bonito on a fly rod—and I never again used my 9- and 10-weight gear for anything but casting off the beach and working the edges of the mangrove lagoon on Isla San Francisco. A 12-weight is a lot of stick—and a lot of stick seemed just about perfect every time another skippie grabbed the fly and line began to melt from the reel.

Of course, no one in his right mind can enjoy casting a 12-weight rod—at least not blind-casting repeatedly, which from a kayak in the midst of the ocean blue is precisely the kind of casting you do. Casting from the seat of your pants, I should add. It's not elegant. It's not fun. And maybe it's not even necessary.

Here's another little secret about kayak fly fishing—a dirty little secret, if you have to know. Almost all of your fishing is done with heavy heads—300, 400, 500 grains of what I call *pure love*. A 500 grain head is more than a tactic or strategic option. Five hundred grains is a commitment, a philosophy, an ideology. The thirty-foot, 500 grain head, with 120 feet of intermediate running line behind it, proclaims allegiance to a new order of fly fishing doctrine that states depth is both the way and the answer—and if you can't double-haul with a double-digit weight rod, that 500 grains of love is going to ask you who's your daddy and probably own you.

But the real secret about kayak fly fishing is that you can catch fish, and catch plenty of them, without ever delivering a cast.

I probably shouldn't say that. Don't we all want to view ourselves as prodigious casters with nothing short of the horizon in our sights? And I recall an old essay by McGuane in which he describes, early in life, paddling around a lake trailing his fly line and a Mickey Finn streamer. "This is about the minimum, fly-wise," he noted. But here's the sober truth: Pitch fly and thirty-foot head in an easy, open loop, strip several dozen yards of line off your reel and shake it out the tip of your rod, then tuck reel and rod butt under one thigh and pick up the paddle and begin heading for the horizon—and the whole way there you're fishing.

It's also called trolling. Don't ask me to take a stand on the ethical probity of such tactics; I'm sure, by now, readers recognize my feel for such slippery arguments. I certainly won't allow that I've ever engaged in anything but my honest share of this kind of primitive sport—enough, however, that I need remind you to make sure your reel handle points away from the deck of your kayak should a skipjack or other line-swilling beast grab the fly, and the reel start spinning like a Skilsaw.

By the time the skipjack's on board, the fly in the corner of its mouth looks like a skeleton, a tiny bird without feathers or skin. Once again, another hastily crafted Clouser Minnow, tied between steelhead outings back home, has disintegrated under attack of the first fish encountered. *Time was short,* I tell myself, hurrying to free the remains. *But I guess you do need epoxy heads—and synthetic hair instead of bucktail.*

The tuna, lying like a weapon across my lap, an elegant missile amidst tangle of line, rod, paddle, and the constricted disorder of most of my kayak landings, offers no more resistance. Its visible eye, opaque as an olive, stares into oblivion with the cold truth of a river stone. I'm worried I've killed the fish, wearing it out beyond revival. Is this the price of . . . sport? What's left of the fly finally free, I grab the skippie by the slender, serrated root of the tail and stab the fish headfirst into the water, then plunge it up and down, trying to fill the gills with oxygen.

One final thrust and the tuna dives like a spear through the shimmering blue below. Will it make it? *Won't be around long if it doesn't,* I conclude—a thought with its own gentle tension that resonates while I gaze across a half-mile of open water, sighting our boat, *El Pato Loco,* seeping into the horizon while surrounding it the *rancheros* in their kayaks look like plastic specks in primary colors stitched lightly atop the sea.

That evening in camp, I watch Bulla feed fist-sized wads of fish guts from a bucket to a moray—not a true eel, but ugly enough to be one, long as a man, a beast the color of motor oil wallowing in the shallows as if an abandoned beach towel. Maybe Bulla got into the thermos of margaritas before the rest of us. He wades in up to his knees, his pants legs billowing, and the fish, it seems, would readily take the viscera directly from his hand, writhing forward in slow motion as if a creature in a bad dream.

"Yiggh," says Bulla, dropping the goods and backing out of the water long before the moray reaches striking range. He holds the beast in the glare of his headlamp. "Imagine if it had your hand," he adds, watching another gory clump disappear.

"Think it would take a fly?" I ask, keeping a rod's length between me and the edge of the water.

"The *Amigo,*" says Bulla. "It'll catch anything."

Or these fish will eat *anything,* I think—a notion that's soon reinforced when Alvaro, the camp cook, comes down to the water and tosses in the carcass of a filleted skipjack, which the moray, having already consumed an entire bucketful of fish guts, immediately grasps by the head and sucks down through its stretched jaws in a fast-motion imitation of a rattlesnake ingesting a rabbit.

Despite Bulla's belief in, and development of, a few choice Baja patterns, I remain an old-school skeptic, convinced the real trick in all of this is finding fish and presenting them with the opportunity to strike the fly. The following morning we break camp and motor to Isla San Francisco, where we again pitch our small tents in a colorful chain stretched to the far reaches of the beach in order to accommodate a pair of newlyweds in the bunch. There remains some question, naturally, whether such flagrant connubial relations automatically disqualify guests from *ranchero* status at all—an unspoken debate that plays out, much like questions about flies, in final claims on territory, with the added allowance made, in this case, for proximity to the outdoor john and one particular guest who, we've all learned, snores like a chainsaw.

The move and midday heat leave several *rancheros* in a quiet heap beneath the freshly staked shade canopy, the sudden siesta a testimony to the benefits of the good life. Then Bulla, drawing in the sand, begins to map out the margins and byways of the nearby mangrove lagoon—and in a swift resurgence of energy we congregate and again follow the now familiar if still somewhat chaotic routine that puts us back aboard *El Pato Loco* and then delivers us, later, digging with paddles through the strong current of an ebb tide pouring out the mouth of the lagoon.

The lagoon offers its own blend of mercurial sport. One moment you're skipping a popper-like Crease Fly into the shade of the mangrove, where the odd snapper explodes from a tangle of roots; the next, you're racing across open water, trying to close the gap between you and a flurry of pelicans and gulls diving into the lacerations of God knows what smashing bait. Most of this action confirms my Baja prejudices: Find fish and get a fly in front of them, and when that doesn't work, string up a heavy head and fish deep.

Yet the next evening even that doesn't work. As the sun leaves the water, I ride the current back toward the mouth of the lagoon, beyond which rests our boat, anchored serenely in a gentle wind swell while Manuel, our captain, stands on the bow practicing casts with the 10-weight Bulla has given him. I drag my kayak over rocks exposed by the falling tide, my legs stiff from disuse. Past the last thicket of mangrove stretches the long arc of a steep beach, pale and sedate in contrast to the lushness of the lagoon. A vigorous shorebreak snaps at the toe of the sandy berm, and after days spent casting from my butt, confined to the yellow skirt of my kayak, I'm drawn to the open beach and tumbling surf as if beckoned by an old lover, her blouse pressed to her by the breeze.

I don't get far. Just where the rocks end, I launch a cast out over the break, and on the second strip I come up tight on something. It's a small fish—but spirited in that way that every fish fought on the level through waves seems energized by its dynamic environment. A green jack, it turns out, that doesn't top even two pounds—yet a jack is a jack, I tell myself, the elegant scimitar of the caudal fin evoking a family of fish that seems perfectly designed for fly rods, if only because they strike the fly so readily, pull like bloodhounds, and often come in bunches.

But it's not only jacks that turn out to be piled up just beyond the surf line. More casts than not I get hit, the line stiffening as if snatched at the same moment a swell's energy compresses to the point that the shorebreak vaults toward the beach. Which is probably pretty much what's happening, I think. Cabrilla, cornetfish, needlefish, triggerfish and more jacks grab the fly as if competing with one another—which, I suspect, swapping out another tattered chartreuse and white Clouser, is also probably the case.

I keep at it long after such sport should hold anyone's interest. The light falls and between casts I see the other *rancheros* squirting out of the lagoon and gather around the boat. Kayaks get pulled aboard, raised against the darkening eastern sky. I see the brief flash of a match or lighter. I make a cast and strip and set the hook again, reminding myself to hold onto the moment, this evening on a beach casting flies again in the Baja surf.

Amigo (by Guy Wright)

Hook: Size 1X–4X long
Thread: Olive Monocord
Eyes: Dumbbell, red, 1/24 oz.
Lateral stripe: 1 peacock herl each side
Body: Crystal Hair, pearl midsection; Super Hair, olive over white
Fins: Crystal Hair and Super Hair extended one-quarter inch tight behind eyes*
Gill plate: Marabou, red
Glue: Krazy glue; 5-minute epoxy

Tuna Tux (created by Gary Bulla)

Hook: Owner Aki, Billy Pate, Varivas 2–4/0
Thread: Black 3/0
Lateral line: Black or gray ultra hair (optional two strands of blue Krystal Flash)
Wing: Black Ocean Hair or other synthetic hair
Belly: White Ultra Hair, Ocean Hair, or bucktail
Eyes: Spirit River red or pearl with black pupils
Weight (optional): Black tungsten cone head
Rib: Two strands yellow Krystal Flash
Throat (optional): Three red marabou tips or strands of red Krystal Flash

Tying Notes

Slip cone head over hook to eye. Place hook in vise. Tie in ribbing at bend of hook. Wind thread from bend to eye, building a small hump behind cone head. Wind ribbing forward and tie off. Tie on top of hook Ultra Hair lateral line so it extends one and a half times the hook length and lies in line with the hook shank. Tie in black hair on top of hook at middle and add another clump directly behind cone head or future builtup thread head. Turn over hook and add a small amount of white belly material that extends just beyond the bend. Turn over fly again and add white material that does not go past bend in hook. Add red throat if desired. Build thread head if no cone used. Glue on eyes with small amount of Goop and set aside. Double coat head and eyes with epoxy.

---

* For the Gill Plate Fins extend midbody Crystal Hair a quarter of an inch and tie in tight behind eyes. Do the same with the white Super Hair underbelly. Then tie in the marabou gills tight behind eyes. Finish the fly by tying the olive Super Hair on top in front of the eyes. Glaze lightly with epoxy.

LESSON 32

ANIMATE
THE FLY

Vendetta is the wrong word.

Redemption seems more like it, the thing you're after on returning to the spot where, a week before, a bunch of trout fed like hungry spaniels without one showing trace of interest in any of your hurriedly swapped flies. The humiliation fuels a rich brew of doubt and self-incrimination, a fresh attack on your meager store of pride. Of course, this has happened before—which is only to say that your heart needs no reminder what it means to beat in vain. You and what hope have ever felt altogether safe? But in angling, at least, one advances toward a kind of immunity to fate, a reckless aim that leaves you vulnerable, in the face of each new failure, to something that's never felt quite so harsh before.

But vendetta is the wrong word. You hope to please these trout, after all—not hurt a one. And despite sensations of intense rejection, you understand, upon reflection, that these are never personal matters, no more so than the fury of a noontime sun or the bite of rain on one's exposed, windswept flesh.

Still, the feeling remains: Something needs to be put right. The culprit, this time, appears to have been the Little Western Weedy-Water Sedge: family *Brachycentridae*, genus *Amiocentrus*, species—give me a break. These are little black caddis, the ones that come out of those slender, finely tapered larval cases, some round, some rectangular, depending on species that you have to be more clever than I am to name. Some oldtimers still refer to these caddis as Grannom, a name that traces the roots of the sport eastward, all the way to England, where it refers to both the insect and a two-century-old wet fly pattern that can still save your bacon during a caddis hatch today.

(Okay, for the record: The *Brachycentridae* caddis family has two significant trout-stream genera, 9+*Amiocentrus*—the caddis we're talking about—and *Brachycentrus*, the American Grannom. *Amiocentrus aspilus*, the Little Western Weedy-Water Sedge, is the only species in the genus, important in many well-known rivers throughout the West. *Brachycentrus*, with over a half-dozen North American species, enjoys the fame and history—plus the confusion that accompanies notoriety. *B. occidentalis* is the species of the illustrious Mother's Day caddis hatch that everyone hopes to catch on the Yellowstone, the Clark's Fork, the Yakima, etc.; *B. americanus*, on the other hand, is found coast to coast and usually receives the generic "Grannom" appellation. East of the Rockies, the *Brachycentrus* genus becomes more complex and convoluted—requiring the kind of snooty, Latinate name-dropping that no one should have to suffer more of than is absolutely necessary. Now where were we?)

Few among us, anyway, remain so articulate in the heat of an unidentified hatch. You recall, from the week before, the phrase "Oh my flipping God!" as you began to comment on the inefficacy of your merrily swinging fly, surrounded by trout behaving like untrained canine. Your eloquence went downhill from there. You failed until dark to pass the test—at which point you felt thoroughly convinced, once more, that your exclusion from the fraternity of Real Guys remains an appropriate curse, no more surprising, really, than the effect your pronounced love of *chorizo* had on the vegan you recently tried dating.

Worse, in the end, was the manner of your pale enlightenment. Stumbling over mossy rocks toward dry ground, stars above the eastern horizon squinting like the eyes of an untoward jury, you noted the headlamp of your buddy sweeping side to side above the knees of his waders—just the depth of river anglers will comfortably stand in while casting futilely to trout rising all around them. Your buddy suggested you come over and take a look.

"What do you think?" he asked, dark bands around both thighs illuminated by the bluish, law-enforcement glow of his lamp.

"I think that's what they were feeding on," you offered inanely. Caddis pupae, the tiny pearlescent shucks of caddis pupae, and even little black caddis adults themselves remained plastered to your buddy's waders—a picture that brought to mind the reverse image of what you find some-times in your teenage son's shower after he's failed to clean the drain, for who knows how long, of his shoulder-length hair.

"I think we suck, too," you added.

But this time you're ready.

Not only have you done your research, identifying the caddis in question beyond a shadow of a doubt, you've also stopped in at the local fly shop to inspect patterns offered to cover the hatch. More than that, you've read about this hatch in the hatch guide written for this very river, and of course you went back to the guru himself, Gary LaFontaine, to see what he had to say about the Little Western Weedy-Water Sedge in his classic opus, *Caddisflies*.

And you tied flies: Good flies—no, *great* flies that reveal that after three decades of serious tying and heaven knows how many thousands and thousands of flies, you really have gotten pretty good at this, flies that are not only technically sound but also subtle, sedate, sophisticated in ways you just don't see in mass-produced, commercially tied flies. Your Emergent Sparkle Pupa has just the right proportions, just enough Antron to form a sparse but distinct overbody, just the right shade of deer hair for the small, sprouting wing. Your adults, as well, are the per-fect size, not the overhackled bottle brushes you normally see. And your Soft-Hackle Diving Caddis, tied with a dark dun hen neck that you were directed to by the cane-rod enthusiast you consider the best trout angler you know? Money, dude.

So prepared are you, in fact, so sure you've got things covered, that it seems peculiarly appropriate when, an hour into the first show of rising trout, you've still failed to stick a fish.

What's going on?

You know it's not some quirk in these rainbows or this particular stretch of water. You've fished here dozens of times, often with unquali-fied success. Drift? No, you know the currents and seams here like the wrinkles in your sun-damaged face. Depth? Nope, you've worked the entire water column, adding minute gradations of lead to your leader so that by now you could practically map the contours and rocks along the bottom.

What is it?

Once more you run your brace of finely tuned flies through the slot. There's a subtle moment when your cast leaves the current and settles deeper in the soft water, right where you know the fish are. Nothing. You shake your head. You scratch it. You squint. You run a hand over your face and beard. What now? you ask yourself, your flies all but dangling in the water.

And then, as you begin a new cast, slowly lifting against the subtle weight of flies and lead, something heavy stops your rod—and the next thing you know your reel is wailing, and somewhere in the distance there's a trout dancing on the end of your line.

Hmm.

You try it again. Drift. Descent. Pause. Slowly lift. And when it works, it makes so much sense that, once again, you feel foolish—although not quite so foolish as when everything you try catches nothing at all.

Everyone has heard about the Leisenring Lift. It's right up there with techniques like the reach cast, the double haul, high-stick nymphing, mending line, or even something so simple as the wet fly swing—yet another skill that makes up an accomplished angler's repertoire of tricks. The Lift works, of course, because caddis pupae—and mayfly nymphs— head to the surface to hatch, and a fly that mimics this perilous journey can prove especially effective. (Some nymphs and pupae also hatch beneath the surface and then finish their ascent as winged adults: hence the efficacy of winged wet flies.) The Lift, in other words, is a classic, time-honored, tradition-bound, empirically proven technique.

But anyone who's tried it knows it's easier said than done.

The difficulty, I believe, begins with the name. The Lift, in reality, is hardly a lift at all, but instead more of a stop, a holding-in-place of the line with the rod tip so that the submerged fly, upon reaching a fish, rides upward in current against the tension of the line. Any actual lifting with the rod must be extremely subtle—so subtle, in fact, that, as is the case with other slack-free line manipulations, the words used to describe the action overstate what the angler actually does, the description verging on metaphor, near the limits of literal language.

Jim Leisenring, by all accounts a hell of a fly fisher, seems himself to have recognized the daunting task of putting into words the subtle techniques he practiced on the water. The Lift was only one of many methods he employed, yet the only one he described in his book, *The Art of Tying the Wet Fly*, coauthored with Pete Hidy. Note the title alone: This was a tying book, not a book about fishing techniques. What Leisenring did was describe just one particular method he used when fishing the subsurface flies he showed the reader how to tie—and ever since then anglers have been trying to mimic that method in the vast array of different situations they face on trout streams of all kinds.

The Leisenring Lift, despite its lovely alliterative lilt, was no more the main component of Jim Leisenring's game than The Ali Shuffle was essential to the Great One's heroic heavyweight prizefighting career. Instead, The Lift exemplified a particular approach to the problem of fooling trout—a mindset, if you will. In the one brief anecdote he uses to help the reader see how he fishes his beloved soft-hackled wet flies, Leisenring reveals his thinking in less than a sentence, surely one of the great lines in all the literature. "I always fish my fly," he wrote, "so that it becomes deadly at the point where the trout is most likely to take his food. . . ."

There it is. *Deadly.* You make the fly deadly. You make the fly become deadly at the moment it matters most. It's not about The Lift. It's not about the lift, the lunge, the loop, the leap. It's not about the this, the that, or the anything—other than *making the fly deadly*, and doing it at the moment a trout can't say no.

Oliver Kite called it the "induced take."

Disciple of the great Frank Sawyer, he of the original famed Pheasant Tail Nymph, Kite shared thinking similar to Leisenring in his 1963 classic, *Nymph Fishing in Practice.* Here and elsewhere during Kite's short life (he died five years later at age forty-eight) he claimed—and proved—that he could catch fish on a bare hook, employing accurate casts and, most important, "the life-like employment of the artificial by the angler." What connects Kite to Leisenring, and both anglers to Sawyer—as well as, over the years, writers as diverse as Pete Hidy and Sylvester Nemes, Polly Rosborough and especially Dave Hughes—is the notion of fishing a slack-free line as a means of imparting realistic movement to the fly. The lift, the lead, the stop, the twitch, the strip, the swing—I'm sure there are a dozen different techniques I've never even heard of or that circles of anglers refer to amongst themselves—all of these are essentially methods in which the angler animates the fly. Sometimes, more than anything else, it's this action—usually subtle, usually accurately timed—

that makes the fly effective, that makes it deadly, that makes it behave in a manner absolutely contrary to the much-heralded "drag-free drift" we've been directed to aim for most of our angling lives.

Maybe vendetta *is* the right word. Unless you've read between the lines, you've been told, over and over again, that the two best ways to catch trout are either on a drag-free drifting dry fly or on a nymph drifting drag-free beneath an indicator. Look around you. Watch how guided clients fish. Read the magazines. Study the books. There's an entire school if not generation of fly fishers who think the drag-free drift is not only the best way to catch trout, but the only way. Doesn't it feel good now and then to prove them wrong?

Animate the fly.

Sometimes the trout like it real well.

Emergent Sparkle Pupa
Hook: TMC 3671, size 16–18
Thread: Camel 8/0
Overbody: Green Antron yarn
Underbody: Highlander green Pearsall's marabou silk floss
Wing: Light speckled tips of deer body hair
Head: Brown squirrel dubbing

Brachycentrus Soft Hackle
Hook: TMC 900BL or TMC 2487, size 16–20
Thread: Camel 8/0
Hackle: Dark brown dun hen hackle
Body: Olive Antron yarn or highlander green Pearsall's marabou silk floss
Thorax: Brown squirrel dubbing

Diving Caddis
Hook: TMC 900BL or 3671, size 16–20
Thread: Camel 8/0
Body: Olive Antron yarn
Underwing: English grouse
Overwing: Black or dark brown antron yarn
Hackle: Dark brown dun hen hackle

LESSON 33

HOMING IN

After two days attempting to service my van's air conditioning system, Walt asks for a $200 advance—cash if I don't mind. I do. One day was lost ordering the wrong expansion valve; the second day—I'm not sure what went wrong. Walt lives in a room you can't help but look into from the shop office; both mornings I've had to bang on the office door and wake him, standing to one side of a stream of condensation pouring from the A/C unit overhead. Already I'm looking at the unexpected cost of the old-style caviar-priced R-12 Freon, which Walt failed to include in his quote, believing the van's age fell just this side of a technology change that predates videogame consoles and DVDs. I can't blame Walt for that. Still, even at my age, I find attention of any kind to auto air conditioning slightly decadent, especially when repair costs will soon rival, by the looks of things, the worth of the vehicle itself.

But I don't back off on trout in the heat of summer like I used to, either.

Day three extends well into the afternoon. Walt has to jerry-rig the mounting bracket for the new dryer, the only other part he needed to make the system good as new. Unless the pump goes out. For the umpteenth time he flips the switches and spins the dials on the one tool you seem to need to become an A/C and cooling specialist, a testing unit that bears a strong resemblance to a souped-up shop vac. Walt points to needles and numbers and nods his head of curly unkempt hair, the bright eyes in his pockmarked face as charming as the smile of a criminal. This long into the job, I feel like Walt's new buddy—despite the $200 check of mine he had to cash after hours God knows where.

"So where you going fishing?" he asks, climbing into the driver's seat. He punches the A/C buttons and thrusts a thermometer through a louvered vent.

"East," I say, gesturing opposite the direction of sunlight flooding the garage bay.

"You ever thought about hanging a sheet here?"

Walt points behind him, the van a big metal box, void of paneling or insulation, that suits my idea of a sport utility vehicle.

"Keep some of that hot air off you."

"Won't be hot now," I try, hopefully.

"Forty-two effing degrees," claims Walt, holding the thermometer at an angle I can't read. "That oughta do it."

When we settle up, Walt promises I don't need to be shy about using my revitalized air conditioning.

"It's a closed system," he explains. "You've already replaced everything that can go wrong."

"Except the pump."

"It's working now," reasons Walt. "Isn't it?"

I meet Bruce and Linda Milhauser early afternoon on a stretch of Wolf River without scrub or cottonwoods or other impediments to the sun. They've parked their camper on a sweep of flattened river stones, the closest thing to a campsite along a mile of water hidden behind a band of willows bent sideways in the wind. Between the pavement and a parking spot of my own, I make every effort to enjoy the last of the effects of Walt's handiwork. By the time I'm done shaking hands with my hosts, I can feel the desert working on me like the fingers of a calloused masseuse.

Linda retreats to the camper. A fan there enhances a kind of white noise I associate with midday desert heat, as if the land has begun to vibrate beneath the force of the sun. Through a break in the willows I watch a piece of river slip by, the smooth surface a vegetative green that seems all but frog water in a broad tailout not yet animated by the next riffle. Bruce and I both catch sight of the inevitable rise, the widening rings passing from view as if an idea no one wrote down.

"We've been getting our share," offers Bruce. "Especially when the sun leaves the water."

"What about that one?" I ask, nodding in the direction of the departed rings.

"You can always try 'em."

Instead I follow Bruce along the backside of the willows to a hidden opening he pushes through knowingly to water's edge. The river here has picked up pace, churning around the flanks of a long narrow island before rejoining directly across from our view. We watch for a few moments until, in the seam just above the melding currents, a dark shape the size of a stray cat tilts up, rises, and takes something from the surface of the quiet, rippled water.

"The ones in here can be a little easier."

I catch myself taking quick, shallow breaths. It's not just the heat. Still, my excitement is only partially a response to the fish, a brown trout that appeared, from what I could tell, about average for what I've seen on the river in the past. In other words a slab, a slob, a pig. Yet beyond the big trout, and the prospects of catching one—or many—just like it, I'm hopped up and even slightly giddy to be on this kind of water with an angler like Bruce Milhauser, who just happens to get the nod in my life as the best trout fisher I know.

It's not just the cane rods and sexy, soft-hackled flies. It's not just the sharp, accurate casts—although I should say that's one of the things I enjoy most about watching Bruce fish, an immediate, unadorned precision of delivery that Joe Warren, another angler who recognizes Bruce's skills, has referred to as "casts on the order of heat-seeking missiles." It's not even the fact that Bruce catches so many good trout. Or it is that, but not just that, or it's that and the combination of untold other things Bruce does so well that makes the trout he catches seem better, bigger, and more numerous, which they usually are, even though that's not what makes him so good.

You know what I mean?

An hour later Bruce and I slip into the river, the pace of an afternoon PMD hatch beginning to rise. Despite the heat the water, even through waders, feels cold; the shadow of the canyon wall casts the warm afternoon in an odd, evening light. From the far side of the river I get a fish on a little yellow parachute dun directly below the seam Bruce pointed out through the willows, a relatively small trout for these waters, although closer to eighteen than sixteen inches. Reluctant, on this river, to pose with any fish under twenty inches, I impatiently allow Bruce a quick snapshot—and by the time the hatch begins to come off in earnest, trout rising at every lie, Bruce has moved off through the willows and vanished somewhere downstream.

Despite the one quick take and confident rises, the fishing proves tougher than it looks. What's new? I put down a couple of fish and then move up into a tongue of broken water, only to find the little parachute all but impossible to keep afloat. I solve that problem with a yellow Humpy, as small as I tie them—and after three good fish and several other shocking but missed rises, I decide to back out and let the pool rest and head downstream to find Bruce.

He's down in some slick water, midstream, casting tight to an overgrown bank where, although I can't see them from this distance, I'm sure there are big fish sipping with fastidious care—the kind of trout that keep most of us from sleeping as well as we'd like. And when Bruce suddenly sets up on a fish, taking an abrupt step backward as he does, the soft cane rod bends to the cork, and the arc it describes seems as elegant a picture as any the sport has to offer.

We finally rejoin at the last press of fast water above this same slick pool, where ribbons of current wend their way through sharp boulders sloughed off from the canyon wall. Trout rise sporadically from several likely lies, and they are all big fish and hard to fool, each drift complicated by eddies and serpentine seams, by moving water rubbing up directly against water quiet if not absolutely still. Bruce does what he does best. With little line but his leader outside his rod tip, he's still able to load the rod and deliver casts directly on the noses of feeding fish. There's virtually no drift. The fly's just there, the fish eats, and Bruce sticks it. He's got on a Hare's Ear Soft Hackle, a size 16, and though I claim I'm fishing the same pattern, trying to match the last of the PMD emergers still trapped or adrift in the film, I can tell my pattern isn't quite right, that, unlike Bruce's, it wasn't tied for this hatch on this river specifically.

But it's his presentation, I think, *not the fly.*

Later, after the PMD show has finally subsided, and while we're waiting for the evening caddis rush to begin, we compare notes. Bruce is surprised when I relate my success with the Humpy—but we both know it goes without saying that it was the swift water that gave the pattern an edge, while in the slow currents, say, before us, the fly would fool no more trout than a tennis ball floating downstream.

Then Linda shows up, the caddis begin to move out of the willows, and for the next two hours we get slammed by more big brown trout, right into dark, than most trout fishers see in a season.

In the morning I'm surprised to learn that Bruce and Linda intend to leave. Something about fishing with and feeding grandkids at a reservoir a few hours west. We're all a little disappointed to break up the fun so quickly. I set off on foot upstream to try a new piece of water, and when they drive by in their camper, headed for a dumpster to unload their trash, I get that funny feeling that tells me I'm on my own now and that's that.

But by this time, I realize, I've got pretty much everything—besides company—I need: a good stretch of river, a handle on the hatches, a pattern I can home in on, a clear mental picture of those short accurate casts Bruce employs to stick the snooty fish. Plus big brown trout up the wazoo. The heat's bound to take its toll, I imagine, but so what? Isn't this fiery canyon and threatening sun part of the appeal? I ask myself, catching sight of Bruce and Linda's rig passing again, this time headed downstream.

And for once this sense of sufficiency, the feeling of having a solid grip on the situation, proves accurate. In two days I settle into the exquisite rhythm of a man with nothing better to do with his life than catch fish. Most mornings, after coffee and oatmeal, I find an excuse—ice, yogurt, wet ones—to drive to the nearest minimart, thirty miles away, for an hour of respite in the comfortable embrace of good buddy Walt's temperature refreshing handiwork. Then, with the van cool and the sun still low, an hour of tying, the vise clamped to the bottom of the steering wheel, tools and materials spread atop the engine well. Nowhere, I'm reminded, offers better light for tying flies than sunlight through a windshield, a conviction that quickly helps me transform my own Wild Hare into a replica of Bruce's Hare's Ear Soft Hackle, a pattern I refine to the point that it seems, eventually, perfectly married to the size, shape, and color of the PMD emergers littering the surface of the river every afternoon from one until four, with big brown trout tipping up to them with ruthless, relentless efficiency. Afterward, the caddis appear, prompting their own brand of madness, low-profile hairwing dries or the Wet

Caddis swung downstream on a tight line, the trout lashing at the surface in heavy explosive rises, so that by the time I finally call it quits for the day I've been in the water eight or nine hours straight, an amount that satisfies my working-class need to put in a full day's effort, even if I have no real responsibilities beyond hydration, releasing my trout quickly, and keeping my campsite clean.

Eight days of this and suddenly it's time to go home. I don't know how this happens. One day you're certain there simply isn't any limit to how many big brown trout you can hold up and measure against your rod, and the next morning you roll out of the cot and you're already placing gear in the van, positioning it for the long drive home. Maybe it's the shower you need, the ripening wading garments, the restless nights filled with dreams made all the more vivid fueled by ground and sharply seasoned animal parts, consumed beneath the star-spangled nights. Maybe you even feel a little guilty, out here by yourself catching all these big trout, although what there is you might be charged with, and by whom, seems more and more a theoretical question, if not also a problem better left to the philosophers in the bunch.

The Stanley thermos is still half full when I pull away from the river. I'm only three hours from home when I notice the air conditioner has stopped working.

PMD Hare's Ear Soft Hackle

Hook: TMC 900BL, size 16
Thread: 8/0 rusty dun or camel
Hackle: Dark brown dun hen
Tail: Barred lemon wood duck flank fibers
Rib: Fine copper wire
Body: Superfine Adams gray dubbing
Thorax: Dark hare's mask

Tying Notes

Step 1: Secure the hook and start the thread. Choose a slightly undersized hackle feather. Strip the webby materials from the lower portion of the feather. Lay the stripped stem along the top of the hook, the convex or shiny side of the hackle toward you, and secure the stem with your thread.

Step 2: Wind your thread to the rear of the hook and create a tail out of five to eight barred lemon wood duck flank fibers.

Step 3: Secure a length of fine copper wire at the root of the tail. Leave it for later.

Step 4: Create a slender tapered abdomen out of the dubbing material—the less dubbing material the better. Stop the abdomen just forward the halfway point of the hook. Rib the abdomen with three or four turns of copper wire.

Step 5: Form a dubbing loop, wax it, and apply a pinch of that precious dark spiky material you get off the ears of a hare's mask. Spin the dubbing loop tight. Form a distinct thorax with two or three turns of the material in the dubbing loop.

Step 6: Affix your hackle pliers to the tip of the hackle feather. Wind the hackle from the eye of the hook back to the thorax, making only one or two turns. Advance the thread through the hackle, making sure to seat the wraps without matting down any hackle fibers. Clip the excess hackle point at its tie-down point. Whip finish and add head cement.

LESSON 34

STEELHEAD LIES

Part One

For a long time Jeff Cottrell didn't believe me. He'd seen me catch steelhead on my Waking Muddler, a fly so sparse it seems to represent a ruined fly, one that's fallen apart, lost much of its dressing. But Jeff caught plenty of fish himself, and though he liked the idea of a slender waking pattern, he didn't believe it held any more promise than countless other dressings you can swing on the surface, eliciting from steelhead those heart-stopping rises that seasoned anglers long for like hope itself.

Then Jeff fell into a slump. Every serious steelheader knows about these spells, when hours turn into days, and days into weeks, and it feels whenever you fish, the river is empty, and nothing you do, nothing you try, makes one bit of difference. The very best steelheaders accept these unproductive periods with the stoic resignation of victims of bad marriages. They figure things will eventually get better. The rest of us, deep in the throes of a steelhead skunk, whine and moan, curse the Fates, wonder what we've done to deserve this treatment—and keep changing flies.

Now Jeff Cottrell is no rookie. Those seventeen seasons guiding on Tierra del Fuego's Rio Grande for sea run browns taught him a thing or two about anadromous fish. So when I gave him one of my Waking Muddlers and suggested he might like to try it, he did what most experienced aficionados of sea run fish will do with someone's favorite fly—he put it in his fly box and went right on fishing with patterns he knows and believes in.

Then, one afternoon deep into Jeff's slump, Marty Sheppard, the guide, found us on a favorite run and stopped to see how we were doing.

"I thought I heard shouting down here," said Marty, pushing through the bankside brush.

"Second rise," I said, my voice still on edge from hollering. "I can't believe it didn't take it."

Later, when Jeff came downstream to watch me land that same fish, two rises after Marty left, he said he'd asked Marty what kind of fly he should be using.

"What he say?"

"Guess."

Jeff pointed an unlit cigarette at the precise spot my little muddler hung from the corner of the hatchery fish's mouth.

But it wasn't until the next afternoon, and only after Jeff had gotten skunked again in the morning, that he knotted on the Waking Muddler I had given him the previous season.

That evening, he called.

"I'm a believer," he said.

But this isn't a story about a steelhead fly. If it were, it wouldn't prove valuable to most experienced steelheaders, who recognize that flies are rarely the key to success, who already have a few choice patterns they rely on, flies that meet the requirements of specific conditions encountered at various times and places throughout the year. Given those conditions, the seasoned steelheader ties on this or that fly, confident it will do the trick should a cast find a fish.

For the truth is, steelheading is a simple game. Note, I didn't say easy. Essentially, you face two problems: finding fish and getting fish to bite your fly. For three weeks Jeff swung sparse little muddlers, first the one I had given him, then ones he fashioned on his own, and in that period he hooked upwards of two dozen fish, landing at least half of them. That's a pretty good stretch of steelheading—especially for a guy with a job. I got a few, too. Yet most of what Jeff and I confirmed during this streak was that we had found ourselves a good lie—a spot in a river's countless approximations of holding water, only a few of which will actually harbor steelhead with any predictable regularity, and fewer still will give up fish in numbers that make a lie seem perfectly suited to one particular style of presentation and fly.

But that is the game—finding or at least recognizing lies, and then knowing how to fish them. The first difficult lesson most steelheaders must learn is that rivers are, by and large, void of steelhead, virtual deserts with but a few sweet spots sprinkled throughout them like good surf breaks along a coast. Just as important, if not more so, is the hard-won lesson that even within runs that are likely to hold fish, steelhead generally get hooked in only a select few places—those specific, articulated lies where fish seem most ready to take the fly or the fly can be presented to them most favorably. Some lies produce fish year after year; others change one year to the next. Some lies produce best in high water, others in low. But what remains consistent in steelheading is that successful anglers keep their flies fishing effectively through specific lies, or holding water, generously sharing the rest of the water with those of us who haven't put in the necessary time and research to unravel a steelhead river's strict but enigmatic truths.

If you're ever fortunate enough to fish with a good steelhead guide, one thing you should pay attention to is when the guide pays attention to you.

Now, Jeff doesn't guide much anymore; he reached a certain age, he says, and his patience ran out. I don't guide much, either, but for the simple reason that I'd starve if my livelihood depended on my fishing success.

Yet if either Jeff or I were guiding, and we had been fishing with clients on that run where we enjoyed such success last fall with our surface muddlers, we would have known just where to begin expecting a steelhead to either rise or grab—or both—and that would have been just after we moseyed over as if to see how this imaginary client was doing.

It's a common guide trick. They wander off while you work your way down a run, inspect the boat, relieve themselves of morning coffee behind the bushes, take a cigarette break far enough away that you're not bothered by the smoke. Or that's what you're supposed to think. But the truth is, your guide doesn't really expect you to get a grab when he's not around you because, unless he's also working on your casts or presentation, he doesn't hang tight until you get to that spot where he knows—from experience—the fish both hold and are willing to grab. Or, viewed another way, the guide leaves you to your own devices in the portions of a run that he knows probably won't matter—and then, like a bird dog moving toward scent, he gravitates toward you as your fly begins to swing toward the probable lie.

It may or may not be worth noting the precise details of the lie Jeff and I so effectively fished last fall. My point here is that there seems to be, in steelheading at least, such an array of variables that make up a good lie that only empirical proof elevates one spot over a dozen others that look more or less the same. The lie in question extended through the broad tailout of a textbook steelhead run—a run similar to ones you could find for miles and miles both up and down the river. Because the depth of the tailout was relatively shallow, the pace of the current even and slow, the lie seemed to beg for the floating line and surface presentations—a conclusion Jeff also reached, but only after seeing me raise several steelhead where his conventional swinging wet flies had moved nothing.

Two aspects of this situation bear special note. First, repeated observations—and success—demonstrated that this particular tailout was unusual on the river in that the bottom was comprised of ledges, slots, and fissures, an assortment of pronounced nooks and crannies in the basalt bedrock rather than the relatively uniform paving of tumbled rock common to most other sections of this typical freestone river. In other words, the lie contained structure—in my mind, the single most important element of prime holding water. Jeff and I floated a section of the John Day the previous fall with Marty Sheppard—a real guide— and he repeatedly pointed out to us runs that looked as good as the ones from which we caught fish, but these unproductive runs lacked the big boulders, sloughed off from the canyon walls, that lie hidden in the runs where Marty, day after day, finds fish.

The other aspect worth noting about the success Jeff and I both eventually achieved at this spot is more subtle—and, for that reason, more problematic. Was it, in fact, the style of fly and presentation that earned us so many grabs? Or, as many steelheaders argue, was it simply a matter of getting the fly to the fish once we had discovered this good lie?

This is slippery territory—and I'm the last one to make any contentions that claim one style of presentation superior to another. The data in this case, however, were conclusive: The little surface muddlers stuck fish in bunches.

Still, it's a tough argument. The notion is that given certain lies, under certain conditions (water temperature, according to steelhead guru Bill Mcmillan, being most important), a surface presentation will elicit more takes from steelhead than any other single method of presentation—more, even, than if you swing or drift a fly down at the level at which steelhead hold. Other steelheaders find such notions heretical. They agree that steelhead will, at times, move to the fly—but they figure why hope for that to happen if you can just as easily put the fly on the fish's nose.

Advocates of surface presentations argue, however, that there's something about a waking, skating, or other tightline surface presentation that stimulates steelhead to move to the fly with greater frequency than other methods, or when other methods fail to work at all. After years of swinging surface muddlers, I'd also suggest that smaller flies with sparse dressings contribute to a surface pattern's efficacy, especially when fished with a riffle hitch in low, clear water, encountered so often in summer and fall steelheading.

This certainly seemed the case for Jeff and me. Of course, I didn't need any convincing. The surface or waking muddler remains for me the consummate summer steelhead fly, capable of moving fish from most lies. Does it always work? Of course not. Do I always fish it? No. Steelheading, I suggested, may be simple—but it isn't easy.

LESSON 35

STEELHEAD LIES

Part Two

This winter I didn't catch any steelhead. I'm serious. Not one. My son Patrick got his first ever right before Christmas, fishing a two-hander at the bottom of a favorite run—but then nothing, nada, el cero. *How can that be?* you wonder. A man of my . . . stature?

Snow fell, and for two months the rivers ran low, lean, and clear. Counts at the nearest dam averaged less than ten fish a day. I was working on three different manuscripts at the same time, churning out chapters and stories with the hint of hysteria writers suffer when they aren't sure who's going to buy their work or if, in fact, it will get published at all.

And I fell in love. Oh, I fell in love all right.

But that's a different story.

Of course, we all understand that winter steelheading can prove tough. Yet a spell like this brings into question everything you know. Or everything you think you know—because obviously if you actually knew much of anything at all, you sense, you wouldn't be getting skunked every time you venture to the water.

Or so it seems to those of us who see ourselves as genuine aficionados of the winter game. No matter what, we think, we ought to be able to catch something. Yet if truth be known, more often than not winter steelheading fails to produce fish—and for this reason alone it qualifies as a form of extreme (some would say masochistic) sport that carries with it its own blend of hopes, attitudes, and techniques. No one goes fishing intending to cast hours on end without any evidence whatsoever that a single fish swims in the river. No one but a steelheader with a fly rod along a Northwest river in winter endures this experience so often.

Deep in the throes of this season of futility, I stumbled into an opportunity to fish a day or two for winter steelhead with John Gierach. Given the status of such company, I figured it may be time I reviewed what I actually know about the sport—especially if I hoped to present myself as an angler in possession of some genuine local knowledge. The fact that I hadn't caught squat of late cast a shadow of doubt over any claims I might make on inside dope—yet it's this persistent doubt, I would argue, that helps define the sport, while gnawing at the core of every serious winter steelheader's game.

The Fish

The first thing to remember about winter steelhead is that they are winter steelhead—unique from the vast majority of steelhead caught throughout the Northwest, even many of the steelhead caught during winter months, with snow on the ground and ice in your rod's guides. Winter steelhead are sexually mature fish that arrive in freshwater and spawn in one great burst of energy—entirely different from summer fish, which migrate upstream for months on end before finally settling down to spawn in their natal waters. The salient point in the life cycles of Northwest steelhead is that there are no true winter runs on Columbia tributaries east of Hood River. Genuine winter steelhead are confined to that relatively narrow corridor of rivers that flow west of the Cascades—or out of the coast ranges from California to Alaska. Like their range, the time winter steelhead spend in rivers seems compressed, circumscribed by the immediacy of their spawning needs. Winter fish suggest a more driven, determined steelhead, less prone to wandering travels and frivolous responses to the fly—and as such they behave, by and large, nothing like their summer cousins that seem, at times, like little more—nor less—than enormous trout.

The Rivers

Pitched along the verdant slopes of the region's maritime mountains, winter steelhead rivers rise and fall in quick response to the season's volatile weather. Steelhead move and hold in their own direct response to fluctuating river flows, and it's a sharp eye on this abrupt rising and falling that keeps local anglers into fish while the rest of us often do little more in winter than practice our casting. The timeless adage is that steelhead "bite best" on a dropping river—and anglers soon learn to recognize the illustrious "steelhead green" of rivers falling back into shape following a spate of high or off-colored water. Thanks to the Internet, anglers now have ready access to graphs and cfs values that eliminate much of the guesswork, although nothing but a visual inspection can tell you if water clarity is sufficient to give fish a chance to see your fly.

Still, on the rivers I fish, I find I'm most successful during periods when the line describing the slope of a dropping river approaches the average historical flows for that same time period. I'm sure this is nothing new to anglers who swung their flies on winter steelhead rivers before the advent of online information. A falling river that still remains higher than during average flows affords steelhead a much broader selection of holding water. Too high, of course, and flows make it difficult to present the fly appropriately. Too low and steelhead retreat from many of the lies fished effectively with flies, ending up in cramped or abysmal quarters where the fly fisher's most effective methods are, if truth be known, an imitation of techniques employed by conventional gear and bait anglers.

Holding Water

The river I fish most often in winter, the Hood, does little to relieve my sense that one day steelhead fishing will drive me absolutely batty. The Hood is small and funky, subject to the same radical fluctuation of flows as rivers pouring directly into the Pacific, with an unstable bed of boulders and sand, sloughed from the flanks of Mount Hood, that allows the river to rearrange itself with the regularity of a coastal California creek. Only the last four miles of river are open to angling—but in that short distance you'll find every type of holding water, from traditional fly friendly runs to the heavy pocket water so conducive to nymphing with indicators, splitshot, and egg patterns.

To be frank, I harbor an open love-hate relationship with the Hood. In a half-dozen winters, I've come to know most of its holding water, guiding a fly, at one time or another, through most of its legal lies, finding fish, now and then, in practically all of them. I can walk up the Hood and point out one lie after another that has produced a fish—some spots obvious, others as subtle or obscure as the face of love itself.

Steelhead lies, however, should be a secret to no one. I remember when I was first starting out, a greenhorn still wet from the California surf, and a guy telling me that steelhead are in the exact same spots you find trout. That's an oversimplification. But not by much—especially on a small, easily readable river like the Hood.

Presentation

Every winter I start out with a new pattern or line or cast or presentation technique that I think is really going to make the difference, that *this* winter I knock them dead. But as the season progresses, things turn out pretty much the same as every other winter: I get one here. I get one there.

And often—more often than I care to admit—I don't get one at all.

What's especially frustrating—hence the *hate* in the relationship—is this remarkable sense I have that it doesn't much matter what I do: I get more or less the same number of winter steelhead across any given stretch of time. Obvious though this may sound, I get my fish by whatever way I'm fishing. I'm trying not to sound facetious. I'm not a fan of indicators and egg-pattern nymphing, but I've cozied up to every style and configuration of nymphing strategy purported to make winter steelhead beg for mercy, and when I do, here and there I get a fish. Likewise, there's nothing more I do like in winter than throwing a big fly on a long line with a double-handed rod—and when I fish this way, here and there I get a fish.

Regardless of how I'm fishing, when I do get a winter steelhead, it always makes perfect sense. Generally, it seems fairly simple: I've done my job, presenting the fly appropriately through likely holding water. According to conventional wisdom, appropriate means slow when you're swinging the fly, and deep on a drag-free drift when you're nymphing. The water is cold; you can't expect winter steelhead to move much off their lies. You keep at it, and now and then, here and there, a fish grabs. *Just like it's supposed to happen*, you think. *I know how to do this.*

Yet often, before the next fish, you'll wonder again if you know anything at all.

Flies

No one who knows anything about winter steelheading will make anything but tentative claims about the value of one fly over another. It's a bittersweet truth that the strength and efficacy of any given pattern extends exactly as far as the fame and fishing prowess of the angler who created and used or popularized the fly. More than anything else, winter steelhead patterns belong to a narrative or history of an angler's career: *This is the fly I used to catch this fish. This is the fly I had on when this or that happened.*

Which isn't to contend your fly doesn't matter. Of course it matters. But the harsh lesson in winter steelheading is that the fly matters most to you. The "best" fly is the one you keep in the water, cast after cast, run after run. The best fly is one you believe in—absolutely—each time you straighten your line. The best fly is the one that catches steelhead—which is precisely what it will do if you keep it in the river in winter while fishing steelhead lies.

It turns out Gierach and a pal, Vince Zounek, would be bunking in a cheap motel in Troutdale, hoping to encounter signs of the "big, late-winter natives" that have long been part of the region's steelhead lore. They had a day lined up on the Sandy with Mark Bachmann; I sent an email to Marty Sheppard, who offered a float from a private launch on a nearby stretch of the river, as long as we covered the cost of the put-in plus expenses. Gierach, I suspect, gets these good ol' boy deals all the time. It's one thing to be a Real Guy—quite another to be one of very few authors who has ever made an actual living writing about the game.

Everything, anyway, came together like it's supposed to. Rain fell hard for a couple of days, and then snow levels dropped and the rivers settled into shape. Bachmann practically owns the Sandy, so I figured John and Vince could get a fish or two under their belts, taking the pressure off our day together on the river. Sheppard is part of a cadre of hotshot guides who started out under the tutelage of Bachmann, and I've been around him enough the past couple of years to know he's a dynamite caster, a steelhead magnet, and a gentleman besides.

And on the first run we fished, I was pleased to see that John and Vince are proficient as can be with double-handed rods.

We had this deal covered. What a great way this would be to come out of my slump and end up with an upbeat conclusion for a winter steelhead piece I'd been assigned to write. It couldn't work out any better. I love it when something as tough even as finding steelhead in winter on the fly suddenly seems like the easiest thing in the world.

Or so I figured. Optimism, you see, is the one trait serious winter steelheaders share. Without it, you might as well stay home.

But I've probably said enough as it is. If there's more to tell, you'll have to hear it from some other guy.

Metal Detector (by Marty Sheppard)

Hook: Gamakatsu Octopus, size 2 or 4, tied behind Waddington shank
Cone (optional): HMH small 3/32-inch ID Nickel
Thread: Blue 6/0
Tail: Black bucktail
Flash: Black Krystal Flash over bucktail
Body: Black Polar Chenille
Collar: Black marabou topped with Guinea fowl dyed blue

LESSON 36

TROUT SCHOOL

If you're fortunate to have good friends you've fished with over the years, and now you only fish with them infrequently, you face the challenge of trying to overlook how old they look each time you see them—especially when you're certain you've hardly changed at all. Clearly your thoughts haven't changed, the iron fist of obsession continuing to pound away at your fragile sense of purpose. But the remedy remains close at hand, and if you can convince a couple of old friends to join you on the water, the mounting case against your angling desires can come to seem so much prudish claptrap—even if the time together does keep bringing up the question of why the years have been so tough on them while hardly touching you at all.

A week on Wolf River with Peter and John Syka, anyway, will be kind of a reunion. Peter goes back further in my fly fishing career than anyone but my father, and John, Peter's brother, has joined us over the decades on a handful of trips, appearing as a comet in the orbital sweep of our angling lives. I should also mention that Peter and John served as models for a couple of characters in a novel I wrote, characters named, squarely enough, Peter and John. Employing friends as characters in a work of fiction is probably ill-advised, however; as time passes, you can begin to lose track of the source of your stories, which memories are based on reality and which belong to something you created. The fiction takes on the aspect of recurring dreams, coloring the truth in hues that seem lifted as much from hallucinations as actual history.

Yet by the time we reach the river, everyone looks and sounds the same again—the friends beneath the lost or graying hair, the wrinkled sun-damaged skin, having emerged as if reflections on quieting waters. And the stories, too, have all been sorted out, or at least the ones that still matter, who said what to whom, where we were, which river, which beach, which year it was. Sixteen hours after Peter and John flew in from different parts of the country, a short night at my house, then the long drive east—by the time we see the Wolf it's as if the years between trips have retreated into brief, insignificant periods of compressed time, leaving behind, by and large, the fishing trips and little more. *What does matter?* you ask yourself—a question that all but answers itself as, driving upstream, we glance furtively at the opaque waters of the Wolf, green as an apple beneath the summer sun, imagining the movement of brown trout the size of house pets eager to rise to our drifting flies.

Camp takes shape in a series of smooth gestures that find each of us accepting roles to an unspoken, improvised mandate. The midday summer heat prompts the inevitable recollections of Baja, and when the big cabin tent rises against a backdrop of blue sky and barren cliffs, someone delivers, as if on cue, the appropriate lines about walls speaking and the stories they could tell. Poles, guy lines, and the emblematic blue shade tarp go up with only minor protests: a stake here that won't hold, a knot there that slips free. Alone, I recall, spending four days fussing with one of these things, returning to camp after fishing to find it, time and again, draped over the cot and cook station in a posture of exhausted defeat. A pleasant, unstated consensus informs our work: Over the years, we've all suffered the frustrations of erecting camps in the company of family members or friends either too young or too helpless or inexperienced to do more than respond, task by task, to directions for a job that seems as straightforward as building a leader and tying on a fly.

But on the water there's a different feel. We slip from the willows into the broad tailout directly below camp, searching for clues that might sharpen our focus tighter than the general aim to "hook some of these mothers." Hardly a moment finds us unable to spot feeding fish, the big browns lifting to the surface with an elegant lack of haste or revealing themselves in delicate gestures that send spasms of concentric shockwaves drifting downstream. Yet in the manner of most such trout, these prove difficult fish, the very stuff of our angling dreams, if not many of our nightmares besides.

Oddly enough, I remain fairly casual about the slow start. Then it occurs to me that I've been doing a lot more of this lately than either Peter or John, hunting big trout in challenging circumstances that demand you to be on top of your game. I suffer a stab of anxiety. I'm a friend, not a guide, in this situation—but when you've invited a couple of old pals to fish some local water, you do hope they can sort things out so that everyone enjoys his fair share of the action. It's not exactly pressure you feel as much as the kind of responsibility a host carries at a party trying to make sure everyone has a good time. At some point, of course, you realize you've done what you can by bringing everyone this far—and if you've learned nothing else about the sport you know it's best to get your head in your own game and trust your buddies will manage soon enough.

My anxieties retreat the moment I see Peter, rod raised, plunging down a swift side channel, a worried look splashed across his face. Whatever's on the end of his line is threatening him with the most severe sort of abuse. My relief is immeasurable. My old friend is getting his butt kicked. John and I offer encouragement, although it's unclear whether we're rooting more for Peter or the fish.

Even before this encounter resolves itself, I'm struck by the promise of what lies ahead. In a rare fit of equanimity, I call to mind a half-dozen distinct kinds of holding water all within shouting distance, such that I realize it's as if we've enrolled for a week at our own little trout school. Peter hooked his fish—which is still intimidating him by size alone—in a narrow pocket perfectly arranged for a class on upstream nymphing. Between that and two different stretches of painfully esoteric dry fly water, where the trout, at times, require casts as sublime as life itself, the Wolf here offers a little bit of everything, from riffles to runs, edges to eddies, water swift, slow, broken, and braided, and some of it as quiet as sleep itself—yet all of it, taken as a whole, affording opportunities to move trout by every manner described in the literature.

My fears, in other words, seem unfounded. The three of us share a moment of disappointment when it turns out Peter has foul hooked his fish—probably after the initial take; probably why the fish proved so difficult to land—but not even this can disturb my sudden sense of confidence. Peter hooked the fish exactly where I'd directed him; it's really not going to get too much tougher than that. There are fish here, they are up and feeding and, despite any rustiness, Peter and John have been fishing plenty long enough to ease their way back into this silly game.

And maybe this, I suddenly consider, is all it really means to be a Real Guy—this quiet confidence that you've got enough of a handle on things that you usually know what's going on, and when you don't, you've got enough experience to fall back on and make something happen rather than submit to the kind of shrill hysteria that the innumerable mysteries of fish and fly fishing can so readily inspire.

Or maybe, I think, while John and Peter, now completely aware of the stakes at hand, slip off in separate directions for their own private studies—maybe it's just me who requires such consideration, and all I'm really sensing is that I've finally started to feel like the kind of fly fisher I've always wanted to be. You would assume it had to eventually happen. Left alone, I stay put alongside a dark seam of calm water between currents sweeping around the tail of an island, the precise juncture where Peter ended up freeing his fish. Everything's quiet; the turbid, jade-colored water reveals no signs of trout. By all evidence, I could be looking at a murky vernal creek carrying irrigation water through this flinty, scalded desert, which seems as close to trout country as it does to a Bahaman bonefish flat.

Unless you happen to know the West like the Real Guys do.

What I know is that there are brown trout as big as rain boots someplace right in front of me, and if I wait here long enough, they'll begin to rise. I also happen to know that there's an evening caddis show ahead that's been coming off about as predictably as these things can happen, an overlapping mix of hatching and mating and egg-laying bugs of a genus whose Latin name I know but that requires no more translation, on the water, than your classic size 14 tan caddis that you find from California to Montana, Washington to Wyoming, and probably a lot of other places where trout live, too. On the Wolf this season, this hatch has proven so reliable that I have close to half a fly box filled with tan caddis, and of these, nearly all fall under one of two simple patterns—a Dry Caddis or a Wet Caddis.

Assumptions, I understand, knotting on the dry, can be dangerous. But experience, and the quiet retreat of afternoon light, suggests that we're soon to enjoy some blistering action—if we keep our wits about ourselves and don't succumb to the temptation to flail the water or start switching flies if a fish or two, or even three or four, ignores our casts. Better casts, I've come to believe, catch more—and better—fish. It's the Dry Caddis that lights right on the trout's nose that seems, most often, to inspire a rise. It's the Wet Caddis fished downstream, on a line so soft that you're not swinging it so much as merely influencing it, that gets those heavy, rod-yanking grabs.

Would the Real Guys agree? Some wouldn't, I suspect. Others might. It seems useful to note, anyway, that no one has all the answers, and none of this is etched in stone. At the edge of the seam I see a trout rise alongside the trace of a submerged rock, leaving behind an impression such that I can't tell if the fish was sixteen inches or six pounds. The cast is less than twenty feet. The take seems absurdly delicate, especially on discovering, sometime later, that the estimate in weight was a lot closer to the one in length. This is when the fish gets a good look at me, too, and it finally starts behaving seriously, boring off into heavy current at the head of seventy-five yards of boulders, plunge pools, and tangles of overhanging willows.

I wade in and follow downstream.

Wet Caddis

Hook: TMC 3671, size 14
Thread: 8/0, camel
Body: Tan, gray, or cinnamon dubbing
Underwing: English grouse
Overwing: Tan or cream Antron yarn
Hackle: Hen hackle, ginger or dark brown dun

Tying Notes

A quick and simple tie. The tan Antron yarn is a great color, although I have no proof that it out-fishes the traditional cream. As when tying many different wet flies, I secure the hackle feather by the stem before tying the rest of the fly. Later, I wind the hackle back toward the wing and then wind the thread through the hackle before finishing at the head, thus making the fly more durable.

Dry Caddis

Hook: TMC 900BL, size 14
Thread: 8/0, brown
Body: Tan, gray, or cinnamon dubbing
Hackle: Brown
Wing: Bleached deer hair

Tying Notes

Again, nothing new here. Keep the wing sparse. Make only a couple turns of hackle. Sometimes I wind it before tying in the wing; sometimes I wind it in front like the Wet Caddis. This is a smooth-water pattern, lacking the palmered hackle of traditional elk or deer hair caddis. I want this fly to ride low in the water, even if it disappears in the film. I know where it is. If a rise shows, I assume it's my fly the fish ate.

LESSON 37

CREASE FLY

Of the countless opportunities in fly fishing for failure and self-reproach, none seems more pregnant with possibility than venturing into bluewater with a Baja panga guide.

Efren, one of Gary Bulla's favored East Cape captains, exudes the untoward nonchalance befitting both youth and his barely concealed disdain for the general foolishness of fly fishing. He scatters bait for Bulla and me across the rhythmic rise and fall of a *chubasco* ground swell, flinging each handful in a manner that suggests an outlaw discarding a cigarette in a black and white movie. Clearly this is all but beneath him, although not for lack of efficacy of effort. About the boat, sudden explosions erupt with startling ferocity, audible blasts from tuna rocketing to the surface and smashing the ill-pitched herring, only to vanish in contracted moments that recall the disjointed movements in an oft-repaired copy of that same old outlaw film.

Yet there's more to Efren's romantic posturing than the habits of age or angling machismo. Shortly before, a minefield of pelagic detonations much like the one now immediately in front of us was strafed by a lone marauding dorado—a beast of such unearthly iridescence and belligerent hydrodynamics that it seemed somehow fitting that it broke off both Bulla and me.

Fitting—but in no way excusable. Bulla's failure, nevertheless, I found easy to overlook. The fish was hooked and gone so quickly that, despite the exclamations from Bulla's station in the bow, I thought the fly must have pulled free—when in fact the twenty-pound tippet had parted. I had no time, however, to offer Bulla my condolences, as the dorado—all greens and blues and yellows, as long as a hippie's VW bumper—immediately appeared off the stern of the boat, the fire in its eyes all but incandescent as it continued to slash recklessly at the weakened bait.

My cast fell in the general vicinity of the target. The fish pivoted and ate the big streamer as though a dog used to scraps pitched from a table. *Oh, for such moments does one often forsake so much*, I warbled, tending the loose line left behind at my feet from the short but sufficient cast.

Now, while Bulla and I stand, rods ready, at opposite ends of the panga, while Efren flings his handfuls of bait into the flexed and recoiling sea, while we all await another dorado, rejecting the prevalent tuna—while all this transpires I suffer the sight of that first flaring dorado headed for the horizon in a series of elegant leaps, each a replica of the first, that ended the moment the last loop of line rose from my feet and slipped round the butt of the rod.

The next dorado arrive in a pack, a tangle of frenetic energy that appears so suddenly amidst the bait it's as if the water has burst into flames. Apropos to some farfetched logic or grade-school metaphysics, the fish, I note, are but half the size of the one Bulla and I mishandled—which has not one iota of effect on our enthusiastic response. Efren, naturally, has spotted the fish well before we have, and he urges them into our wheelhouse, shortening the swath of the scattered bait.

I haul against the weight of the heavy head and drop my fly in the path of the approaching mayhem. A dorado darts forward and comes so close to the offering that its dizzy eyes cross. *Oh, doctor*, I think. *Strip, strip. You're mine.*

But the dorado remains detached from the fly, following it without eating. As the fish approaches the boat, the distance between it and the fly gradually increases until, with what seems to me a shrug of its radiant shoulders, the dorado abruptly veers off and vanishes.

There is too much commotion blistering the immediate water for me to pause and reflect on this stern rejection. Yet I also can't help but notice Efren eyeing me, as if the dorado's refusal to take the fly offers further evidence of my declining status, now so far beneath that of a real fisherman that I might well be kin to a village pariah dog. Dorado vector in and out of casting range, coursing through the bait as if psychedelic sharks with attention deficit disorders. I know better than to "shoot the covey"—that it's always better to select a fish, take aim, and cast—but both knowing what's right and doing it remain two steps I've yet to master in any number of dances accompanied by sparking riffs and wailing horns.

I pitch my fly into the fray and, as soon as I begin stripping, a dorado again comes up cross-eyed behind the black and white Tuna Tux, so close it appears as if it's preparing to balance the fly on its nose. If it had a nose. The head of the dorado, slicing the water, presents the strong suggestion of an oversized meat cleaver wielded by graffiti artists in a tough part of town. I give the fly several quick, violent tugs, trying to incite the fish into striking, a ploy that leaves the dorado's eyes crossed and cold, as if those of a woman refusing to kiss.

But when the fly approaches the boat and this dorado, too, suddenly jags off course and disappears, Efren steps forward and leans against the gunwale as if finally fed up with my failure to fasten myself to a fish. I understand his frustration. I also recognize the hint of despair I inevitably feel when feeding fish repeatedly refuse my fly, a kind of psychic nausea that seems invigorated to the point of dementia when—

"Crease fly."

?

"*Crease fly!*"

It's only after Efren repeats himself—the first words I've heard him speak in English—it's only then that I understand he wants me to change flies. I swing the tip of the rod toward the boat and allow him to wrap a hand around the line, slide it down to the leader, and grab the Tuna Tux, which he takes hold of as if it's an offensive little toy we should have never played with in the first place. With his teeth Efren clips the heavy tippet material; he hands me the fly as though it's a problem I need to deal with. Then, in a series of gestures that bring to mind the hero in a film assembling a firearm while the bad guy is heard approaching up the stairs, Efren rifles through Bulla's cache of flies in a tackle box on the floor of the panga, finds what he's looking for, and affixes it to the leader with a modified Palomar knot that he completes as fast as I could staple together two sheets of paper.

Off in the distance at the far end of the panga I see Bulla fighting a fish—skipjack, yellowfin, dorado, I can't tell which. By the configuration of his rod, it might well be Moby Dick. Somewhere between me and the rigid vanishing point of Bulla's line I spot two dorado, side by side, racing toward the boat like a pair of dueling thoroughbreds. Just before I release my cast, Bulla hollers at me to cast beyond the dorado, that in doing so the fish will grab going away, affording a better chance for a solid hookup. The cast seems counterintuitive, aiming the fly to a spot opposite the direction the pair of dorado are headed—but when the Crease Fly lands, and one of the dorado immediately wheels as if a dog hitting the end of its chain, I consider the notion, yet again, that grace remains a possibility whenever and wherever the fly—by any means—is in the water.

The folded foam-bodied Crease Fly belongs to that category of so-called new and unique patterns that do in fact seem, once you get past the hype and hyperbole, new and unique and not yet another variation on an old theme. Often I resist such patterns; they suggest an element of extravagance and impropriety that I view as simply too much. But of course nothing is "too much" that belongs on the end of a leader and fly line and catches fish. Whether such a fly is required for catching the fish we're after, or whether we simply believe we need it, is more or less the same question, our answer to which will determine whether we keep refusing a pattern on grounds of too-much-ness or we finally get around to learning to tie them for ourselves.

The Crease Fly was apparently created by Captain Joe Bladdos, who seems to be some kind of East Coast art wizard when he's not chasing stripers, bluefish, and false albacore. I say *apparently* because claims regarding a fly's origins often prove messier than the accepted version of the story. Bladdos's artwork certainly reflects a fertile mind, and he's put together Crease Fly kits that you can track down online and then start right in tying. The other step you might want to take is to get a cutting tool or two from River Road Creations for making the foam bodies that are the signature element of the pattern. You don't need this tool any more than you need these flies. But they work.

Tying a Crease Fly is part actual fly tying and part assembly on the order of building model cars. The finished fly, in fact, is really fairly close to something you might call a jig, but because it looks and acts like a popper as well, no one seems to badmouth it much. Of course, when you get out in bluewater and start flinging hard-bodied flies and 500 grain heads over baitfish chum, few anglers gripe about what goes on, for the simple reason that everyone's pretty much agreed you do what it takes, and if you can come up with a better way to hook fish than the other guy, more power to you.

That raises a few questions that I'm going to have to ignore right now. My notion of Real Guys in fly fishing grew out of a sense that the sport contains inner circles of fly fishers who succeed, time and again, where the rest of us find failure, frustration, and seemingly random moments of grace. Now and then we get it right; Real Guys, on the other hand, have achieved a level of expertise that makes them all but immune to the kinds of foibles other fly fishers suffer. Real Guys, I'm suggesting, reflect an ideal—and as such, they might not actually exist.

Fly fishing, too, is an ideal, one born on the slick and orderly Old World streams where brown trout sipped mayfly duns on the other side of the ocean where all kinds of bad shit was always coming down. I sound like a yokel but that's okay right now. My point is, even Real Guys, if they're not careful, turn into Old Guys—which is fine as long as you're happy right where you are. That's probably a good attitude, although despite what Lao Tzu and plenty of others have said, you can end up wading through a lot of crap that way when all you might need to do is dump some ballast and drift into a different, clearer part of the stream. Real Guys, it turns out, aren't so much located in any inner circles, but they seem to belong to these interconnected orbits, always migrating to better water, better casts, better flies, better ideas. No one ever gets anywhere other than where he or she is. *There* is not some place or level of expertise where the Real Guys are. *There* is the path they're on.

A life of fly fishing entails innumerable steps—a countless number of lessons—from those early casts on a small stream you found yourself on way back when. You learn flies. You learn bugs. You learn fish and rivers and casts and runs. You learn how to catch fish. Most of all, you learn how to catch fish.

Floating atop the surface of the ocean blue, the angler who hopes to catch fish with a fly rod and flies faces a fairly daunting challenge. Real Guys have figured out a few ways to get the job done; Real Guys are the men and women who will continue to discover new methods and new flies, and Real Guys will refine those patterns and techniques until they filter down to the rest of us who want to enjoy the same level of sport that Real Guys enjoy. Some of us, of course, will become Real Guys ourselves. Most of us will just keep doing the best we can.

The Crease Fly may or may not prove an essential pattern for your blue-water fly fishing. Lord knows we could all get by with a little less shit on the water. But if there's an absolutely genuine Real Guy anywhere in this tale, it's Efren Lucero, the stern and youthful panga captain trying to guide a couple of dizzy gringos into a dance with dazzling dorado. Efren made the call; I managed a cast—and by the time the dorado takes the fly in its mouth, I've taken two steps backwards, preparing to bury the hook.

I lean back against the anticipated pull and weight of the fish. But as the backs of my thighs hit the gunwale, and my own weight and momentum carry me over the edge, the line remains void of the dorado's energy. *I'm going in*, I think, glancing over my shoulder to see where in the water I'll fall.

But then the line goes immediately taut, I feel the fish, and I'm tugged upright and back into the middle of the boat, shuffling my bare feet as line leaps about them and upwards through the reel.

Off to one side of me, Efren and Bulla shake their heads laughing, disappointed, I imagine, they didn't get to see my feet pitch over my head.

Once the fish is on the reel, unchecked by pressure applied to the whirling spool by my right hand, I consider how close I came to going in. There's something in that moment, I sense, that may be worth looking at more closely—that place we find ourselves, headed over the edge, only to be saved by the grace of a good fish grabbing the fly.

But that's probably another story.

CREASE FLY

Hook: Mustad 34011 or any conventional long-shanked saltwater hook, size 2–3/0
Thread: Danville's 140 Denier, olive
Tail: White bucktail, fluorescent chartreuse Krystal Flash, chartreuse yak hair, chartreuse bucktail
Body: 2mm foam with Crease Fly transfer film and foil
Eyes: Flat stick-on eyes, 3/16"; green with black pupils

Tying Notes

Step 1: Assemble materials, tools, the works. That should be your first step regardless of which pattern you're tying—but in this case it seems worth the reminder.

Step 2: If you get a Capt. Bladdos Crease Fly Kit, it includes a roll of transfer film. Run a strip of it across the top portion of the face of a sheet of foam. Peel off the protective, wax-paper-like liner material. To this sticky surface, apply one of the iridescent Mylar-like foils, dull side to the adhesive. Peel the cellophane off the foil.

Step 3: Cut out several bodies from the foil-covered foam. I use the Capt. Joe Bladdos's Crease Fly Popper cutter, size 2/0, available from River Road Creations. Scissors work as well. Experiment with sizes and shapes. When you find something you like, make your own pattern.

Step 4: Secure a hook in your vise. Start your thread. Tie in a sparse tail about the length of the foam body. I try to replicate the colors that will make up the body—in this case a thin layer of white bucktail, four to six strands of Krystal Flash, a bit of chartreuse yak hair, and finally some chartreuse bucktail.

Step 5: Cover the entire hook with thread, then continue to build up the thread until it approaches the thickness of the tie-in wraps at the tail. Whip finish behind the eye of the hook and cut the thread.

Step 6: Remove the thread-covered hook from the vise. Cover the thread with a thin layer of cyanoacrylate glue. Fold the foam body, foil side out, and squeeze the bottom edge along the hook shank, making sure to avoid glue on your fingers. Hold the edge of the foam tight to the hook for about a minute, until the bond is strong enough to keep the folded foam in place.

Step 7: Use colored Sharpies to detail the fly. For example: along the top portion of both sides, make a thin stripe of yellow, followed by lime green, followed by olive green along the spine or top of the fly. Add red along the front edge of the fly to suggest gills.

Step 8: Apply eyes.

Step 9: After building a few flies, mix a small batch of five-minute epoxy. Fill any gap that still exists between the bottom edges of the foam along the hook shank. Cover the entire body with a thin coat of epoxy.